POETRY AND DRAMA
LITERARY TERMS AND CONCEPTS

POETRY AND DRAMA

LITERARY TERMS AND CONCEPTS

EDITED BY **KATHLEEN KUIPER**, MANAGER, ARTS AND CULTURE

Britannica
Educational Publishing

IN ASSOCIATION WITH

ROSEN
EDUCATIONAL SERVICES

Published in 2012 by Britannica Educational Publishing
(a trademark of Encyclopædia Britannica, Inc.)
in association with Rosen Educational Services, LLC
29 East 21st Street, New York, NY 10010.

Distributed exclusively by Rosen Educational Services.
For a listing of additional Britannica Educational Publishing titles, call toll free (800) 237-9932.

First Edition

Britannica Educational Publishing
Michael I. Levy: Executive Editor
J.E. Luebering: Senior Manager
Adam Augustyn, Assistant Manager, Encyclopaedia Britannica
Marilyn L. Barton: Senior Coordinator, Production Control
Steven Bosco: Director, Editorial Technologies
Lisa S. Braucher: Senior Producer and Data Editor
Yvette Charboneau: Senior Copy Editor
Kathy Nakamura: Manager, Media Acquisition
Kathleen Kuiper: Manager, Arts and Culture

Rosen Educational Services
Heather M. Moore Niver: Editor
Nelson Sá: Art Director
Cindy Reiman: Photography Manager
Nicole Russo: Designer
Matthew Cauli: Cover Design
Introduction by Kathleen Kuiper

Library of Congress Cataloging-in-Publication Data

Poetry and drama : literary terms and concepts/edited by Kathleen Kuiper.—1st ed.
 p. cm.—(The Britannica guide to literary elements)
"In association with Britannica Educational Publishing, Rosen Educational Services."
Includes bibliographical references and index.
ISBN 978-1-61530-490-5 (lib. bdg.)
1. Poetry--History and criticism. 2. Drama--History and criticism. 3. Poetics. I. Kuiper,
Kathleen.
PN1031.P546 2011
809.1—dc22

                                        2010045788

Manufactured in the United States of America

Cover, pp. 1, 67, 103, 122, 137, 171, 197 Shutterstock.com

CONTENTS

2

6

21

50

53

Lord, who createdst man in wealth and sto
Though foolishly he lost the same,
Decaying more and more
Till he became
Most poor:
With thee
O let me rise
As larks, harmoniously,
And sing this day thy victories;
Then shall the fall further the flight in m

62

Rose kissed me to-day.
Will she kiss me to-morrow?
Let it be as it may,
Rose kissed me to-day,
But the pleasure gives way
To a savour of sorrow;—
Rose kissed me to-day,—
Will she kiss me to-morrow?

CHAPTER 2: PROSODY 67

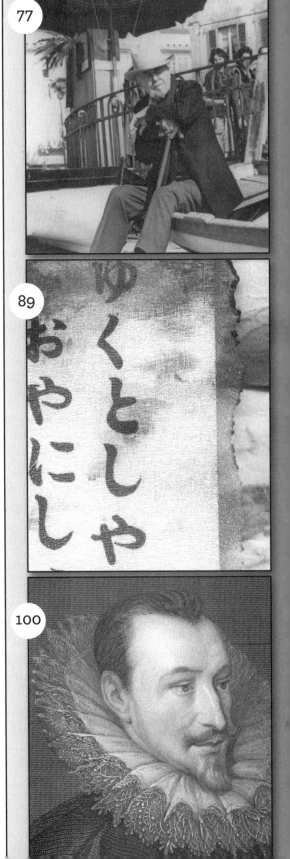

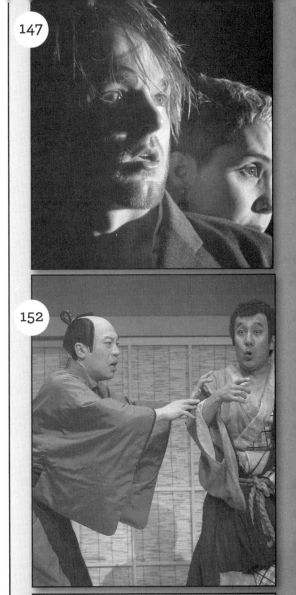

147

152

164

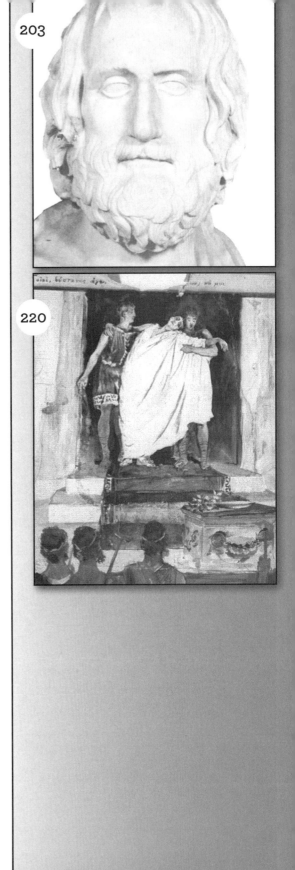

INTRODUCTION

Let us celebrate the word! Whether it is spoken and bears the gnarled barnacles of age or recently written and mingles with our own experiences to evoke sounds (the din of cicadas), or smells (the air after a heavy rain), or painful feelings that we recognize, words are wondrous.

We cannot know with certainty how the cave dwellers of millennia ago conveyed information to their clans. We know they drew animals on cave walls and that these animals were portrayed with sensitivity and a sense of awe. But did they also describe them as "noble" or even "lip-smackin' tasty"? When, in the course of human history, did the early hunters and gatherers begin to relate their adventures? Did one woman turn to another and say, "You know, Uta, this plant produced well for us this year. If we plant seeds from it next year, maybe it will do the same thing . . ."

In the 21st century we can only theorize. All we know for certain is that early humans—Neanderthals and *Homo sapiens* at least—migrated out of Africa, spread out, and populated the Earth. Languages developed and, as populations grew, people of the same clan who lived at opposite ends of the territory, though they still understood each other, spoke slightly differently and developed their own words for a few items and ideas.

As languages evolved, the primacy of the word as a means of conceptualizing, storing, and transmitting experience became evident. People began to tell stories in a particular way. Sometimes these people had a specific social function and performed at a specific place. Among other purposes, this ritual storytelling passed on legend and history. This was a good way of keeping track of things—who had married whom in the past generation, why one person didn't speak to another, how the group had come to live where they were.

This tradition persists among many peoples living in the present century. The Australian Aborigines are one of the best known of these contemporary cultures. These indigenous peoples navigated their territory through series of short songs popularly known as songlines. As John Miles Foley put it in Britannica's article on the oral tradition, "In addressing a network of both mythical and tangible landmarks, the songlines together constitute a catalogue of local route systems—in essence, a map delineating the geographical, spiritual, social, and historical contour, of their environment." Other cultures also—in South Asia and Kazakhstan, for example—record and celebrate their cultures in this fashion, with bards memorizing enormous quantities of material.

It's clear from these persistent traditions that poetry and performance have always had significance to humanity. This book deals chiefly with the subjects

Poetry can be written or spoken in any language. Gyro Photography/Getty Images

of poetry and drama, though there is considerable overlap in many genres and styles. These two forms are the most ancient means of literary communication. They represent a moving beyond the mere counting of goods and other types of reckoning. Storytelling itself—a communal exchange that continues today in countries throughout the world—is a sort of performance that diverged long ago into several streams, including drama, stand-up comedy, and fiction.

In the introduction to her book *Soul Says: On Recent Poetry* (1995), the American critic and academic Helen Vendler discusses the difference between reading a novel and reading poetry:

> *At first, I found it hard to understand when such categories were ritually invoked, why people felt that they could only respond to literature that replicated their own experience of race, class, or gender … The last thing I wanted from literature was a mirror of my experiences. What I wanted was a mirror of my feelings, and that I found in poetry . . . Metaphor, not mimesis [imitation, mimicry], was my realm.*

What then makes poetry a distinctive genre? And why is it that people either love it or hate it? The critical difference lies in our ability to find a way in, and with a bit of will and the use of the correct set of keys, we can not only unlock the meaning of a particular poem but can provide the foundation for a lifetime of pleasurable and immensely rewarding reading. Are you lovesick, lost, uncertain about your direction? Who can clarify those feelings quite like Shakespeare? If you are humiliated, misunderstood, in pain, or angry, certain works by Langston Hughes may be the perfect remedy.

Just how is it that these poets and tens of thousands of others can create what they do? What tools do they use? The acoustic and rhythmic effects of poetry (and also prose) are gathered under the umbrella term *prosody*. They include such elements as scansion (a combination of rhythm and sound), meaning, pace, and a variety of sonic effects such as consonance, assonance, and alliteration. Each of these is to some degree at the mercy of the poet's native tongue. Germanic and Romance languages, for example, specialize in somewhat different types, which is why poetry is more difficult to translate than other genres.

A poet determines the length and nature of the poem depending on his or her intent. Will it be a long narrative poem? Will it be epic, dramatic? A short fixed verse form, such as a sonnet? Or should one prefer a clerihew, deliberately lame and achieving its hilarious effect by its very limping quality? Will it reflect simply the poet's voice or (as in a dramatic monologue by Robert Browning) the voice of some figure the poet chooses as a vehicle? How does that person sound—lyrical and eloquent? Or, like Gollum in *Lord of the Rings*, with a tendency toward drawn-out, snake-like sibilants?

The competent use of these ingredients contributes to a poet's success in communicating with readers. By the same token, a reader's awareness of how poets achieve their effects makes the experience richer and fuller.

Although Homer may not be the first name English-language readers think of when we think about poetry, he is surely one of the greatest. It is doubtful he created the narratives of *Iliad* and the *Odyssey*, but he certainly shaped them. These two epics provided the basis of Greek education and culture throughout the Classical age and formed the backbone of humane education down to the time of the Roman Empire and the spread of Christianity.

It was probably through their impact on Classical Greek culture itself that the *Iliad* and the *Odyssey* most subtly affected Western standards and ideas. The Greeks looked on the distinguished epics as far more than works of literature. They knew much of them by heart, and they held them to be a symbol of Hellenic unity and heroism as well as an ancient source of moral and even practical instruction.

Both prose and poetry translations of these works have been made since the 17th century. Their effect on Western culture remains strong today, as we can see in the Coen brothers' movie *O, Brother, Where Art Thou?* Too, James Joyce's *Ulysses*, one of the most acclaimed works of the 20th century, follows the narrative scheme of Homer's *Odyssey*. Odysseus's years-long journey home is the model for Leopold Bloom's day-long meander through Dublin.

The epic mode—which is present in prose as well as poetry—provides one of the main threads of literature. Written examples abound not only in Western literature, where they can be traced through Virgil's *Aeneid* to John Milton's *Paradise Lost* and beyond, but also in other traditions including those of the Middle East and East Asia. African epics are less well known in the West.

Like the epic, the form of poetry known as the ballad also has its roots in the oral tradition. Despite its similarly ancient origins, the ballad diverges from the epic in a number of ways. For one thing, the ballad is often associated with music. For another, its emphasis is on the decisive moment rather than a larger narrative or the overall story. Ballads such as "Frankie and Johnnie" or The Beatles' "Rocky Raccoon" exhibit many of the usual traits of the genre, such as incremental repetition, plain language, conventional imagery, and an impersonal speaker. Typically, the ballad is driven by economical means to a dramatic end. It gains emotional weight with the use of short words, formulaic language (the phrase *blood red*, for example, is often used in place of simply *red*), and an abrupt or unexpected end, such as a breathtaking betrayal or a hair-raising revelation.

From drama in a turn of phrase we move to drama as a genre. The play shares with the ballad the element of performance. To be sure, the texts of plays can be read privately—and certainly can still bring a tear to the eye or a broad laugh—yet they are most effective when performed by actors for an audience and in a communal setting.

Traditionally, plays have been identified as falling into one of two categories: tragedy or comedy. Broadly stated, the difference between the two is that comedies end happily, while tragedies end unhappily—often in the main character's disgrace or death.

Why would people write or watch tragedies? The ancient Greek philosopher Aristotle suggested in his theory of catharsis that tragedy purges or releases our emotions. Its events arouse pity for the victim, with whom we the audience identify. As the play closes we are washed clean of these emotions, feeling unburdened and morally improved.

A classical tragedy portrays a high-born or noble person who struggles and fails in a conflict with some superior force—whether it be fate, the gods, or his own "tragic flaw," a weakness in his own character. A domestic tragedy concerns the lives of ordinary people rather than heroic figures.

Comedies likewise take different forms. A romantic comedy is a love story that ends with the main characters, the lovers, united. The secondary characters are comic ones. Farce is comedy at its broadest, featuring boisterous fun and clever silliness. A comedy of manners is subtle, witty, and often mocking, poking fun at the flaws or insincere behaviour of a particular class or circle of people. Sentimental comedy mixes sappy or syrupy emotion with its humour. Melodrama has a plot filled with overblown emotion, extreme situations, and menacing threats by a villain, but it also includes comic relief and has a happy ending. It depends on physical action rather than on character development. Modern plays are not always easily labeled "comedy" or "tragedy," however. Many combine elements of both modes.

Both poetry and drama, as we have noted, were born of the oral tradition. In the earliest examples we know of as well as in the forms written in the 21st century, they represent the efforts of the human attempt to connect. People write poetry to make a connection, to say in a new way what all humans understand at some level. We read it to gain new insight into ourselves and the world in which we live. In a more public and discursive way, this same observation applies to drama.

What would we do without the word? Would we understand the relationship between the sadness of autumn leaves falling and the decline of a human life (as in Gerard Manley Hopkins, "Spring and Fall: To a Young Child")? Would we know that the comfort of friendship can help heal the pain of disappointment and the feeling of inadequacy (as in Shakespeare's Sonnet 29)?

Maybe it wouldn't make much difference. After all, our pets seem happy enough without words. Our dogs still manage to goof around with their canine friends (and sometimes with us). They get by. It's true that we don't know how different our lives would be without words, without an organizing principle. But there's no denying that our lives are richer with the stories of our families, our communities, and our multicultural world. Think about that when you're sitting around a holiday feast and the stories begin. Or when your friends start telling you about their latest exploits. Think about it.

CHAPTER 1

POETRY

Poetry is a genre of literature that evokes a concentrated imaginative awareness of experience or a specific emotional response through language chosen and arranged for its meaning, sound, and rhythm.

Poetry is a vast subject, as old as history and older, present wherever religion is present, and possibly—under some definitions—the primal and primary form of languages themselves. The present chapter means only to describe in as general a way as possible certain properties of poetry and poetic thought regarded as in some sense independent modes of the mind. Naturally, not every tradition nor every local or individual variation can be—or need be—included, but the chapter illustrates by examples of poetry ranging between nursery rhyme and epic. This chapter considers the difficulty or impossibility of defining poetry; our nevertheless familiar acquaintance with it; the differences between poetry and prose; the idea of form in poetry; poetry as a mode of thought; and what little may be said in prose of the spirit of poetry.

ATTEMPTS TO DEFINE POETRY

Poetry is the other way of using language. Perhaps in some hypothetical beginning of things it was the only way of using language or simply was language *tout court*, prose being the derivative and younger rival. Both poetry and language are

Poems hanging from an outdoor poetry line during the annual International Festival of Poetry in Trois-Rivières, Que., Can. Christiane St-Pierre, Festival International de la Poesie

fashionably thought to have belonged to ritual in early agricultural societies. And poetry in particular, it has been claimed, arose at first in the form of magical spells recited to ensure a good harvest. Whatever the truth of this hypothesis, it blurs a useful distinction: by the time there begins to be a separate class of objects called poems, recognizable as such, these objects are no longer much regarded for their possible yam-growing properties, and such magic as they may be thought capable of has retired to do its business upon the human spirit and not directly upon the natural world outside.

Formally, poetry is recognizable by its greater dependence on at least one more parameter, the *line*, than appears in prose composition. This changes its appearance on the page. And it seems clear that people take their cue from this changed appearance, reading poetry aloud in a very different voice from their habitual voice, possibly because, as Ben Jonson said, poetry "speaketh somewhat above a mortal mouth." If, as a test of this description, people are shown poems printed as prose, it most often turns out that they will read the result as prose simply because it looks that way; which is to say that they are no longer guided in their reading by the balance and shift of the line in relation to the breath as well as the syntax.

That is a minimal definition but perhaps not altogether uninformative. It may be all that ought to be attempted in the way of a definition: poetry is the way it is because it looks that way, and it looks that way because it sounds that way and vice versa.

POETRY AND PROSE

People's reason for wanting a definition is to take care of the borderline case, and this is what a definition, as if by definition, will not do. That is, if an individual asks for a definition of poetry, it will most certainly not be the case that he has never seen one of the objects called poems that are said to embody poetry. On the contrary, he is already tolerably certain what poetry in the main is, and his reason for wanting a definition is either that his certainty has been challenged by someone else or that he wants to take care of a possible or seeming exception to it: hence the perennial squabble about distinguishing poetry from prose, which is rather like distinguishing rain from snow—everyone is reasonably capable of doing so, and yet there are some weathers that are either-neither.

Sensible things have been said on the question. The American-English poet T.S. Eliot suggested that part of the difficulty lies in the fact that there is the technical term *verse* to go with the term *poetry*, while there is no equivalent technical term to distinguish the mechanical part of prose and make the relation symmetrical. The French poet Paul Valéry said that prose was walking, poetry dancing. Indeed, the original two terms, *prosus* and *versus*, meant, respectively, "going straight forth" and "returning." That distinction does point up the tendency of poetry to incremental repetition, variation, and the treatment of many matters and different themes in a single recurrent form such as couplet or stanza.

American poet Robert Frost shrewdly said that poetry was what got left behind in translation, which suggests a criterion of almost scientific refinement: when in doubt, translate; whatever comes through is prose, the remainder is poetry. And yet to even so acute a definition the obvious exception is startling and formidable: some of the greatest poetry in the world is in the Authorized or King James Version of the Bible, which is not only a translation but also, as to its appearance in print, identifiable neither with verse nor with prose in English but rather with a cadence owing something to both.

There may be a better way of putting the question by the simple test alluded to previously. When people are presented with a series of passages drawn indifferently from poems and stories but all printed as prose, they will show a dominant inclination to identify everything they possibly can as prose. This will be true, surprisingly enough, even if the poem rhymes and will often be true even if the poem in its original typographical arrangement would have been familiar to them. The reason seems to be absurdly plain: readers recognize poetry by its appearance on the page, and they respond to the convention whereby they recognize it by reading it aloud in a quite different tone of voice from that which they apply to prose (which, indeed, they scarcely read aloud at all). It should be added that they make this distinction also without reading aloud. Even in silence they confer upon a piece of poetry an attention that differs from what they give to prose in two ways especially: in tone and in pace.

Major Differences

In place of further worrying over definitions, it may be both a relief and an illumination to exhibit certain plain and mighty differences between prose and poetry by a comparison. In the following passages a prose writer and a poet are talking about the same subject, growing older.

> *Between the ages of 30 and 90, the weight of our muscles falls by 30 percent and the power we can exert likewise . . . . The number of nerve fibres in a nerve trunk falls by a quarter. The weight of our brains falls from an average of 3.03 lb. to 2.27 lb. as cells die and are not replaced . . . .* (Gordon Rattray Taylor, *The Biological Time Bomb*, 1968)

> *Let me disclose the gifts reserved for age*
> *To set a crown upon your lifetime's effort.*
> *First, the cold friction of expiring sense*

> *Without enchantment, offering no promise*
> *But bitter tastelessness of shadow fruit*
> *As body and soul begin to fall asunder.*
> *Second, the conscious impotence of rage*
> *At human folly, and the laceration*
> *Of laughter at what ceases to amuse.*
> *And last, the rending pain of*
>   *re-enactment*
> *Of all that you have done, and been . . . .*
>   (T.S. Eliot, *Four Quartets*)

Before objecting that a simple comparison cannot possibly cover all the possible ranges of poetry and prose compared, the reader should consider for a moment what differences are exhibited. The passages are oddly parallel, hence comparable, even in a formal sense. Both consist of the several items of a catalog under the general title of growing old. The significant differences are of tone, pace, and object of attention. If the prose passage interests itself in the neutral, material, measurable properties of the process, while the poetry interests itself in what the process will signify to someone going through it, that is not accidental but of the essence. If one reads the prose passage with an interest in being informed, noting the parallel constructions without being affected by them either in tone or in pace, while reading the poetry with a sense of considerable gravity and solemnity, that too is of the essence. One might say as tersely as possible that the difference between prose and poetry is most strikingly shown in the two uses of the verb "to fall":

*The number of nerve fibres in a
nerve trunk falls by a quarter*

*As body and soul begin to fall
asunder*

It should be specified here that the important differences exhibited by the comparison belong to the present age. In each period, speaking for poetry in English at any rate, the dividing line will be seen to come at a different place. In Elizabethan times the diction of prose was much closer to that of poetry than it later became, and in the 18th century authors saw nothing strange about writing in couplets about subjects that later would automatically and compulsorily belong to prose—for example, horticulture, botany, even dentistry. Here is not the place for entering into a discussion of so rich a chapter in the history of ideas. But the changes involved in the relation of poetry and prose are vast, and the number of ways people can describe and view the world are powerfully influenced by developments in science and society.

POETIC DICTION AND EXPERIENCE

Returning to the comparison, it is observable that though the diction of the poem is well within what could be commanded by a moderately well-educated speaker, it is at the same time well outside the range of terms in fact employed by such a speaker in daily occasions. It is a diction quite conscious, as it were, of its power of choosing terms with an effect of peculiar precision and of combining the terms into phrases with the same effect of peculiar precision and also of combining sounds with the same effect of peculiar precision. Doubtless the precision of the prose passage is greater in the more obvious property of dealing in the measurable. But the poet attempts a precision with respect to what is not in the same sense measurable nor even in the same sense accessible to observation. The distinction is perhaps just that made by the French scientist and philosopher Blaise Pascal in discriminating the spirits of geometry and finesse. And if one speaks of "effects of precision" rather than of precision itself, that serves to distinguish one's sense that the artwork is always somewhat removed from what people are pleased to call the real world, operating instead, in German philosopher Immanuel Kant's shrewd formula, by exhibiting "purposefulness without purpose." To much the same point is what English poet Samuel Taylor Coleridge remembers having learned from his schoolmaster:

*I learnt from him, that Poetry,
even that of the loftiest and, seemingly, that of the wildest odes, had
a logic of its own, as severe as
that of science; and more difficult,
because more subtle, more complex, and dependent on more, and
more fugitive causes. In the truly
great poets, he would say, there is
a reason assignable, not only for*

every word, but for the position of every word.

(*Biographia Literaria*, chapter 1)

Perhaps this is a somewhat exaggerated, as it is almost always an unprovable, claim, illustrating also a propensity for competing with the prestige of science on something like its own terms—but the last remark in particular illuminates the same author's terser formulation: "prose = words in the best order, poetry = the best words in the best order." This attempt at definition, impeccable

SAMUEL TAYLOR COLERIDGE

(b. Oct. 21, 1772, Ottery St. Mary, Devonshire, Eng.—d. July 25, 1834, Highgate, near London)

The English lyrical poet, critic, and philosopher Samuel Taylor Coleridge is known for two works in particular. His Lyrical Ballads *(1798), written with William Wordsworth, heralded the English Romantic movement, and his* Biographia Literaria *(1817) is the most significant work of general literary criticism produced in the English Romantic period.*

Coleridge studied at the University of Cambridge, where he became closely associated with the poet Robert Southey. In his poetry he perfected a sensuous lyricism that was echoed by many later poets. Among his best-known poems are the famous "Rime of the Ancient Mariner" and "Frost at Midnight," both of which are often anthologized. Other poems in the unusual style of the "Mariner" include the unfinished "Christabel" and the celebrated "Pleasure Dome of Kubla Khan." While in an unhappy marriage and addicted to opium, he produced "Dejection: An Ode" (1802), in which he laments the loss of his power to produce poetry. Later, partly restored by his revived Anglican faith, he produced the two-volume Biographia Literaria, *a rambling and discursive but highly stimulating and influential work in which he outlined the evolution of his thought and developed an extended critique of Wordsworth's poems. Coleridge was imaginative and complex, possessed of a unique intellect, and he led a restless life full of turmoil and unfulfilled possibilities.*

Samuel Taylor Coleridge, detail of an oil painting by Washington Allston, 1814; in the National Portrait Gallery, London. *Courtesy of The National Portrait Gallery, London*

because uninformative, was derived from Jonathan Swift, who had said, also impeccably and uninformatively, that style in writing was "the best words in the best order." This may be much to the same effect as jazz trumpeter and singer Louis Armstrong's saying, on being asked to define jazz, "Baby, if you got to ask the question, you're never going to know the answer;" or the French artist Marcel Duchamp's elegant remark on what psychologists call "the problem of perception:" "If no solution, then maybe no problem?" This species of gnomic, riddling remark may be determinate for the artistic attitude toward definition of every sort; and its skepticism is not confined to definitions of poetry but extends to definitions of anything whatever, directing one not to dictionaries but to experience and, above all, to use: "Anyone with a watch can tell you what time it is," said Valéry, "but who can tell you what is time?"

Happily, if poetry is almost impossible to define, it is extremely easy to recognize in experience. Even untutored children are rarely in doubt about it when it appears:

> Little Jack Jingle,
> He used to live single,
> But when he got tired of this kind of life,
> He left off being single, and liv'd with
>   his wife.

It might be objected that this little verse is not of sufficient import and weight to serve as an exemplar for poetry. It ought to be remembered, though, that it has given people pleasure so that they continued to say it until and after it was written down, nearly two centuries ago. The verse has survived, and its survival has something to do with pleasure, with delight. And while it still lives, how many more imposing works of language—epic poems, books of science, philosophy, theology—have gone down, deservedly or not, into dust and silence. It has, obviously, a form, an arrangement of sounds in relation to thoughts that somehow makes its agreeable nonsense closed, complete, and decisive. But this somewhat muddled matter of form deserves a heading and an instance all to itself.

FORM IN POETRY

People who speak of form in poetry almost always mean such externals as regular measure and rhyme, and most often they mean to get rid of these in favour of the freedom they suppose must follow upon the absence of form in this limited sense. But in fact a poem having only one form would be of doubtful interest even if it could exist. In this connection, the American poet J.V. Cunningham speaks of "a convergence of forms, and forms of disparate orders," adding: "It is the coincidence of forms that locks in the poem." For a poem is composed of internal and intellectual forms as well as forms externally imposed and preexisting any particular instance, and these may be sufficient without regular measure and rhyme. If the intellectual forms are absent, as in greeting-card verse and advertising jingles, no amount of thumping and banging will supply the want.

Form, in effect, is like the doughnut that may be said to be nothing in a circle of something or something around nothing. It is either the outside of an inside, as when people speak of "good form" or "bourgeois formalism," or the inside of an outside, as in the scholastic saying that "the soul is the form of the body." Taking this principle, together with what Cunningham says of the matter, one may now look at an extremely short and powerful poem with a view to distinguishing the forms, or schemes, of which it is made. It was written by Rudyard Kipling—a great English poet somewhat sunken in reputation, probably on account of misinterpretations having to do more with his imputed politics than with his poetry—and its subject, one of a series of epitaphs for the dead of World War I, is a soldier shot by his comrades for cowardice in battle.

> I could not look on Death, which being
> known,
> Men led me to him, blindfold and alone.

The aim of the following observations and reflections is to distinguish as clearly as possible—distinguish without dividing—the feelings evoked by the subject, so grim, horrifying, tending to helpless sorrow and despair, from the feelings, which might better be thought of as meanings, evoked by careful contemplation of the poem in its manifold and somewhat subtle ways of handling the subject, leading the reader on to a view of the strange delight intrinsic to art, whose mirroring and shielding power allows him to contemplate the world's horrible realities without being turned to stone.

There is, first, the obvious external form of a rhymed, closed couplet in iambic pentameter (that is, five poetic "feet," each consisting of an unstressed followed by a stressed syllable, per line). There is, second, the obvious external form of a single sentence balanced in four grammatical units with and in counterpoint with the metrical form. Third, there is the conventional form belonging to the epitaph and reflecting back to antiquity. It is terse enough to be cut in stone and tight-lipped also, perhaps for other reasons, such as the speaker's shame. There is, fourth, the fictional form belonging to the epitaph, according to which the dead man is supposed to be saying the words himself. Fifth, and especially poignant in this instance, there is the real form behind or within the fictional one, for the reader is aware that in reality it is not the dead man speaking, nor are his feelings the only ones the reader is receiving, but that the comrades who were forced to execute him may themselves have made up these two lines with their incalculably complex and exquisite balance of scorn, awe, guilt, and consideration even to tenderness for the dead soldier. There is, sixth, the metaphorical form, with its many resonances ranging from the tragic through the pathetic to irony and apology: dying in battle is spoken of in language relating it to a social occasion in drawing room or court. The coward's fear is implicitly represented as merely the timorousness and embarrassment one might feel about being introduced to a somewhat superior and majestic person, so that the soldiers responsible for killing him are seen as sympathetically helping him through a difficult moment in the realm of manners. In addition, there is, seventh, a linguistic or syntactical form, with at least a couple of tricks to it: the second clause, with its reminiscence of Latin construction, participates in the meaning by conferring a Roman stoicism and archaic gravity on the saying; remembering that the soldiers in the poem had been British schoolboys not long before, the reader might hear the remote resonance of a whole lost world built upon Greek and Roman models; and the last epithets, "blindfold and alone," while in the literal acceptation they clearly refer to the coward, show a distinct tendency to waver over and apply mysteriously to Death as well, sitting there waiting "blindfold and alone." One might add another form, the eighth, composed of the balance of sounds, from the obvious likeness in the rhyme down to subtleties and refinements beneath the ability of coarse analysis to discriminate. And even there one would not be quite at an end. An overall principle remains, the compression of what might have been epic or five-act tragedy into two lines, or the poet's precise election of a single instant to carry what the novelist—if he did his business properly—would have been hundreds of pages arriving at.

It is not at all to be inferred that the poet composed his poem in the manner of the above laborious analysis of its strands. The whole insistence, rather, is that he did not catalog 8 or 10 forms and assemble them into a poem. More likely it "just came to him." But the example may serve to indicate how many modes of the mind go together in this articulation of an implied drama and the tension among many possible sentiments that might arise in response to it.

In this way, by the coincidence of forms that locks in the poem, one may see how to answer a question that often arises about poems: though their thoughts are commonplace, they themselves mysteriously are not. One may answer on the basis of the example and the inferences produced from it that a poem is not so much a thought as it is a mind: talk with it, and it will talk back, telling you many things that you might have thought for yourself but somehow didn't until it brought them together. Doubtless a poem is a much simplified model for the mind. But it might still be one of the best models available. On this great theme, however, it will be best to proceed not by definition but by parable and interpretation.

POETRY AS A MODE OF THOUGHT: THE PROTEAN ENCOUNTER

In the fourth book of the *Odyssey* Homer tells the following strange tale. After the war at Troy, Menelaus wanted very much to get home but was held up in Egypt for want of a wind because, as he later told Telemachus, he had not sacrificed enough to the gods. "Ever jealous the Gods are," he said, "that we men mind their dues." But because the gods work both ways, it was on the advice of a goddess, Eidothea, that Menelaus went to consult Proteus, the old one of the sea, as one might consult a travel agency.

Proteus was not easy to consult. He was herding seals, and the seals stank in spite of the ambrosia Eidothea had provided. And when Menelaus crept up close, disguised as a seal, and grabbed him, Proteus turned into a lion, a dragon, a leopard, a boar, a film of water, and a high-branched tree. But Menelaus managed to hang on until Proteus gave up and was himself again; whereupon Menelaus asked him the one great question: How do I get home? And Proteus told him: You had better go back to Egypt and sacrifice to the gods some more.

This story may be taken as a parable about poetry. A man has an urgent question about his way in the world. He already knows the answer, but it fails to satisfy him. So at great inconvenience, hardship, and even peril, he consults a powerful and refractory spirit who tries to evade his question by turning into anything in the world. Then, when the spirit sees he cannot get free of the man, and only then, he answers the man's question, not simply with a commonplace but with the same commonplace the man had been dissatisfied with before. Satisfied or not, however, the man now obeys the advice given him.

A foolish story? All the same, it is to be observed that Menelaus did get home. And he was heroic to have hung onto Proteus through those terrifying changes and compelled him to be himself and answer up. Nor does it matter in the least to the story that Menelaus personally may have been a disagreeable old fool as well as a cuckold.

A poet also has one great and simple question, simple though it may take many forms indeed. The 14th-century English poet Geoffrey Chaucer, author of *Canterbury Tales*, put it as well as anyone could in a mere three lines:

> *What is this world? what asketh men*
> *to have?*
> *Now with his love, now in his colde grave,*
> *Allone, with-outen any companye.*
> ("The Knight's Tale")

And a poet gets the simple answer he might expect, the one the world grudgingly gives to anyone who asks such a question: the world is this way, not that way, and you ask for more than you will be given, which the poet, being scarcely more fool than his fellowmen, knew already. But on the path from question to answer, hanging onto the slippery disguiser and shape-shifter Proteus, he will see many marvels. He will follow the metamorphoses of things in the metamorphoses of their phrases. And he will be so elated and ecstatic in this realm of wonders that the voice in which he speaks these things, down even to the stupid, obvious, and commonplace answer, will be to his hearers a solace and a happiness in the midst of sorrows:

When I do count the clock that tells
    the time,
And see the brave day sunk in
    hideous night;
When I behold the violet past prime,
And sable curls, all silver'd o'er with white;
When lofty trees I see barren of leaves,
Which erst from heat did canopy the herd,
And summer's green all girded up in
    sheaves,
Borne on the bier with white and
    bristly beard,
Then of thy beauty do I question make,
That thou among the wastes of time
    must go,
Since sweets and beauties must them-
    selves forsake
And die as fast as they see others grow;
And nothing 'gainst Time's scythe can
    make defence
Save breed, to brave him when he takes
    thee hence.
            (Shakespeare, Sonnet 12)

Like Menelaus, the poet asks a simple question, to which, moreover, he already knows the unsatisfying answer. Question and answer, one might say, must be present, although of themselves they seem to do nothing much; but they assert the limits of a journey to be taken. They are the necessary but insufficient conditions of what really seems to matter here, the Protean encounter itself, the grasping and hanging on to the powerful and refractory spirit in its slippery transformations of a single force flowing through clock, day, violet, graying hair, trees dropping their leaves, the harvest in which, by a peculiarly ceremonial transmutation, the grain man lives by is seen without contradiction as the corpse he comes to. As for the answer to the question, it is not surprising nor meant to be surprising; it is only just.

On this point—that the answer comes as no surprise—poets show an agreement that quite transcends the differences of periods and schools. The English Augustan poet and satirist Alexander Pope's formula, "What oft was thought, but ne'er so well expresst," sometimes considered as the epitome of a shallow and parochial decorum, is not in essence other than this offered by English Romantic poet John Keats:

I think Poetry should surprise by a fine excess, and not by Singularity—it should strike the Reader as a wording of his own highest thoughts, and appear almost a Remembrance.
            (Letter to John Taylor, 1818)

In the 20th century, American poet Robert Frost was strikingly in agreement:

A word about recognition: In literature it is our business to give people the thing that will make them say, "Oh yes I know what you mean." It is never to tell them something they dont know, but something they know and hadnt thought of saying. It must be something they recognize.
        (Letter to John Bartlett, in *Modern Poetics*, ed. James Scully, 1965)

And the American poet and critic John Crowe Ransom gives the thought a cryptically and characteristically elegant variation: "Poetry is the kind of knowledge by which we must know that we have arranged that we shall not know otherwise." Perhaps this point about recognition might be carried further, to the extreme at which it would be seen to pose the problem of how poetry—which at its highest has always carried, at least implicitly, a kind of Platonism and claimed to give, if not knowledge itself, what was more important, a "form" to knowledge—can survive the triumph of scientific materialism and a positivism minded to skepticism about everything in the world except its own self (where it turns credulous, extremely). Over two or three centuries, the poet has had to adjust to a Newtonian cosmos, Kantian criticism, and the spectral universe portrayed by physics. This circumstance has led alternately or simultaneously to the extremes of rejection of reason and speaking in tongues on the one hand and the hysterical claim that poetry will save the world on the other. But of this let the Protean parable speak as it will.

There is another part to the story of Menelaus and Proteus, for Menelaus asked another question: What happened to my friends who were with me at Troy? Proteus replies, "Son of Atreus, why enquire too closely of me on this? To know or learn what I know about it is not your need: I warn you that when you hear all the truth your tears will not be far behind . . . ." But he tells him all the same: "Of those others many went under; many came through . . . ." And Menelaus does indeed respond with tears of despair, until Proteus advises him to stop crying and get started on the journey home. So it sometimes happens in poetry, too: the sorrowful contemplation of what is, consoles, in the end, and heals, but only after the contemplative process has been gone through and articulated in the detail of its change:

> When to the sessions of sweet silent
>   thought
> I summon up remembrance of things past,
> I sigh the lack of many a thing I sought,
> And with old woes new wail my dear
>   time's waste;
> Then can I drown an eye, unused to flow,
> For precious friends hid in death's date-
>   less night,
> And weep afresh love's long since
>   cancell'd woe,
> And moan the expense of many a
>   vanish'd sight.
> Then can I grieve at grievances foregone,
> And heavily from woe to woe tell o'er
> The sad account of fore-bemoaned moan,
> Which I new pay as if not paid before.
> But if the while I think on thee, dear friend,
> All losses are restor'd and sorrows end.
>
> (Shakespeare, Sonnet 30)

This poem, acknowledged to be a masterpiece by so many generations of readers, may stand as an epitome and emblem for the art altogether, about which it raises a question that must be put, although it cannot be satisfactorily and unequivocally answered: the question of whether poetry is a sacrament or a confidence game or both or neither. To reply firmly that poetry is not religion and must not promise what religion does is to preserve a useful distinction. Nevertheless, the religions of the world, if they have nothing else in common, seem to be based on collections of sacred poems. Nor, at the other extreme, can any guarantee that poetry is not a confidence game be found in the often-heard appeal to the poet's "sincerity." One will never know whether Shakespeare wept all over the page while writing the 30th sonnet, though one inclines to doubt it, nor would it be to his credit if he did, nor to the reader's that he should know it or care to know it.

For one thing, the sonnet is obviously artful—that is, full of artifice—and even the artifice degenerates here and there into being artsy. "Then can I drown an eye, unused to flow." Surely that is poesy itself, at or near its worst, where the literal and the conventional, whatever their relations may have been for Shakespeare and the first reader of these sugar'd sonnets among his friends, now live rather uncomfortably together (English Stuart dramatist Ben Jonson's "Drink to me only with thine eyes" is a similar example of this bathetic crossing of levels), though perhaps it has merely become unattractive as a result of changing fashions in diction.

Moreover, while the whole poem is uniquely Shakespearean, the bits and pieces are many of them common property of the age, what one writer called "joint stock company poetry." And the tricks are terribly visible, too. Art is not used to conceal art in such goings-on as "grieve at grievances" and "fore-bemoaned moan." "He who thus grieves will excite no sympathy," as the great English critic Samuel Johnson sternly wrote of John Milton's style in the elegy "Lycidas," "he who thus praises will confer no honour."

Nor is that the worst of it. This man who so powerfully works on the reader's sympathies by lamenting what is past contrives to do so by thinking obsessively about litigation and, of all things, money; his hand is ever at his wallet, bidding adieu. He cannot merely "think" sweet silent thoughts about the past. No, he must turn them into a court in "session," whereto he "summons" the probable culprit "remembrance." When he "grieves," it is at a "grievance"—in the hands of the law again. Finally, as with the sinners in Dante's *Divine Comedy*, his avarice and prodigality occupy two halves of the one circle: he bemoans his expenses while paying double the asking price.

And still, for all that, the poem remains beautiful. It continues to move both the young who come to it still innocent of their dear time's waste and the old who have sorrows to match its sorrows. As between confidence game and sacrament there may be no need to decide, as well as no possibility of deciding: elements of play and artifice, elements of true feeling, elements of convention both in the writing and in one's response to it, all combine to veil the answer. But the poem remains.

If it could be plainly demonstrated by the partisans either of unaided reason or revealed religion that poetry was metaphorical, mythological, and a delusion, while science, say, or religion or politics were real and true, then one might throw poetry away and live honestly though poorly on what was left. But, for better or worse, that is not the condition of human life in the world. And perhaps people care for poetry so much—if they care at all—because, at last, it is the only one of many mythologies to be aware, and to make us aware, that it, and the others, are indeed mythological. The English literary critic I.A. Richards, in a deep and searching consideration of this matter, concludes: "It is the privilege of poetry to preserve us from mistaking our notions either for things or for ourselves. Poetry is the completest mode of utterance."

The last thing Proteus says to Menelaus is strange indeed:

You are not to die in Argos of the fair horse-pastures, not there to encounter death: rather will the Deathless Ones carry you to the Elysian plain, the place beyond the world . . . . There you will have Helen to yourself and will be deemed of the household of Zeus.

So the greatest of our poets have said—or not so much said, perhaps, as indicated by their fables—though nowadays people mostly sing a different tune. To be as the gods, to be rejoined with the beloved, the world forgotten . . . . Sacrament or con game? Homer, of course, is only telling an old story and promises humankind

nothing; that is left to the priests to do. And in that respect poetry, as one critic puts it, must always be "a ship that is wrecked on entering the harbor." And yet the greatest poetry sings always, at the end, of transcendence. While seeing clearly and saying plainly the wickedness and terror and beauty of the world, it is at the same time humming to itself, so that one overhears rather than hears: All will be well.

POETRY: TERMS AND CONCEPTS

Multiple styles and types of poetry are discussed in classrooms and living quarters. Some are limited to particular periods or regions of the world, while others straddle the centuries and continents. The following selection of terms offers a sampling of types and clarifies details of origins and development of specific styles.

ABSTRACT POEM

The English poet Edith Sitwell coined the term *abstract poem* to describe a poem in which the words are chosen for how they sound rather than for their sense or meaning. An example from "Popular Song" in Sitwell's *Façade* (1923) follows:

*The red retriever-haired satyr
Can whine and tease her and flatter,
But Lily O'Grady,
Silly and shady,
In the deep shade is a lazy lady;
Now Pompey's dead, Homer's read,*

ROBERT FROST

(b. March 26, 1874, San Francisco, Calif., U.S.—
d. Jan. 29, 1963, Boston, Mass.)

Robert Frost, 1954. Ruohomaa/Black Star

The American poet Robert Frost was much admired for his depictions of the rural life of New England, his command of American colloquial speech, and his realistic verse portraying ordinary people in everyday situations.

Frost's family moved to New England early in his life. After stints at Dartmouth College and Harvard University and a difficult period as a teacher and farmer, he moved to England and published his first collections, A Boy's Will *(1913) and* North of Boston *(1914). At the outbreak of war he returned to New England. He closely observed rural life and in his poetry endowed it with universal, even metaphysical, meaning, using colloquial language, familiar rhythms, and common symbols to express both its pastoral ideals and its dark complexities. His collections include* New Hampshire *(1923, Pulitzer Prize),* Collected Poems *(1930, Pulitzer Prize),* A Further Range *(1936, Pulitzer Prize), and* A Witness Tree *(1942, Pulitzer Prize). He was unique among American poets of the 20th century in simultaneously achieving wide popularity and deep critical admiration. Many of his poems, including "Stopping by Woods on a Snowy Evening," "Birches," "The Death of the Hired Man," "Dust of Snow," "Fire and Ice," and "Home Burial," continued to be published in anthologies and learned by heart in the 21st century.*

Heliogabalus lost his head,
And shade is on the brightest wing,
And dust forbids the bird to sing.

ALLITERATIVE VERSE

Alliterative verse is a significant early type of poetry prevalent in the Germanic languages in which alliteration—the repetition of consonant sounds at the beginning of words or stressed syllables—is a basic structural principle rather than an occasional embellishment. Although alliteration is a common device in almost all poetry, the only Indo-European languages that used it (along with strict rules of accent and quantity—the relative duration of speech sounds) as a governing principle are Old Norse, Old English, Old Saxon, Old Low German, and Old

High German. The Germanic alliterative line consists of two hemistichs (half lines) separated by a caesura (pause). There are one or two alliterating letters in the first half line preceding the medial caesura; these also alliterate with the first stressed syllable in the second half line. Alliteration falls on accented syllables; unaccented syllables are ineffective, even if they begin with the alliterating letter.

The introduction of rhyme, derived from medieval Latin hymns, contributed to the decline of alliterative verse. In Low German, pure alliterative verse is not known to have survived after 900. And by that time, in Old High German, rhymed verse already replacing it. In England, alliteration as a strict structural principle is not found after 1066 (the date of the Norman-French conquest of Britain), except in the western part of the country. Although alliteration was still extremely important, the alliterative line became freer: the second half line often contained more than one alliterating word, and other formalistic restrictions were gradually disregarded. The early 13th-century poetry of Lawamon and later poems such as *Piers Plowman, Sir Gawayne and the Grene Knight,* and *The Pearl* use end rhyme extensively. Sometimes all the verses rhyme, and sometimes the succession of alliterative verses is broken by rhymed verses grouped at roughly regular intervals. The last alliterative poem in English is usually held to be "Scottish Fielde," which deals with the Battle of Flodden (1513).

Later Norse poets (after 900) also combined many forms of rhyme and assonance with alliteration in a variety of stanzaic forms. After 1000, Old Norse alliterative verse became practically confined to the Icelanders, among whom it continues to exist.

In Celtic poetry, alliteration was from the earliest times an important, but subordinate, principle. In Welsh poetry it gave rise to the *cynghanedd,* an intricate bardic verse.

Alphabet Rhyme

Mnemonic verses or songs used to help children learn an alphabet are known as alphabet rhymes. Such devices appear in almost every alphabetic language. Some early English favourites are about three hundred years old and have served as models for countless variations. One is a cumulative rhyme to which there is a printed reference as early as 1671. It often appeared in 18th-century chapbooks under the imposing name *The Tragical Death of A, Apple Pye Who was Cut in Pieces and Eat by Twenty-Five Gentlemen with whom All Little People Ought to be Very well acquainted.* It begins:

> *A was an apple-pie;*
> *B bit it,*
> *C cut it,*
> *D dealt it, etc.*

Another, known as "Tom Thumb's Alphabet," enjoyed continuous popularity. The earliest printed record of it is from *c.* 1712. In its most familiar version, the rhyme begins:

A was an archer, who shot at a frog.
B was a butcher, and had a great dog.

These early rhymes showed little discrimination in subject matter. Lines such as "D was a drunkard, and had a red face," "U was a Usurer took Ten *per* Cent," or "Y was a youth, that did not love school" were later considered to have a harmful effect on children. They were replaced by the widely taught alphabet rhyme of the *New-England Primer*, published by the English bookseller and writer Benjamin Harris in the late 17th century. This volume combined moral messages with the learning of letters:

In Adam's fall
We sinned all.

A simplified version of English alphabet rhyme, still popular, is sung to the tune of "Twinkle, Twinkle, Little Star."

A B C D E F G
H I J K L M N O P
Q and R and S and T
U V W X Y Z
Now I've said my ABC's,
Tell me what you think of me.

BARD

A poet, especially one who writes impassioned, lyrical, or epic verse, may also be called a bard. Bards were originally Celtic composers of eulogy and satire.

The word came to mean more generally a tribal poet-singer gifted in composing and reciting verses on heroes and their deeds. As early as the 1st century CE, the Latin author Lucan referred to bards as the national poets or minstrels of Gaul and Britain. In Gaul the institution gradually disappeared, whereas in Ireland and Wales it survived. Through chanting, the Irish bard preserved a tradition of poetic eulogy. In Wales, where the word *bardd* has always been used for poet, the bardic order was codified into distinct grades in the 10th century. Despite a decline of the order toward the end of the European Middle Ages, the Welsh tradition has persisted and is celebrated in the annual eisteddfod, a national assembly of poets and musicians.

BLANK VERSE

Blank verse is unrhymed iambic pentameter, and it is the preeminent dramatic and narrative verse form in English and also the standard form for dramatic verse in Italian and German. Its richness and versatility depend on the skill of the poet in varying the stresses and the position of the caesura (pause) in each line, in catching the shifting tonal qualities and emotional overtones of the language, and in arranging lines into thought groups and paragraphs.

Adapted from unrhymed Greek and Latin heroic verse, blank verse was introduced in 16th-century Italy along with other classical metres. The Italian humanist Francesco Maria Molza attempted the writing of consecutive unrhymed verse in 1514 in his translation of Virgil's *Aeneid*. Other experiments in 16th-century Italy were the tragedy *Sofonisba* (written 1514–15) by Gian Giorgio Trissino, and the didactic poem *Le api* (1539) by Giovanni Rucellai. The latter poet was the first to use the term *versi sciolti*, which was translated into English as "blank verse." It soon became the standard metre of Italian Renaissance drama, used in such major works as the comedies of Ludovico Ariosto, *L'Aminta* of Torquato Tasso, and the *Il pastor fido* of Battista Guarini.

Henry Howard, earl of Surrey, introduced the metre, along with the sonnet and other Italian humanist verse forms, to England in the early 16th century. Thomas Sackville and Thomas Norton used blank verse for the first English tragic drama, *Gorboduc* (first performed 1561), and Christopher Marlowe developed its musical qualities and emotional power in *Tamburlaine, Doctor Faustus,* and *Edward II*. William Shakespeare transformed the line and the instrument of blank verse into the vehicle for the greatest English dramatic poetry. In his early plays, he combined it with prose and a 10-syllable rhymed couplet. Later he employed a blank verse dependent on stress rather than on syllabic length. Shakespeare's poetic expression in his later plays, such as *Hamlet, King Lear, Othello, Macbeth,* and *The Winter's Tale,* is supple, approximating the rhythms of speech, yet capable of conveying the subtlest human delight, grief, or perplexity.

After a period of debasement, blank verse was restored to its former grandeur by John Milton in *Paradise Lost* (1667). Milton's verse is intellectually complex, yet flexible, using inversions, Latinized words, and all manner of stress, line length, variation of pause, and paragraphing to gain descriptive and dramatic effect. In the 18th century, James Thomson used blank verse in his long descriptive poem *The Seasons,* and Edward Young's *Night Thoughts* uses it with power and passion. Later, William Wordsworth wrote his autobiography of the poetic spirit, *The Prelude* (completed 1805–06; published 1850), in blank verse; Percy Bysshe Shelley used it in his drama *The Cenci* (1819), as did John Keats in *Hyperion* (1820). The extreme flexibility of blank verse can be seen in its range from the high tragedy of Shakespeare to the low-keyed, conversational tone of Robert Frost in *A Masque of Reason* (1945).

Blank verse was established in German drama by Gotthold Lessing's *Nathan der Weise* (1779). Examples of its use are found in the writings of Johann Wolfgang von Goethe, Friedrich Schiller, and Gerhart Hauptmann. It was also used extensively in Swedish, Russian, and Polish dramatic verse.

BOUTS-RIMÉS

Rhymed words or syllables to which verses are written are bouts-rimés (French: "rhymed ends"). They are best known from a literary game of making verses from a list of rhyming words supplied by another person. The game, which requires that the rhymes follow a given order and that the result make a modicum of sense, is said to have been invented by the minor French poet Dulot in the early 17th century. Its wide popularity inspired at least one notable tour de force, an extended satirical poem by the French poet Jean-François Sarasin, entitled *Dulot vaincu* (1654; "Dulot Defeated"). The fad was revived in the 19th century when Alexandre Dumas *père* invited French poets and versifiers to try their skill with given sets of rhymes and published the results in 1865.

In 19th-century England, John Keats is said to have produced his charming poem "On the Grasshopper and Cricket" (1816) in a bouts-rimés competition with his friend the essayist and editor Leigh Hunt. Dante Gabriel Rossetti (1828–82) and his brother William tested their ingenuity and improved their rhyming facility by filling in verses from bouts-rimés. Most of William's poems in the Pre-Raphaelite magazine *The Germ* were bouts-rimés experiments.

Breton Lay

A poetic form, the Breton lay (Middle English: Lai Breton) was so called because Breton professional storytellers supposedly recited similar poems, though none are extant. A short, rhymed romance recounting a love story, it includes supernatural elements, mythology transformed by medieval chivalry, and the Celtic idea of faerie, the land of enchantment. Derived from the late 12th-century French lais of Marie de France, it was adapted into English in the late 13th century and became very popular. The few existing English Breton lays include *Sir Gowther* (c. 1400), a version of the story of Robert the Devil; the incomplete, early 14th-century *Lai le Freine; Sir Orfeo,* a recasting of the Orpheus and Eurydice story; the 14th-century *Sir Launfal,* or *Launfalus Miles,* an Arthurian romance by Thomas Chestre; *Sir Emare,* of the late 14th or early 15th century, on the theme of the constant wife; and the 15th-century *Sir Landeval,* a variant of *Sir Launfal.* Some of Chaucer's *Canterbury Tales* are derived from Breton lays.

Canto

A major division of an epic or other long narrative poem is known as a canto. An Italian term, derived from the Latin *cantus* ("song"), it probably originally indicated a portion of a poem that could be sung or chanted by a minstrel at one sitting. Though early oral epics, such as Homer's, are divided into discrete sections, the name canto was first adopted for these divisions by the Italian poets Dante, Matteo Boiardo, and Ludovico Ariosto. The first long English poem to be divided into cantos was Edmund Spenser's *The Faerie Queene* (1590–1609). Lord Byron structured his long poems *Childe Harold's Pilgrimage* (1812) and *Don Juan*

(1819–24) in cantos. An ambitious, unfinished epic by the American poet Ezra Pound is known simply as *The Cantos*.

CI

The *ci* (also spelled *tz'u*) is a Chinese song form characterized by lines of unequal length with prescribed rhyme schemes and tonal patterns, each bearing the name of a musical air. The varying line lengths are comparable to the natural rhythm of speech and therefore are easily understood when sung. First sung by ordinary people, they were popularized by professional women singers and attracted the attention of poets during the Tang dynasty (618–907). It was not, however, until the transitional period of the Five Dynasties (907–960), a time of division and strife, that *ci* became a major vehicle for lyrical expression. Of *ci* poets in this period, the greatest was Li Yu, last monarch of the Nan Tang (Southern Tang) dynasty. The *ci* served as the predominant form for verse of the Song dynasty (960–1279).

CLERIHEW

One of the more risible forms of light verse, the clerihew is a quatrain (consisting of four lines) having lines usually of varying length, rhyming *aabb*, and usually dealing with a person named in the initial rhyme.

This type of comic biographical verse form was invented by Edmund Clerihew Bentley, who introduced it in *Biography for Beginners* (1905) and continued it in *More Biography* (1929) and *Baseless Biography* (1939). The humour of the form lies in its purposefully flat-footed inadequacy: in addition to clumsy rhythm and rhyme, the verse's treatment of the subject is either off the mark or totally beside the point, as though it were the work of a reluctant schoolchild. Clerihews are written as four-line verses of two rhyming couplets, the first line almost invariably ending with the name of the subject:

> *After dinner, Erasmus*
> *Told Colet not to be "blas'mous"*
> *Which Colet, with some heat*
> *Requested him to repeat.*

The number of accents in the line is irregular, and one line is usually extended to tease the ear. Another requisite of the successful clerihew is an awkward rhyme, as in Bentley's "Aeschylus":

> *"Steady the Greeks!" shouted Aeschylus.*
> *"We won't let such dogs as these kill us!"*
> *Nothing, he thought, could be bizarrer than*
> *The Persians winning at Marathon.*

Another example is Bentley's "Cervantes":

> *The people of Spain think Cervantes*
> *Equal to half-a-dozen Dantes:*
> *An opinion resented most bitterly*
> *By the people of Italy.*

Some of the funniest of clerihews were written by Sir Francis Meynell, W.H. Auden, and Clifton Fadiman.

Illustration by G.K. Chesterton for the clerihew "Cervantes" by Edmund Clerihew Bentley.

CONCRETE POETRY

When a poet's intent is conveyed by graphic patterns of letters, words, or symbols rather than by the meaning of words in conventional arrangement, the resultant poem is considered concrete poetry. The writer of concrete poetry uses typeface and other typographical elements in such a way that chosen units—letter fragments, punctuation marks, graphemes (letters), morphemes (any meaningful linguistic unit), syllables, or words (usually used in a graphic rather than denotative sense)—and graphic spaces form an evocative picture.

The origins of concrete poetry are roughly contemporary with those of *musique concrète*, an experimental technique of musical composition. The Swiss graphic artist Max Bill and Swiss-Bolivian poet Eugen Gomringer were among the early practitioners of concrete poetry. The Vienna Group of Hans Carl Artmann, Gerhard Rühm, and Konrad Bayer also promoted concrete poetry, as did Austrian writers Ernst Jandl and Friederike Mayröcker. The movement drew inspiration from Dada, Surrealism, and other nonrational 20th-century movements. Concrete poetry has an extreme visual bias and in this way is usually distinguished from pattern poetry. It attempts to move away from a purely verbal concept of verse toward what its proponents call "verbivocovisual expression," incorporating geometric and graphic elements into the poetic act or process. It often cannot be read aloud

to any effect, and its essence lies in its appearance on the page, not in the words or typographic units that form it. At the turn of the 21st century, concrete poetry was produced in many countries. Among the most notable concrete poets of the time were the Brazilian brothers Haroldo de Campos and Augusto de Campos. Many contemporary examples of animated concrete poetry can be found on the Internet.

COUPLET

Couplets consist of a pair of end-rhymed lines of verse that are self-contained in grammatical structure and meaning. A couplet may be formal (or closed), in which case each of the two lines is end-stopped, or it may be run-on (or open), with the meaning of the first line continuing to the second (this is called enjambment). Couplets are most frequently used as units of composition in long poems, but, because they lend themselves to pithy, epigrammatic statements, they are often composed as independent poems or function as parts of other verse forms, such as the Shakespearean sonnet, which is concluded with a couplet. In French narrative and dramatic poetry, the rhyming alexandrine (12-syllable line) is the dominant couplet form, and German and Dutch verse of the 17th and 18th centuries reflects the influence of the alexandrine couplet. The term *couplet* is also commonly substituted for *stanza* in French versification. A "square" couplet, for example, is a stanza of eight lines, with each line composed of eight syllables. The preeminent English couplet is the heroic couplet, or two rhyming lines of iambic pentameter with a caesura (pause), usually medial, in each line. Introduced by Chaucer in the 14th century, the heroic couplet was perfected by John Dryden and Alexander Pope in the late 17th and early 18th centuries. An example is

Then share thy pain, allow that sad relief;
Ah, more than share it, give me all thy grief.
　(Alexander Pope, "Eloisa to Abelard")

Couplets were also frequently introduced into the blank verse of Elizabethan and Jacobean drama for heightened dramatic emphasis at the conclusion of a long speech or in running dialogue, as in the following example:

Think what you will, we seize into
　　our hands
His plate, his goods, his money, and
　　his lands.
　　　(William Shakespeare, *Richard II*)

CYWYDD

The *cywydd* (plural *cywyddau*) is a Welsh verse form, a kind of short ode in rhyming couplets in which one rhyme is accented and the other unaccented. Each line is composed of seven syllables and contains some form of *cynghanedd* (a complex system of alliteration and internal rhyme). Developed in the 14th century in south Wales by Dafydd ap Gwilym, the *cywydd* shows affinities with forms used by the earlier *bardd teulu* ("bard of the [king's] war band"), the second grade in the Welsh bardic system, and with those of the French trouvères and jongleurs. It was the leading Welsh verse form from the 14th to the early 17th century. The golden age of the *cywydd* was from the mid-14th to the mid-15th century, and its silver age, when excessive concern with stylistic rules hampered free poetic expression, from about 1500 to 1650. It was revived, with other bardic forms, by the classical school of Welsh poets in the mid-18th century, and again in the 19th century. It remains in use by those modern Welsh poets who prefer strict (i.e., classical) forms to the free metres that are derived from Welsh folk song and from English verse.

DITHYRAMB

A choral song in honour of the wine god Dionysus is called a dithyramb. The form was known as early as the 7th century BCE in Greece, where an improvised lyric was sung by banqueters under the leadership of a man who, according to the poet Archilochus, was "wit-stricken by the thunderbolt of wine." It was contrasted with the more sober paean, sung in honour of Apollo. The word's etymology is uncertain, although, like other words that end in *amb*, it seems to be of pre-Hellenic origin.

　The dithyramb began to achieve literary distinction about 600 BCE, when, according to the Greek historian

Herodotus, the poet Arion composed works of this type, named the genre, and formally presented them at Corinth. In the last decades of the 6th century BCE in Athens, during the tyranny of Peisistratus, a dithyrambic competition was officially introduced into the Great Dionysia by the poet Lasus of Hermione. Dithyrambs were also performed at other festivals. The performance of dithyrambs was grandiose and spectacular: after a prologue spoken by the group's leader, two choruses in expensive apparel—one of 50 men and the other of 50 boys—sang and performed circle dances around the altar of Dionysus. *Auloi* (a pair of single- or double-reed pipes with three or four finger holes) provided the instrumental accompaniment.

The great age of the dithyramb was also the period of the flourishing of the Greek choral lyric in general. Simonides, Pindar, and Bacchylides all composed them. Little is known of the dithyrambs of Simonides, whom a Hellenistic epigram credited with 56 victories, but papyrus discoveries have supplied two complete dithyrambs of Bacchylides along with considerable fragments of Pindar's work. Bacchylides' ode 18 is unusual because it includes a dialogue between a chorus and a soloist. At one time scholars associated the dramatic and mimetic structure of this ode with Aristotle's famous assertion in *Poetics* that tragedy originated from improvisation by the leaders of the dithyramb. However, many contemporary scholars see the poem's use of dialogue for dramatic interest as a sign of the dithyramb's surrender to the more vivid methods of tragedy.

From about 450 BCE onward, dithyrambic poets such as Timotheus, Melanippides, Cinesias, and Philoxenus employed ever more startling devices of language and music until for ancient literary critics *dithyrambic* acquired the connotations of "turgid" and "bombastic." True dithyrambs are rare in modern poetry, although John Dryden's "Alexander's Feast" (1697) may be said to bear a coincidental resemblance to the form. The poets of the French Pléiade (16th century CE) used the term to describe some of their poetry, as did the Italian physician and poet Francesco Redi for his "Bacco in Toscana" (1685; "Bacchus [Dionysus] in Tuscany").

The term may also refer to any poem in an inspired irregular strain, or to a statement or piece of writing in an exalted impassioned style, usually in praise of a particular subject. Modern examples include Friedrich Nietzsche's *Dithyrambs of Dionysus* (1891) and Gabriele d'Annunzio's "Alcyone" (1904).

DOGGEREL

A verse form that is low, or trivial, loosely constructed and often irregular, but effective because of its simple mnemonic rhyme and loping metre is called doggerel. It appears in most literatures and societies as a useful form for comedy and satire. It is characteristic of children's game rhymes from ancient times to the present and of most nursery rhymes.

One of the earliest uses of the word is found in the 14th century in the works of Geoffrey Chaucer, who applied the term *rym doggerel* to his "Tale of Sir Thopas," a burlesque of the long-winded medieval romance.

John Skelton, caught in the transition between Chaucer's medieval language and the beginning of the English Renaissance, wrote verse long considered to be almost doggerel. He defended himself in *Colin Clout:*

For though my rhyme be ragged,
Tattered and jagged,
Rudely rain-beaten,
Rusty and moth-eaten,
If ye take well therewith,
It hath in it some pith.

Since then, doggerel has been employed in most English comic verse, from that of Samuel Butler and Jonathan Swift to the American poet Ogden Nash.

The German version, called *Knüttelvers* (literally "cudgel verse"), was popular during the Renaissance and was later used for comic effect by such poets as Goethe and Friedrich Schiller. Doggerel verse is still commonly heard in limericks and nonsense verse, popular songs, and commercial jingles.

DRAMATIC MONOLOGUE

A poem written in the form of a speech of an individual character, the dramatic monologue compresses into a single vivid scene a narrative sense of the speaker's history and psychological insight into his character. Though the form is chiefly associated with Robert Browning, who raised it to a highly sophisticated level in such poems as "My Last Duchess," "The Bishop Orders His Tomb at St. Praxed's Church," "Fra Lippo Lippi," and "Andrea del Sarto," it is actually much older. Many Old English poems are dramatic monologues—for instance, "The Wanderer" and "The Seafarer." The form is also common in folk ballads, a tradition that Robert Burns imitated with broad satiric effect in "Holy Willie's Prayer." Browning's contribution to the form is one of subtlety of characterization and complexity of the dramatic situation, which the reader gradually pieces together from the casual remarks or digressions of the speaker. The subject discussed is usually far less interesting than what is inadvertently revealed about the speaker himself. The aristocratic speaker in "My Last Duchess," while showing off a painted portrait of his late wife, reveals his cruelty to her. The form parallels the novelistic experiments with point of view in which the reader is left to assess the intelligence and reliability of the narrator. Later poets who successfully used the form were Ezra Pound ("The River Merchant's Wife: A Letter"), T.S. Eliot ("Love Song of J. Alfred Prufrock"), and Robert Frost ("The Pauper Witch of Grafton").

ECLOGUE

An eclogue is a short pastoral poem, usually in dialogue, on the subject of rural life and the society of shepherds, depicting rural life as free from the complexity and corruption of more civilized life. The eclogue first appeared in the *Idylls* of the Greek poet Theocritus (*c.* 300–*c.* 260 BCE), generally recognized as the inventor of pastoral poetry. The Roman poet Virgil (70–19 BCE) adopted the form for his 10 *Eclogues,* or *Bucolics.*

The eclogue, along with other pastoral forms, was revived during the Renaissance by the Italians Dante, Petrarch, Boccaccio, and Battista Spagnoli (Mantuanas), whose neo-Latin *Eclogues* (1498) were read and imitated for more than a century.

Edmund Spenser's series of 12 eclogues, *The Shepheardes Calender* (1579), is considered the first outstanding pastoral poem in English. By the 17th century less formal eclogues were written by such poets as Richard Lovelace, Robert Herrick, and Andrew Marvell. Marvell's "Nymph Complaining for the Death of her Fawn" (1681) climaxed the eclogue tradition of combining rural freshness with learned imitation. In the 18th century English poets began to use the eclogue for ironic verse on nonpastoral subjects, such as Jonathan Swift's "A Town Eclogue. 1710. Scene, The Royal Exchange."

The poets of the Romantic period rebelled against the artificiality of the older pastoral, and the eclogue fell from favour. The form has occasionally been revived for special purposes by modern poets, as in Louis MacNeice's ironic eclogues in his *Collected Poems, 1925–1948* (1949).

ELEGY

A meditative lyric poem lamenting the death of a public personage or a friend or loved one is an elegy. By extension, the term can be applied to any reflective lyric on the broader theme of human mortality. In classical literature an elegy was simply any poem written in the elegiac metre (alternating lines of dactylic hexameter and pentameter) and was not restricted as to subject. Though some classical elegies were laments, many others were love poems. In some modern literatures, such as German, in which the classical elegiac metre has been adapted to the language, the term *elegy* refers to this metre, rather than to the poem's content. Thus, Rainer Maria Rilke's famous *Duino Elegies* (1912–22) are not laments; they deal with the poet's search for spiritual values in an alien universe. But in English literature since the 16th century, an elegy has come to mean a poem of lamentation. It may be written in any metre the poet chooses.

A distinct kind of elegy is the pastoral elegy, which borrows the classical convention of representing its subject as an idealized shepherd in an idealized pastoral background and follows a rather formal pattern. It begins with an expression of grief and an invocation to the Muse to aid the poet in expressing his suffering. It usually contains a funeral procession, a description of sympathetic mourning throughout nature, and musings on the unkindness of death. It ends with acceptance, often a very affirmative justification, of nature's law. The outstanding example of the English pastoral elegy is John Milton's "Lycidas" (1638), written on the death of Edward King, a college friend. Other notable pastoral elegies are Percy Bysshe Shelley's "Adonais" (1821), on the death of the poet John Keats, and Matthew Arnold's "Thyrsis" (1867), on the death of the poet Arthur Hugh Clough.

Other elegies observe no set patterns or conventions. In the 18th century the English graveyard school of poets wrote generalized reflections on death and immortality, combining gloomy, sometimes ghoulish imagery of human impermanence with philosophical speculation.

Representative works are Edward Young's *Night Thoughts* (1742–45) and Robert Blair's *Grave* (1743), but the best known of these poems is Thomas Gray's more tastefully subdued creation "An Elegy Written in a Country Church Yard" (1751), which pays tribute to the generations of humble and unknown villagers buried in a church cemetery. In the United States, a counterpart to the graveyard mode is found in William Cullen Bryant's "Thanatopsis" (1817). A wholly new treatment of the conventional pathetic fallacy of attributing grief to nature is achieved in Walt Whitman's "When Lilacs Last in the Dooryard Bloom'd" (1865–66).

In modern poetry the elegy remains a frequent and important poetic statement. Its range and variation can be seen in such poems as A.E. Housman's "To an Athlete Dying Young" (1896), W.H. Auden's "In Memory of W.B. Yeats" (1939), E.E. Cummings's "my father moved through dooms of love" (1940), John Peale Bishop's "Hours" (1940; on F. Scott Fitzgerald), and Robert Lowell's "The Quaker Graveyard in Nantucket" (1947).

ENVELOPE

In poetry, an envelope is a device in which a line or a stanza is repeated so as to enclose a section of verse, as in Sir Thomas Wyatt's "Is it Possible?":

Is it possible
That so high debate,
So sharp, so sore, and of such rate,
Should end so soon and was begun so late?
Is it possible?

EPIGRAM

Originally an epigram was an inscription suitable for carving on a monument, but for centuries the term has been applied to any brief and pithy verse, particularly if astringent and purporting to point a moral. By extension the term is also applied to any striking sentence in a novel, play, poem, or conversation that appears to express a succinct truth, usually in the form of a generalization. Catullus (*c.* 84–*c.* 54 BCE) originated the Latin epigram, and it was given final form by Martial (40–103 CE) in some 1,500 pungent and often indecent verses that served as models for French and English epigrammatists of the 17th and 18th centuries.

The epigram was revived by Renaissance scholars and poets, such as the French poet Clément Marot, who wrote epigrams in both Latin and the vernacular. In England the form took shape somewhat later, notably in the hands of Ben Jonson and his followers, among whom was Robert Herrick, writer of such graceful examples as the following:

> *I saw a Flie within a Beade*
> *Of Amber cleanly buried:*
> *The Urne was little, but the room*
> *More rich than Cleopatra's Tombe.*

As the century progressed, the epigram became more astringent and closer to Martial in both England and France. The *Maximes* (1665) of François VI, Duke de La Rochefoucauld marked one of the high points of the epigram in French, influencing such later practitioners as Voltaire. In England, John Dryden, Alexander Pope, and Jonathan Swift produced some of the most memorable epigrams of their time.

Samuel Taylor Coleridge, writing at the beginning of the 19th century, produced an epigram that neatly sums up the form:

> *What is an Epigram? A dwarfish*
> *whole,*
> *Its body brevity, and wit its soul.*

The *Sinngedicht*, or sententious epigram, engaged German taste in the 18th and early 19th centuries, culminating in Goethe's *Zahme Xenien* (1820; "Gentle Epigrams"). Among the later masters of the English epigram were Oscar Wilde and George Bernard Shaw. Wilde became famous for such remarks as "A cynic is a man who knows the price of everything and the value of nothing." Shaw, in his *Annajanska* (1919), commented that "All great truths begin as blasphemies."

EPINICION

An epinicion, or epinician, is a lyric ode honouring a victor in one of the great Hellenic games. The epinicion was performed usually by a chorus, or on occasion by a solo singer, as part of the celebration on the victor's triumphal return to his city. A less elaborate form was offered on the site of his triumph immediately after his victory. The word derives from the Greek adjective meaning "for a victory," and *melos* (song) is understood as the modified noun.

Although the epinicion originated in improvised celebration, the form of surviving works is highly literary. Twentieth-century papyrus finds identified the 6th-century-BCE poet Ibycus as the earliest known author of epinicia. The first datable example is an ode composed in 520 BCE by Simonides of Ceos for the victory of Glaucus of Carystus in the boxing match for youths at Olympia. The genre's structure was not rigidly fixed, but there was a typical uniformity in content and arrangement. The occasion demanded the mention of the victor, as well as the nature and place of his victory. References to victories by members of his family and compliments to his trainer could be added. Generally a more or less relevant myth would be narrated. Finally, a gnomic element of wise sayings and reflections on life served as a bridge between the myth and the description of events surrounding the victory.

The poets did not use traditional lines or stanzas for epinicia. Instead, the metre was formed afresh for each poem and was never used again in exactly the same form. The strophes, or stanzas—either single or in systems of three—were repeated throughout the poem, and often their form was related to the accompanying dance. The performance of epinicia called for a choir trained by a teacher of song and dance (*chorodidaskalos*), and the singers were accompanied by skilled musicians playing lyres. If the poet sent the poem to the victor, then the text would function as a kind of score that contained indications of rhythm and musical modes, with perhaps some hints for appropriate dance steps.

The genre reached its zenith in the odes of Pindar and his contemporary Bacchylides in the 5th century BCE. The epinicion flourished when the Greek world considered athletic competition to be one of the most significant events of social, political, and religious life. Greek aristocrats and rulers saw in the epinicion, as in the figurative arts, an irreplaceable means of persuasion in the service of their personal prestige and political power. Poets began to work freelance, receiving from patrons a conspicuous honorarium. Disputes over fees were sometimes public, as was documented by celebrated cases. For example, Simonides of Ceos agreed to compose a victory ode for Anaxilas, tyrant of Rhegium, for his victory in the mule-drawn-chariot race at the Olympian games only after Anaxilas agreed to pay Simonides more than he had originally offered. The poet could retaliate with ridicule if his terms were not met.

EPITHALAMIUM

A song or poem to the bride and bridegroom at their wedding is called an epithalamium (also epithalmion, or epithalamy). In ancient Greece, the singing of such songs was a traditional way of invoking good fortune on the marriage and often of indulging in ribaldry. By derivation, the epithalamium should be sung at the marriage chamber, but the word is also used for the song sung during the wedding procession, containing repeated invocations to Hymen (Hymenaeus), the Greek god of marriage. No special metre has been associated with the epithalamium either in antiquity or in modern times.

The earliest evidence for literary epithalamiums are the fragments from Sappho's seventh book (*c.* 600 BCE). The earliest surviving Latin epithalamiums are three by Catullus (*c.* 84–*c.* 54 BCE). In the most original, Catullus tried to fuse the native Fescennine verse (a jocular, often obscene form of sung dialogue sometimes used at wedding feasts) with the Greek form of marriage song.

Epithalamiums based on classical models were written during the Renaissance by Torquato Tasso in Italy and Pierre de Ronsard in France. Among English poets of the same period, Richard Crashaw, John Donne, Sir Philip Sidney, and Ben Jonson used the form. Edmund Spenser's *Epithalamion,* written for his second marriage in 1595, is considered by some critics to be the finest example of the form in English.

Anonymous 17th-century epithalamiums are extant. In the 19th century, epithalamiums were written by Gerard Manley Hopkins and Edmund Gosse; and in the 20th century, by Witter Bynner, A.E. Housman, and Dannie Abse.

FABLIAU

The fabliau (plural fabliaux) is a short metrical tale and was made popular in medieval France by the jongleurs, or professional storytellers. Fabliaux were characterized by vivid detail and realistic observation and were usually comic, coarse, and often cynical, especially in their treatment of women.

About 150 fabliaux are extant. Many of them are based on elementary jokes or puns—such as one called *Estula,* which can either be a person's name or mean "Are you there?"—or on wry situations, such as one tale in which a man is rescued from drowning but has his eye put out by the boat hook that saves him.

The majority of fabliaux are erotic, and the merriment provoked often depends on situations and adventures that are sometimes obscene. Recurring characters include the cuckold and his wife, the lover, and the naughty priest. The theme of guile is often treated, frequently to show the deceiver deceived.

It was once widely held that fabliaux represented the literature of the bourgeois and common people. This, however, is unlikely, since they contain a substantial element of burlesque (or mockery and parody) that depends, for its appreciation, on considerable knowledge of courtly society, love, and manners. They also presuppose something like scorn for those of humble rank who ape their betters.

Some of the subject matter in the fabliaux can be paralleled in other times and other countries: many of the plots stem from folklore, some have classical affinities, and a few can be traced to Asian sources. But many of the tales are so simple that they could have arisen spontaneously. The earliest fabliau, *Richeut,* dates from approximately 1175, but the main period of fabliau composition was the 13th century, with an extension into the first half of the 14th. Most fabliaux are two hundred to four hundred lines in length, though there are extremes of fewer than 20 lines and of more than 1,300. Their authors included amateur writers (notably Philippe de Beaumanoir) and professionals (e.g., Jehan Bodel and Rutebeuf). Verse tales analogous to the fabliaux exist in other languages. Geoffrey

Chaucer's "Reeve's Tale," for example, is based on a known fabliau, and several of the other comic tales in *The Canterbury Tales* may trace their origins to fabliaux.

FESCENNINE VERSE

Early native Italian jocular dialogue in Latin verse are known as Fescennine verses. At vintage and harvest, and probably at other rustic festivals, these were sung by masked dancers. They were similar to ribald wedding songs and to the obscene *carmina triumphalia* sung to victorious generals during their triumph, or victory parade. It is clear from the literary imitations by Catullus, that they were very free, even obscene, in language. Horace states that they became so abusive that a law that forbade a *malum carmen* ("evil song"—i.e., charm intended to hurt) was invoked against them.

It was believed that the verses averted the evil eye. For that reason, some ancient scholarship connected the name with *fascinum* (an emblem of a phallus that was worn to drive away evil spirits). Linguists reject this interpretation. The true derivation, which is also ancient, may be from Fescennia, an Etruscan city. In their origin they may have had a magico-religious intent—abuse, buffoonery, and obscenity being well-known fertility or luck charms. Whether they developed into the dramatic *satura* (medley, or hodgepodge) that was the forerunner of Roman drama, as Horace suggests, has been debated by some scholars.

FLYTING

The poetic competition of the Scottish *makaris* (poets) of the 15th and 16th centuries is known as a flyting, which in Scots means "quarreling," or "contention." The flyting has two highly skilled rivals engaging in a contest of verbal abuse, remarkable for its fierceness and extravagance. Although contestants attacked each other spiritedly, they actually had a professional respect for their rival's vocabulary of invective. The tradition seems to have derived from the Gaelic *filid* (a class of professional poets), who composed savage tirades against persons who slighted them. A Scandinavian counterpart is the *Lokasenna* ("Flyting of Loki"), a poem in the *Poetic (Elder) Edda* in which the trickster-god Loki bandies words with the other gods, taunting them with coarse jests. Although true flyting became obsolete in Scottish literature after the Middle Ages, the tradition itself never died out among writers of Celtic background. The style and language of Robert Burns's "To a Louse" ("Ye ugly, creepin, blastit wonner / Detested, shunn'd by saunt an' sinner") parodies earlier Scots flyting, and James Joyce's poem "The Holy Office" is a bard's curse on the society that spurns him.

Examples of true flyting are *The Flyting of Dunbar and Kennedie* (a contest between the poets William Dunbar and Walter Kennedy) and *Flyting betwixt Montgomerie and Polwart* (involving the poets Alexander Montgomerie and Sir Patrick Hume of Polwarth).

FOUND POEM

A poem consisting of words found in a nonpoetic context (such as a product label) and usually broken into lines that convey a verse rhythm is known as a found poem. Both the term and the concept are modeled on the *objet trouvé* (French: "found object"), an artifact not created as art or a natural object that is held to have aesthetic value when taken out of its context.

FREE VERSE

The term *free verse* refers to poetry organized to the cadences of speech and image patterns rather than according to a regular metrical scheme. It is "free" only in a relative sense. It does not have the steady, abstract rhythm of traditional poetry. Its rhythms are based on patterned elements such as sounds, words, phrases, sentences, and paragraphs, rather than on the traditional prosodic units of metrical feet per line. Free verse, therefore, eliminates much of the artificiality and some of the aesthetic distance of poetic expression and substitutes a flexible formal organization suited to the modern idiom and more casual tonality of the language.

Although the term is loosely applied to the poetry of Walt Whitman and even earlier experiments with irregular metres, it was originally a literal translation of vers libre, the name of a movement that originated in France in the 1880s. Free verse became current in English poetics in the early 20th century. The first English-language poets to be influenced by vers libre, notably T.E. Hulme, F.S. Flint, Richard Aldington, Ezra Pound, and T.S. Eliot, were students of French poetry. The Imagist movement, started

AMY LOWELL

(b. Feb. 9, 1874, Brookline, Mass., U.S.— d. May 12, 1925, Brookline)

American critic and lecturer Amy Lowell was a leading poet of the Imagist school. Born into the prominent Lowell family of Boston, she devoted herself to poetry at age 28 but published nothing until 1910. Her first volume, A Dome of Many-Coloured Glass, *was published in 1912. On a visit to England in 1913 Lowell met Ezra Pound and discovered his circle, the Imagists. He included one of her poems in his anthology* Des Imagistes *(1914), and in that year she published her second book,* Sword Blades and Poppy Seed *(1914), which included her first poems in free verse and what she called "polyphonic prose." She became a leader of Imagism and was noted for her vivid and powerful personality and her scorn of conventional behaviour. Lowell edited the three numbers of* Some Imagist Poets *(1915–17). Subsequent volumes of her own work include* Men, Women, and Ghosts *(1916), which contains her well-known poem "Patterns;"* Can Grande's Castle *(1918); and* Legends *(1921). The volumes* What's O'Clock *(1925),* East Wind *(1926), and* Ballads for Sale *(1927) were published posthumously. Her critical works include* Six French Poets *(1915),* Tendencies in Modern American Poetry *(1917), and the two-volume biography of* John Keats *(1925).*

in England in 1912 by Aldington, Pound, Flint, and Hilda Doolittle ("H.D."), was concerned with more than versification, but one of its principles was "to compose in sequence of the musical phrase, not in sequence of the metronome." Almost from the beginning, the free-verse movement split into two groups, one led by Amy Lowell and a more formal one led by Pound. Eliot's early experimentations with free verse influenced the loosening of formal metrical structures in English-language poetry. Carl Sandburg, William Carlos Williams, Marianne Moore, and Wallace Stevens all wrote some variety of free verse. The versification of Williams and Moore most closely resembles that of the vers libre poets of France.

Fu

The *fu* is a Chinese literary form combining elements of poetry and prose. The form developed during the Han dynasty (206 BCE–220 CE) from its origins in the long poem *Lisao* ("On Encountering Sorrow") by Qu Yuan (*c.* 339–*c.* 278 BCE). The *fu* was particularly suitable for description and exposition, in contrast to the more subjective, lyrical *sao*. Its prosody was freer than that of the *sao*, the rhyme pattern being less restrictive. The elements of the *fu* form include a long line, caesura, and the use of balanced parallel phrases. The use of rhyme places it somewhere between poetry and prose.

While some Han writers used the form quite skillfully, it was often abused for purposes of trivial and hackneyed description and was generally characterized by an endless piling up of words. Hundreds of years later, during the Song dynasty (960–1279), the *fu* was enriched by the skill of Ouyang Xiu and Su Dongpo, who used it to express philosophical concerns.

GEORGIAN POETRY

The variety of lyrical poetry produced in the early 20th century by an assortment of British poets was named Georgian poetry. These poets included Lascelles Abercrombie, Hilaire Belloc, Edmund Charles Blunden, Rupert Brooke, William Henry Davies, Ralph Hodgson, John Drinkwater, James Elroy Flecker, Wilfred Wilson Gibson, Robert Graves, Walter de la Mare, Harold Monro (editor of *The Poetry Review*), Siegfried Sassoon, Sir J.C. Squire, and Edward Thomas.

Brooke and Sir Edward Marsh, wishing to make new poetry accessible to a wider public, with Monro, Drinkwater, and Gibson, planned a series of anthologies. To this series they applied the name "Georgian" to suggest the opening of a new poetic age with the accession in 1910 of George V. Five volumes of *Georgian Poetry*, edited by Marsh, were published between 1912 and 1922.

The real gifts of Brooke, Davies, de la Mare, Blunden, and Hodgson should not be overlooked, but, taken as a whole, much of the Georgians' work was lifeless. It took inspiration from the countryside and nature, and in the hands of less gifted poets, the resulting poetry was diluted and middlebrow conventional verse of late Romantic character. "Georgian" came to be a pejorative term, used in a sense not intended by its progenitors: rooted in its period and looking backward rather than forward.

GHAZAL

In Islamic literature, the ghazal (also spelled ghazel, gasal, or gazel) is a genre of lyric poem, generally short and graceful in form and typically dealing with themes of love. As a genre the ghazal developed in Arabia in the late 7th century from the *nasib*, which itself was the often amorous prelude to the qasida (ode). Two main types of ghazal can be identified, one native to Hejaz (Arabia), the other to Iraq.

The ghazals by 'Umar ibn Abī Rabī'ah of the Quraysh tribe of Mecca are some of

ḤĀFEẒ

(b. 1325/26, Shīrāz, Iran—d. 1389/90, Shīrāz)

Born Muḥammad Shams al-Dīn Ḥāfiẓ, the poet known simply as Ḥāfeẓ (or Ḥāfiẓ) is one of the finest lyric poets of Persia. Ḥāfeẓ received a classical religious education, lectured on Qur'ānic and other theological subjects ("Ḥāfeẓ" designates one who has learned the Qur'ān by heart), and wrote commentaries on religious classics. As a court poet, he enjoyed the patronage of several rulers of Shīrāz.

About 1368–69 Ḥāfeẓ fell out of favour at the court and did not regain his position until 20 years later, just before his death. In his poetry there are many echoes of historical events as well as biographical descriptions and details of life in Shīrāz. One of the guiding principles of his life was Sufism, the Islamic mystical movement that demanded of its adherents complete devotion to the pursuit of union with the ultimate reality.

Ḥāfeẓ's principal verse form, one that he brought to a perfection never achieved before or since, was the ghazal, a lyric poem of 6 to 15 couplets linked by unity of subject and symbolism rather than by a logical sequence of ideas. Traditionally the ghazal had dealt with love and wine, motifs that, in their association with ecstasy and freedom from restraint, lent themselves naturally to the expression of Sufi ideas. Ḥāfeẓ's achievement was to give these conventional subjects a freshness and subtlety that completely relieves his poetry of tedious formalism.

The extraordinary popularity of Ḥāfeẓ's poetry in all Persian-speaking lands stems from his simple and often colloquial though musical language, free from artificial virtuosity, and his unaffected use of homely images and proverbial expressions. Above all, his poetry is characterized by love of humanity, contempt for hypocrisy and mediocrity, and an ability to universalize everyday experience and to relate it to the mystic's unending search for union with God. His appeal in the West is indicated by the numerous translations of his poems. Ḥāfeẓ is most famous for his Dīvān; among the many partial English translations of this work are those by Gertrude Bell and H. Wilberforce Clarke.

the oldest. Umar's poems, based largely on his own life and experiences, are realistic, lively, and urbane in character. They continue to be popular with modern readers.

What became a classic theme of the ghazal was introduced by Jamīl, a member of the 'Udhrah tribe from Hejaz. Jamīl's lyrics tell of hopeless, idealistic lovers pining for each other unto death. These enormously popular works were imitated not only in Arabic but also in Persian, Turkish, and Urdu poetry until the 18th century.

Of additional note is the work of Ḥāfeẓ, considered among the finest lyric poets of Persia, whose depth of imagery and multilayered metaphors revitalized the ghazal and perfected it as a poetic form.

GNOMIC POETRY

The Greek word *gnomē* means "moral aphorism" or "proverb," and it is the origin of gnomic poetry, aphoristic verse containing short, memorable statements of traditional wisdom and morality. The aphorism may be either imperative, as in the famous command "know thyself," or indicative, as in the English adage "Too many cooks spoil the broth." Gnomes are found in the literature of many cultures. Among the best known examples are those contained in the biblical book of Proverbs. They are found in early Greek literature, both poetry and prose, from the time of Homer and Hesiod onward. Gnomic poetry is most commonly associated with the 6th-century-BCE poets Solon and Simonides and with the elegiac couplets of Theognis and Phocylides. Their aphorisms were collected into anthologies, called *gnomologia,* and used in instructing the young. One of the best known *gnomologia* was compiled by Stobaeus in the 5th century CE, and such collections remained popular in the Middle Ages.

Gnomes appear frequently in Old English epic and lyric poetry. In *Beowulf* they are often interjected into the narrative, drawing a moral from the hero's actions with such phrases as "Thus a man ought to act." The main collections of Old English gnomes are to be found in the Exeter Book and the 11th-century Cotton Psalter.

Alexander Pope's *Essay on Man* (1733–34) offers a more modern example of the use of couplets of distilled wisdom interspersed through a long poem.

HAIKU

The unrhymed Japanese poetic form consisting of 17 syllables arranged in three lines of 5, 7, and 5 syllables, respectively, is known as haiku. The term *haiku* is derived from the first element of the word *haikai* (a humorous form of *renga,* or linked-verse poem) and the second element of the word *hokku* (the initial stanza of a *renga*). The *hokku,* which set the tone of a *renga,* had to mention in its three lines such subjects as the season, time of day, and the dominant features of the landscape, making it almost an independent poem. The *hokku* (often interchangeably called *haikai*) became known as the haiku late in the 19th century, when it was entirely divested of its original function of opening a sequence of verse. Today even the earlier *hokku* are usually called haiku.

Originally, the haiku form was restricted in subject matter to an objective description of nature suggestive of

BASHŌ

(b. 1644, Ueno, Iga province, Japan—d. Nov. 28, 1694, Ōsaka)

Bashō, also called Matsuo Bashō, was the greatest practitioner of haiku. Born Matsuo Munefusa, he was interested in haiku from an early age. In 1666, after the death of the feudal lord whose service he had entered, Bashō gave up his samurai status to devote himself to poetry. Moving to the capital city of Edo (now Tokyo), he gradually acquired a reputation as a poet and critic. In 1679 he wrote his first verse in the "new style" for which he came to be known:

> *On a withered branch*
> *A crow has alighted:*
> *Nightfall in autumn.*

The simple descriptive mood evoked by this statement and the comparison and contrast of two independent phenomena became the hallmark of Bashō's style. Following the Zen philosophy he studied, he attempted to compress the meaning of the world into the simple pattern of his poetry, disclosing hidden hopes in small things and showing the interdependence of all objects.

In 1684 Bashō made the first of many journeys that figure so importantly in his work. His accounts of his travels are prized not only for the haiku that record various sights along the way but also for the equally beautiful prose passages that furnish the backgrounds. Oku no hoso-michi (1694; The Narrow Road to the Deep North), describing his visit to northern Japan, is one of the loveliest works of Japanese literature.

A term frequently used to describe Bashō's poetry is sabi, *which means the love of the old, the faded, and the unobtrusive, a quality found in the following verse:*

> *Scent of chrysanthemums . . .*
> *And in Nara*
> *All the ancient Buddhas.*

Here the musty smell of the chrysanthemums blends with the visual image of the dusty, flaking statues in the old capital. Living a life that was in true accord with the gentle spirit of his poetry, Bashō maintained an austere, simple hermitage that contrasted with the general flamboyance of his times. On occasion he withdrew from society altogether, retiring to Fukagawa, site of his Bashō-an ("Cottage of the Plantain Tree"), a simple hut from which the poet derived his pen name.

one of the seasons, evoking a definite, though unstated, emotional response. The form gained distinction in the 17th century, during the Tokugawa period, when the great master Bashō elevated the *hokku*, as it was then known, to a highly refined and conscious art. Haiku has since remained the most popular form in Japanese poetry. Later its subject range was broadened, but it remained an art of expressing much and suggesting more in the fewest possible words. Other outstanding haiku masters were Buson in the 18th century, Issa in the late 18th and early 19th centuries, Masaoka Shiki in the later 19th century, and Takahama Kyoshi and Kawahigashi Hekigotō in the late 19th and early 20th centuries. At the turn of the 21st century there were said to be a million Japanese who composed haiku under the guidance of a teacher.

A poem written in the haiku form or a modification of it in a language other than Japanese is also called a haiku. In English, the haiku composed by the Imagists were especially influential during the early 20th century. The form's popularity beyond Japan expanded significantly after World War II, and today haiku are written in a wide range of languages.

HALF RHYME

The device called half rhyme, near rhyme, slant rhyme, or oblique rhyme uses two words that have only their final consonant sounds and no preceding vowel or consonant sounds in common (such as *stopped* and *wept,* or *parable* and *shell*). Half rhyme was common in Welsh, Irish, and Icelandic verse years before it was introduced to English verse by the Anglo-Welsh poet and mystic Henry Vaughan. It was not used regularly in English until English poet and Jesuit priest Gerard Manley Hopkins and Irish poet and dramatist William Butler Yeats began to do so.

HEROIC POETRY

Heroic poetry is narrative verse that is elevated in mood and uses a dignified, dramatic, and formal style to describe the deeds of aristocratic warriors and rulers. It is usually composed without the aid of writing and is chanted or recited to the accompaniment of a stringed instrument. It is transmitted orally from bard to bard over generations.

The extant body of heroic poetry ranges from quite ancient to modern works, produced over a widespread geographic area. It includes what are probably the earliest forms of this verse—panegyrics praising a hero's lineage and deeds, and laments on a hero's death. Homer relates that when Hector's body was brought home "they laid it upon the bed and seated minstrels round it to lead the dirge." Another type of heroic poem is the short, dramatic lay devoted to a single event, such as the Old English "Battle of Maldon" (c. 991), describing a Viking raid on Essex, or the Old High German *Hildebrandslied* (c.

800), dealing with a duel between father and son. The mature form of heroic poetry is the full-scale epic, such as the *Iliad* or *Odyssey*.

Most heroic poetry looks back to a dimly defined "heroic age" when a generation of superior beings performed extraordinary feats of skill and courage. The heroic age varies in different native literatures. The epics of Homer created in the 8th century BCE centre on a war with Troy that may have occurred about 1200 BCE. The heroic poetry of the German, Scandinavian, and English peoples deals chiefly with a period from the 4th to the 6th century CE, the time of the great migrations (*Völkerwanderung*) of the Germanic people. Though some of the heroes portrayed are historical personages, their actions are often combined and related for artistic purposes, with no regard for actual historical chronology.

Nevertheless, a heroic tale is assumed by the poet and his listeners to be somehow true. Its style is impersonal and objective, and the graphic realism of its detail gives it an air of probability that outweighs the occasional intrusion of marvelous elements. None of the mundane details of the hero's acts and none of the amenities connected with them are slighted. The listener is told how the hero looks, what he wears, what he eats, and how he sleeps. Thus, Homer's careful description of how Achilles dresses for battle, how he dons each piece of armour, how he mounts his chariot and addresses his horses, has a verisimilitude that remains undestroyed when his horse converses with him.

Much ancient heroic poetry has been wholly lost, but the tradition is still alive among certain illiterate and semiliterate peoples living in remote communities. In the late 19th and 20th centuries, a wealth of new heroic literature was collected from native storytellers in the Balkans, Russia, Estonia, and Greece. In Central Asia heroic poems have been collected from Tatar peoples speaking Turkish dialects, and some particularly fine examples come from the Kyrgyz of the Tien Shan. The Sakha of northern Siberia, the Ainu of northern Japan, and some tribes of Arabia have also composed heroic poetry in modern times.

Research by modern scholars among these people has resolved any doubt that long epics could be composed orally and has shed light on the methods of oral composition that must have been used by ancient poets such as Homer. Knowing the essentials of a number of traditional stories, and armed with a stock of ready-made formulaic expressions to describe common occurrences such as meetings, partings, passages of time, and victories or defeats, the oral bard improvises a tale. The bard, whose art is a skillful blend of familiar scenes with new incident and detail, does not memorize the tale and usually cannot repeat exactly the same version again. In 1934 the American Homeric scholar Milman Parry transcribed an epic poem of 12,000 lines (the length of the *Odyssey*) from an illiterate bard in southern Serbia. Equally astonishing feats of memory and improvisation were reported by Russian scholars working among Uzbek and Kyrgyz bards.

HORATIAN ODE

Any short lyric poem written in stanzas of two or four lines in the manner of the 1st-century-BCE Latin poet Horace is considered to be a Horatian ode. In contrast to the lofty, heroic odes of the Greek poet Pindar, most of Horace's odes are intimate and reflective. They are often addressed to a friend and deal with friendship, love, and the practice of poetry.

Horace introduced early Greek lyrics into Latin by adapting Greek metres, regularizing them, and writing his Romanized versions with a discipline that caused some loss of spontaneity and a sense of detachment but produced elegance and dignity. But he cautioned Latin writers not to attempt to emulate Pindar, a task that he likened to Icarus' presumptuous flight. Horace's carmina, written in stanzas of two or four lines, are now universally called odes, but they have nothing in common with the passionate brilliance of Pindaric odes. Horace's tone is generally serious and serene, often touched with irony and melancholy but sometimes with gentle humour. His urbane Epicureanism and personal charm, his aphoristic philosophy and studied perfection won him recognition as Rome's leading poet after the death of his friend Virgil.

In later periods when technical felicity was more highly regarded than imagination and spontaneity, Horace's odes were prized and imitated. Among the poets of the Pléiade in 16th-century France, Pierre de Ronsard attempted to model his first odes on Pindar. Defeated, he contented himself with being, in his opinion, better than Horace. Nicolas Boileau and Jean de La Fontaine in the 17th century preserved the Horatian tradition.

Michael Drayton, in *Poems Lyric and Pastoral* (1606), acknowledged his indebtedness to Horace, and Andrew Marvell produced one of the finest English Horatian odes in 1650 on Cromwell's return from Ireland. In the early 18th century, Matthew Prior, Jonathan Swift, and Samuel Johnson revived the Horatian spirit, as did Giacomo Leopardi and Giosuè Carducci in Italy in the 19th century. Since the odes of the Romantic period, which were successful imitations of the manner but not the form of Pindar, few English poets have attempted to return to the classical forms.

IDYLL

The idyll (or idyl; from Greek *eidyllion*, "little picture") is a short poem of a pastoral or rural character in which something of the element of landscape is depicted or suggested. The term was used in Greco-Roman antiquity to designate a variety of brief poems on simple subjects in which the description of natural objects was introduced. The conventions of the pastoral were developed by the

Alexandrian school of poetry, particularly by Theocritus, Bion, and Moschus, in the 3rd century BCE, and the *Idylls* of Theocritus are the source of the popular idea of this type of poem.

The word was revived during the Renaissance, when some poets employed it to distinguish narrative pastorals from those in dialogue. The general use, or misuse, of the word arose in the 19th century from the popularity of two works, the *Idylles héroïques* (1858) of Victor-Richard de Laprade and the *Idylls of the King* (1859) of Alfred, Lord Tennyson, neither of which was related to the pastoral tradition. Thereafter the word was used indiscriminately to refer to works on a variety of subjects.

Although it is impossible to define the idyll as a definite literary form, the adjective *idyllic* has come to be synonymous with the rustic, pastoral, and tranquil, the mood first created by the Alexandrian poets.

JAZZ POETRY

Any poetry that is read to the accompaniment of jazz music is called jazz poetry. Authors of such poetry attempt to emulate the rhythms and freedom of the music in their poetry. Forerunners of the style included the works of Vachel Lindsay, who read his poetry in a syncopated and rhythmic style for audiences, and Langston Hughes, who collaborated with musicians. Later poets known for their interest in combining the two forms included Kenneth Patchen, Kenneth

Rexroth, Amiri Baraka, and Christopher Logue, as well as many of the poets of the Beat movement.

JUEJU

A Chinese verse form that was popular during the Tang dynasty (618–907), the *jueju* (also spelled *chüeh-chü*) was an outgrowth of a form called *lüshi*, which consists of eight lines of five or seven syllables. The *jueju* (meaning "severed sentence") is a four-line poem, each line of which consists of five or seven words. It omits either the first four lines, the last four lines, the first two and the last two lines, or the middle four lines of the *lüshi*. Thus, it retains the tonal quality of the *lüshi*, but the antithetical structure typical of the *lüshi* is optional. Much like the Persian *robāʻī* and the Japanese haiku, *jueju* are judged by their suggestiveness and economy.

LAUDA

The *lauda* (*laude*; plural *laude* or *laudi*) is a type of Italian poetry or a nonliturgical devotional song in praise of the Virgin Mary, Christ, or the saints. The poetic *lauda* was of liturgical origin, and it was popular from about the mid-13th to the 16th century in Italy, where it was used particularly in confraternal groups and for religious celebrations. The first *lauda* in Italian was St. Francis's moving canticle in praise of "Sir Brother Sun," "Sister Moon," "Brother Wind," "Sister Water," "Brother Fire," and

"Mother Earth"—a work that has been called *Laudes creaturarum o Cantico del Sole* ("Praises of God's Creatures or the Canticle of the Sun"). Another outstanding early master of the *lauda* was the gifted 13th-century Franciscan poet Jacopone da Todi, who wrote many highly emotional and mystical *laudi spirituali* ("spiritual canticles") in the vernacular. Jacopone is also the reputed author of a famous Latin *lauda,* the *Stabat mater dolorosa,* which, with another 13th-century *lauda* in Latin, the *Dies irae,* has been part of Roman Catholic liturgy for centuries.

Laude were frequently written in ballata form for recitation by religious confraternities, their content usually consisting of exhortations to a moral life or of events in the lives of Christ and the saints. These recitations evolved into dialogues and eventually became part of the Italian version of the miracle play, the *sacra rappresentazione,* a form of religiously inspired drama, which became secularized during the Renaissance. Later in the Renaissance some *laude* were written for musical settings.

Laude songs were first associated with the early Franciscan friars (early 13th century). Later, to encourage devotional singing, confraternities (Laudisti) were founded in Florence and the rest of northern Italy.

Although there were many writers of *lauda* poetry, the composers were often unknown. *Laude* were simple and popular in style. Their musical form depended on that of the period, and at times folk melodies were used to set *lauda* texts. The earliest *laude,* from the 13th century, were monophonic (single-line) compositions. By the 16th century the *laude* appear in polyphonic (several-voice) settings, usually in chordal style. Collections of *laude* from the secular Congregazione dell'Oratorio, founded by St. Philip Neri (d. 1595), are extant, because the singing of *laude* formed an essential part of their meetings. The 16th-century *lauda* was important as a step in the development of the oratorio. The *lauda* remained important in Italian devotional life until the 19th century.

LIGHT VERSE

Poetry on trivial or playful themes that is written primarily to amuse and entertain and that often involves the use of nonsense and wordplay is categorized under the general term *light verse.* Frequently distinguished by considerable technical competence, wit, sophistication, and elegance, light poetry constitutes a considerable body of verse in all Western languages. The term is general and can be applied to nonsense verse, limerick, clerihew, epigram, and mock-epic.

The Greeks were among the first to practice light verse, examples of which may be found in The Greek Anthology, which includes work composed between the 7th century BCE and the early 11th century CE. Such Roman poets as Catullus, singing of his love's sparrow, and Horace, inviting friends to share his wine, set patterns in light poetry that were followed to the end of the 19th century.

Medieval light verse, mainly narrative in form, was often satirical, bawdy, and irreverent but nonetheless sensible and essentially moral, as can be seen in the 12th-century Latin songs of the goliards, the often indecent French fabliaux, and mock-epics, such as the *Roman de Renart*.

French light poetry of the 14th and 15th centuries was written largely in ballades and rondeaux, challenging such poets as Clément Marot and Pierre de Ronsard to great displays of virtuosity. A vein of light melancholy runs through the witty verse of many English Renaissance poets, from Sir Thomas Wyatt to Richard Lovelace. The more cheerful poetry of Ben Jonson and Robert Herrick sometimes celebrated food and simple pleasures.

Late 17th-century examples of light verse include Samuel Butler's *Hudibras* (1663), which satirized the English Puritans, and the *Fables* (1668, 1678–79, 1692–94) of Jean de La Fontaine, which create a comprehensive picture of society and minutely scrutinize its behaviour.

The great English light poem of the 18th century is Alexander Pope's *The Rape of the Lock* (1712–14), a mock-epic in which the polite society of his day is shown by innuendo to be a mere shadow of the heroic days of old. Lord Byron's verse novel *Don Juan* (1819–24), sardonic and casual, combined the colloquialism of medieval light verse with a sophistication that inspired a number of imitations.

Light verse proliferated in the later 19th century with the rise of humorous periodicals. Among the best-known light works of the period are the limericks of Edward Lear's *Book of Nonsense* (1846), W.S. Gilbert's *Bab Ballads* (1869), and the inspired nonsense of Lewis Carroll's *Hunting of the Snark* (1876). The American poet Charles G. Leland exploited the humorous possibilities of immigrant jargon in *The Breitmann Ballads* (1871; also published as *Hans Breitmann's Ballads*).

In the 20th century the distinction between light and serious verse was obscured by the flippant, irreverent tone used by many modern poets, the nonsense verse of the Dadaists, Futurists, and Surrealists, and the primitivistic techniques of such writers as the Beat poets and E.E. Cummings. In spite of their seeming lightness, the works of such poets as Vladimir Mayakovsky, W.H. Auden, Louis MacNiece, Theodore Roethke, and Kenneth Fearing are usually seriously intended. They may begin by being amusing but often end in terror or bitterness. Though light verse in the traditional manner was occasionally produced by major poets—for example, Ezra Pound's delightful Middle English parody "Ancient Music" ("Winter is icummen in") and T.S. Eliot's *Old Possum's Book of Practical Cats* (1939)—it came to be associated with exclusive or frequent practitioners of the genre: in

DOROTHY PARKER

(b. Aug. 22, 1893, West End, near Long Beach, N.J., U.S.—d. June 7, 1967, New York, N.Y.)

The reputation of U.S. short-story writer and poet Dorothy Parker is based largely on her oft-quoted witty remarks. She grew up in affluence in New York City. From 1916 to 1920 she was a drama critic for Vanity Fair, *from which she was fired for the acerbity of her reviews. Thereafter she became a freelance writer. Her first book of light, witty, and sometimes cynical verse,* Enough Rope, *was a best-seller when it appeared in 1926. Two other books of verse,* Sunset Gun *(1928) and* Death and Taxes *(1931), were collected with it in* Collected Poems: Not So Deep as a Well *(1936). From 1927 to 1933 she wrote book reviews (as "Constant Reader") for* The New Yorker, *and she was associated with that magazine as a staff writer or contributor for much of the rest of her career.*

Early in the 1920s she had been one of the founders of the famous Algonquin Round Table at the Algonquin Hotel in Manhattan and was by no means the least of a group of dazzling wits that included Robert Benchley, Robert E. Sherwood, and James Thurber. It was there, in conversations that frequently spilled over from the offices of The New Yorker, *that Parker established her reputation as one of the most brilliant conversationalists in New York. Her rapier wit became so widely renowned that quips and mots were frequently attributed to her on the strength of her reputation alone. She came to epitomize the liberated woman of the 1920s.*

In 1929 Parker won the O. Henry Award for the best short story of the year with "Big Blonde," a compassionate account of an aging party girl. Laments for the Living *(1930) and* After Such Pleasures *(1933) are collections of her short stories, combined and augmented in 1939 as* Here Lies. *Characteristic of both the stories and Parker's verses is a view of the human situation as simultaneously tragic and funny. In addition to her literary writing, Parker (with her second husband, Alan Campbell) also wrote more than a dozen screenplays.*

Parker's witty remarks are legendary. When told of the death of the taciturn U.S. president Calvin Coolidge, she is said to have asked, "How can they tell?" Of Katharine Hepburn's performance in a 1934 play, Parker said she "ran the gamut of emotions from A to B." She also is responsible for the couplet "Men seldom make passes / at girls who wear glasses."

the United States, Ogden Nash, Dorothy Parker, Phyllis McGinley, and Morris Bishop were especially known during the 20th century; in England, Sir John Betjeman and Hilaire Belloc; and in Germany, Christian Morgenstern and Erich Kästner.

LIMERICK

The limerick is a popular form of short, humorous verse that is often nonsensical and frequently ribald. It consists of five lines, rhyming *aabba,* and the dominant metre is anapestic, with two metrical feet in the third and fourth lines and three feet in the others. The origin of the limerick is unknown, but it has been suggested that the name derives from the chorus of an 18th-century Irish soldiers' song, "Will You Come Up to Limerick?" To this were added impromptu verses crowded with improbable incident and subtle innuendo.

The first collections of limericks in English date from about 1820. Edward Lear, who composed and illustrated those in his *Book of Nonsense* (1846), claimed to have gotten the idea from a nursery rhyme beginning "There was an old man of Tobago." A typical example from Lear's collection is this verse:

There was an Old Man who supposed
That the street door was partially closed;
But some very large rats
Ate his coats and his hats,
While that futile Old Gentleman dozed.

Toward the end of the 19th century, many noted men of letters indulged in the form. W.S. Gilbert displayed his skill in a sequence of limericks that Arthur Sullivan set as the familiar song in *The Sorcerer* (1877):

My name is John Wellington Wells,
I'm a dealer in magic and spells,
In blessings and curses,
And ever-fill'd purses,
In prophecies, witches, and knells.

The form acquired widespread popularity in the early years of the 20th century, and limerick contests were often held by magazines and business houses. Many variations of the form were developed, as can be seen in the following tongue twister:

A tutor who taught on the flute
Tried to teach two tooters to toot.
Said the two to the tutor,
"Is it harder to toot, or
To tutor two tooters to toot?"

Other variations are written in French or Latin, some exploit the anomalies of English spelling, and still others use the form to make pithy observations upon serious philosophical concerns.

LÜSHI

This form of Chinese poetry, also spelled *lü-shih*, flourished in the Tang dynasty (618–907). It consists of eight lines of five or seven syllables, each line set down in accordance with strict tonal patterns.

Exposition (*qi*) was called for in the first two lines; the development of the theme (*cheng*), in parallel verse structure, in the middle, or second and third, couplets; and the conclusion (*he*) in the final couplet. *Lüshi* provided a new, formal alternative to the long-popular free *gushi* ("ancient-style poetry"). The poet Du Fu was particularly associated with *lüshi*, and Bai Juyi also frequently used the form.

The symmetry and lyricism of *lüshi* inspired *jueju*, a condensed form of *lüshi* consisting of quatrains. Another variation, *pailü*, followed most of the rules of *lüshi* but also allowed the poet to alter the rhyme and elongate the poem.

BAI JUYI

(b. 772, Xinzheng, China—d. 846, Luoyang)

The Chinese poet Bai Juyi (also spelled Po Chü-i) of the Tang dynasty used his elegantly simple verse to protest the social evils of his day, including corruption and militarism.

He began composing poetry at age five, and at age 28 he passed the examinations for the Chinese civil service. In 807 Bai became a member of the prestigious Hanlin Academy in Chang'an, the capital, and he rose steadily in official life, except for his banishment in 814 to a minor post at Jiujiang, which arose from the slander of rival courtiers. He assumed the important posts of governor of Zhongzhou (818), Hangzhou (822), and, later, Suzhou. In 829 he became mayor of Luoyang, the eastern capital, but he retired from that post in 842 because of illness.

He became the informal leader of a group of poets who rejected the courtly style of the time, believing that poetry should have a moral and social purpose. His satirical ballads and poems of social protest often took the form of free verse based on old folk ballads. He was revered in both China and Japan, where his poems, notably the "Song of Everlasting Sorrow," became material for other literary works. Many of Bai's poems are quoted in the Japanese classic The Tale of Genji.

LYRIC

The lyric poem is a verse or poem that is, or supposedly is, susceptible of being sung to the accompaniment of a musical instrument (in ancient times, usually a lyre) or that expresses intense personal emotion in a manner suggestive of a song. Lyric poetry expresses the thoughts and feelings of the poet and is sometimes contrasted with narrative poetry and verse drama, which relate events in the form of a story. Elegies, odes, and sonnets are all important kinds of lyric poetry.

In ancient Greece an early distinction was made between the poetry chanted by a choir of singers (choral lyrics) and the song that expressed the sentiments of a single poet. The latter, the *melos*, or song proper, had reached a height of technical perfection in "the Isles of Greece, where burning Sappho loved and sung," as early as the 7th century BCE. That poet, together with her contemporary Alcaeus, were the chief Doric poets of the pure Greek song. By their side, and later, flourished the great poets who set words to music for choirs, Alcman, Arion, Stesichorus, Simonides, and Ibycus, who were followed at the close of the 5th century by Bacchylides and Pindar, in whom the tradition of the dithyrambic odes reached its highest development.

Latin lyrics were written by Catullus and Horace in the 1st century BCE. And in medieval Europe the lyric form can be found in the songs of the troubadours, in Christian hymns, and in various ballads. In the Renaissance the most finished form of lyric, the sonnet, was brilliantly developed by Petrarch, Shakespeare, Edmund Spenser, and

John Milton. Especially identified with the lyrical forms of poetry in the late 18th and 19th centuries were the Romantic poets, including such diverse figures as Robert Burns, William Blake, William Wordsworth, John Keats, Percy Bysshe Shelley, Lamartine, Victor Hugo, Goethe, and Heinrich Heine. With the exception of some dramatic verse, most Western poetry in the late 19th and the 20th century may be classified as lyrical.

Macaronic

The macaronic was originally a comic Latin verse form characterized by the introduction of vernacular words with appropriate but absurd Latin endings. Later variants apply the same technique to modern languages. The form was first written by Tisi degli Odassi in the late 15th century and popularized by Teofilo Folengo, a dissolute Benedictine monk who applied Latin rules

Sappho

(fl. 610–c. 570 BCE, Lesbos, Asia Minor)

Sappho is a Greek lyric poet greatly admired in all ages for the beauty of her writing style. She ranks in the top tier of Greek poets for her ability to impress readers with a lively sense of her personality. Her phrasing is concise, direct, and picturesque. She has the ability to stand aloof and judge critically her own ecstasies and grief, and her emotions lose nothing of their force by being recollected in tranquility.

Although legends about her abound, little is known of her life. She was born on the island of Lesbos and became the leader of a thiasos, an informal female community, whose purpose was the education of young women, especially for marriage. The principal themes of her poetry are personal and reflect the activities and atmosphere of the thiasos. The goddess Aphrodite (who represents sexual love and beauty) is the group's tutelary divinity and inspiration. Sappho is the intimate and servant of the goddess and her intermediary with the girls. In the ode to Aphrodite, the poet invokes the goddess to appear, as she has in the past, and to be her ally in persuading a girl she desires to love her. Frequent images in Sappho's poetry include flowers, bright garlands, naturalistic outdoor scenes, altars smoking with incense, perfumed unguents to sprinkle on the body and bathe the hair—that is, all the elements of Aphrodite's rituals. In the thiasos the girls were educated and initiated into grace and elegance for seduction and love.

Sappho's poetry, mostly vernacular and not formally literary, is concise, direct, picturesque, and various. It includes nuptial songs and an expression of her love for other women, which produced the word lesbian (from the island's name). Though she was much admired in antiquity, most of her work was lost by the early Middle Ages. Only the ode to Aphrodite—28 lines long—is complete.

of form and syntax to an Italian vocabulary in his burlesque epic of chivalry, *Baldus* (1517). He described the macaronic as the literary equivalent of the Italian dish, which, in its 16th-century form, was a crude mixture of flour, butter, and cheese. The *Baldus* soon found imitators in Italy and France, and some macaronics were even written in mock Greek.

The outstanding British poem in this form is the *Polemo-Middinia inter Vitarvam et Nebernam* (published 1684), an account of a battle between two Scottish villages, in which William Drummond subjected Scots dialect to Latin grammatical rules. A modern English derivative of the macaronic pokes fun at the grammatical complexities of ancient languages taught at school, as in A.D. Godley's illustration of declension in "Motor Bus":

> *Domine defende nos*
> *Contra hos Motores Bos*

("Lord protect us from these motor buses").

The form has survived in comic combinations of modern languages. The German-American Breitmann medleys of Charles G. Leland are later examples of the macaronic, in particular his warning "To a Friend Studying German":

> *Vill'st dou learn die Deutsche Sprache?*
> *Den set it on your card*
> *Dat all de nouns have shenders,*
> *Und de shenders all are hard.*

METAPHOR

A metaphor is a figure of speech that implies comparison between two unlike entities, as distinguished from simile, an explicit comparison signalled by the words *like* or *as*. The distinction is not simple. The metaphor makes a qualitative leap from a reasonable, perhaps prosaic comparison, to an identification or fusion of two objects, to make one new entity partaking of the characteristics of both. Many critics regard the making of metaphors as a system of thought antedating or bypassing logic.

Metaphor is the fundamental language of poetry, although it is common on all levels and in all kinds of language. Many words were originally vivid images, although they exist now as dead metaphors whose original aptness has been lost—for example, *daisy* (day's eye). Other words, such as *nightfall*, are dormant images. In addition to single words, everyday language abounds in phrases and expressions that once were metaphors. "Time flies" is an ancient metaphorical expression. When a poet says "The Bird of Time has but a little way / To flutter—and the Bird is on the Wing" (*The Rubáiyát of Omar Khayyam*), he is constructing a new metaphor on the foundations of an older, stock metaphor. When Tennessee Williams entitled his play *Sweet Bird of Youth*, he, too, was referring to that Bird of Time that flies. Thus, metaphorical language develops continuously in complexity just as ordinary language does.

In poetry a metaphor may perform varied functions from the mere noting of a likeness to the evocation of a swarm of associations. It may exist as a minor beauty or it may be the central concept and controlling image of the poem. The familiar metaphor "Iron Horse," for train, for example, becomes the elaborate central concept of one of Emily Dickinson's poems, which begins

I like to see it lap the Miles,
And lick the Valleys up,
And stop to feed itself at Tanks;
And then prodigious step . . .

A mixed metaphor is the linking of two or more disparate elements, which often results in an unintentionally comic effect produced by the writer's insensitivity to the literal meaning of words or by the falseness of the comparison. A mixed metaphor may also be used with great effectiveness, however, as in *Hamlet's*

Whether 'tis nobler in the mind to suffer
The slings and arrows of outrageous
fortune
Or to take arms against a sea of
troubles . . .

in which *sea* should be replaced by *host* for the strictly correct completion of the metaphor.

MUWASHSHAḤ

Arabic for "ode," the *muwashshaḥ* is an Arabic poetic genre in strophic form developed in Muslim Spain in the 11th and 12th centuries. From the 12th century onward, its use spread to North Africa and the Muslim Middle East.

The *muwashshaḥ* is written in Classical Arabic, and its subjects are those of Classical Arabic poetry—love, wine, court figures. It sharply differs in form, however, from classical poetry, in which each verse is divided into two metric halves and a single rhyme recurs at the end of each verse. The *muwashshaḥ* is usually divided into five strophes, or stanzas, each numbering four, five, or six lines. A master rhyme appears at the beginning of the poem and at the end of the strophes, somewhat like a refrain. It is interrupted by subordinate rhymes. A possible scheme is *ABcdcdABefefABghghABijijABklklAB*. The last *AB*, called *kharjah*, or *markaz*, is usually written in vernacular Arabic or in the Spanish Mozarabic dialect. Nomally, it is rendered in the voice of a girl and expresses her longing for her absent lover. Such verses make it probable that the *muwashshaḥ* was influenced by some kind of European Romance oral poetry or song. Jewish poets of Spain also wrote *muwashshaḥ*s in Hebrew, with *kharjah*s in Arabic and Spanish.

NONSENSE VERSE

The humorous or whimsical verse known as nonsense verse differs from other comic verse in its resistance to any rational or allegorical interpretation. Though it often makes use of coined, meaningless words, it is unlike the ritualistic gibberish of children's counting-out rhymes in that it makes these words sound purposeful.

Skilled literary nonsense verse is rare. Most of it has been written for children and is modern, dating from the beginning of the 19th century. The cardinal date could be considered 1846, when *The Book of Nonsense* was published. This was a collection of limericks composed and illustrated by the artist Edward Lear, who first created them in the 1830s for the children of the earl of Derby. This was followed by the inspired fantasy of Lewis Carroll, whose *Alice's Adventures in Wonderland* (1865) and *Through the Looking-Glass* (1872) both contain brilliant nonsense rhymes. "Jabberwocky," from *Through the Looking-Glass*, may be the best-known example of nonsense verse. It begins thus:

'Twas brillig, and the slithy toves
Did gyre and gimble in the wabe;
All mimsy were the borogoves,
And the mome raths outgrabe.

Another of Carroll's poems, *The Hunting of the Snark* (1876), has been called the longest and best sustained nonsense poem in the English language.

Hilaire Belloc's volume *The Bad Child's Book of Beasts* (1896) holds an honoured place among the classics of English nonsense verse, while, in the United States, Laura E. Richards, a prolific writer of children's books, published verses in *Tirra Lirra* (1932) that have been compared to those of Edward Lear.

Nursery Rhyme

Nursery rhymes are, as the name suggests, verses customarily told or sung to small children. The oral tradition of nursery rhymes is ancient, but new verses have steadily entered the stream. A French poem numbering the days of the month, similar to "Thirty days hath September," was recorded in the 13th century; but such latecomers as "Twinkle, Twinkle, Little Star" (by Ann and Jane Taylor; pub. 1806) and "Mary Had a Little Lamb" (by Sarah Josepha Hale; pub. 1830) seem to be just as firmly established in the repertoire.

Some of the oldest rhymes are probably those accompanying babies' games, such as "Handy, dandy, prickly, pandy, which hand will you have?" (recorded 1598) and its German equivalent, "Windle, wandle, in welchem Handle, oben oder unt?" The existence of numerous European parallels for "Ladybird, ladybird [or, in the United States, "Ladybug, ladybug"], fly away home" and for the singing game "London Bridge is falling down" and for the riddle-rhyme "Humpty-Dumpty" suggests the possibility that these rhymes come down from very ancient sources, since direct translation is unlikely.

Such relics of the past are exceptional. Most nursery rhymes date from the 16th, 17th, and, most frequently, the 18th centuries. Apparently most were originally composed for adult entertainment. Many were popular ballads and songs. "The frog who would a-wooing go" first appeared in 1580 as *A Moste Strange weddinge of the ffrogge and the mowse.* "Oh where,

Nursery rhymes, such as that of the unfortunate small shepherdess, Little Bo Peep, are often recited to children from birth. The Bridgeman Art Library/Getty Images

oh where, ish mine little dog gone?" was a popular song written in 1864 by the Philadelphia composer Septimus Winner.

Although many ingenious theories have been advanced attributing hidden significance, especially political allusions, to nursery rhymes, there is no reason to suppose they are any more arcane than the popular songs of the day. Some were inspired by personalities of the time, and occasionally these can be identified. Somerset tradition associates "Little Jack Horner" (recorded 1725) with a Thomas Horner of Mells who did well for himself during the dissolution of the monasteries.

The earliest known published collection of nursery rhymes was *Tommy Thumb's (Pretty) Song Book,* 2 vol. (London, 1744). It included "Little Tom Tucker," "Sing a Song of Sixpence," and "Who Killed Cock Robin?" The most influential was *Mother Goose's Melody: or Sonnets for the Cradle,* published by the firm of John Newbery in 1781. Among its 51 rhymes were "Jack and Jill," "Ding Dong Bell," and "Hush-a-bye baby on the tree top." An edition was reprinted in the United States in 1785 by Isaiah Thomas. Its popularity is attested by the fact that these verses are still commonly called "Mother Goose rhymes" in the United States.

ODE

An ode is a ceremonious poem on an occasion of public or private dignity in which personal emotion and general meditation are united. The Greek word *ōdē,*

which has been accepted in most modern European languages, meant a choric song, usually accompanied by a dance. Alcman (7th century BCE) originated the strophic arrangement of the ode, which is a rhythmic system composed of two or more lines repeated as a unit. Stesichorus (7th–6th centuries BCE) invented the triadic, or three-part, structure (strophic lines followed by antistrophic lines in the same metre, concluding with a summary line, called an epode, in a different metre) that characterizes the odes of Pindar and Bacchylides. Choral odes were also an integral part of the Greek drama. In Latin the word was not used until about the time of Horace, in the 1st century BCE. His carmina ("songs"), written in stanzas of two or four lines of polished Greek metres, are now universally called odes, although the implication that they were to be sung to the accompaniment of a lyre is probably only a literary convention. Both Pindaric and Horatian ode forms were revived during the Renaissance and continued to influence lyric poetry into the 20th century. The first version of Allen Tate's widely acclaimed "Ode to the Confederate Dead," for example, was published in 1926.

In pre-Islamic Arabic poetry, the ode flourished in the form of the *qaṣīdah.* Two great collections date from the 8th and 9th centuries.

OTTAVA RIMA

The Italian stanza form that is composed of eight 11-syllable lines, rhyming *abababcc* is known as the ottava rima. It originated in the late 13th and early 14th centuries and was developed by Tuscan poets for religious verse and drama and in troubadour songs. The form appeared in Spain and Portugal in the 16th century. It was used in 1600 in England (where the lines were shortened to 10 syllables) by Edward Fairfax in his translation of Torquato Tasso. In his romantic epics *Il filostrato* (written *c.* 1338) and *Teseida* (written 1340–41) Boccaccio established ottava rima as the standard form for epic and narrative verse in Italy. The form acquired new flexibility and variety in Ludovico Ariosto's *Orlando furioso* (*c.* 1507–32) and Tasso's *Gerusalemme liberata* (published 1581). In English verse ottava rima was used for heroic poetry in the 17th and 18th centuries but achieved its greatest effectiveness in the work of Byron. His *Beppo* (1818) and *Don Juan* (1819–24) combined elements of comedy, seriousness, and mock-heroic irony. Percy Bysshe Shelley employed it for a serious subject in *The Witch of Atlas* (1824).

PANEGYRIC

Panegyrics are eulogistic orations or laudatory discourses that originally were delivered at an ancient Greek general assembly (*panegyris*), such as the Olympic and Panathenaic festivals. Speakers frequently took advantage of these occasions, when Greeks of various cities were gathered together, to advocate Hellenic unity. With this end in view and also to gratify their audience, they tended to expatiate on the former glories of Greek cities. Hence came the encomiastic associations that eventually clung to the term *panegyric*. The most famous ancient Greek panegyrics to survive intact are the *Panegyricus* (*c.* 380 BCE) and the *Panathenaicus* (*c.* 340 BCE), both by Isocrates.

Akin to panegyric was the *epitaphion,* or funeral oration, such as Pericles' funeral speech as recorded by Thucydides, a panegyric both on war heroes and on Athens itself.

In the 2nd century CE, Aelius Aristides, a Greek rhetorician, combined praise of famous cities with eulogy of the reigning Roman emperor. By his time panegyric had probably become specialized in the latter connection and was, therefore, related to the old Roman custom of celebrating at festivals the glories of famous men of the past and of pronouncing *laudationes funebres* at the funerals of eminent persons.

Another kind of Roman eulogistic speech was the *gratiarum actio* ("thanksgiving"), delivered by a successful candidate for public office. The *XII Panegyrici Latini*, an ancient collection of these speeches, includes the *gratiarum actio* delivered by Pliny the Younger when he was nominated consul by the emperor Trajan in 100 CE. Late Roman writers of the 3rd to the 5th century indiscriminately praised and flattered the emperors in panegyrics that were sometimes written in verse.

Although primarily a literary form associated with classical antiquity, panegyric continued to be written on occasion in the European Middle

Ages, often by Christian mystics in praise of God, and in the Renaissance and Baroque periods, especially in Elizabethan England, in Spain during the Golden Age, and in France under the reign of Louis XIV.

PATTERN POEM

The pattern poem, in which the typography or lines are arranged in an unusual configuration, usually to convey or extend the emotional content of the words, is also called figure poem, shaped verse, or carmen figuratum. Of ancient (probably Eastern) origin, pattern poems are found in *The Greek Anthology*, which includes work composed between the 7th century BCE and the early 11th century CE. A notable later example is the wing-shaped "Easter Wings" of the 16th-century English Metaphysical poet George Herbert:

> *Lord, who createdst man in wealth and store,*
> *Though foolishly he lost the same,*
> *Decaying more and more*
> *Till he became*
> *Most poor:*
> *With thee*
> *O let me rise*
> *As larks, harmoniously,*
> *And sing this day thy victories;*
> *Then shall the fall further the flight in me.*

In the 19th century, the French Symbolist poet Stéphane Mallarmé employed different type sizes in *Un Coup de dés* (1897; "A Throw of Dice").

Representative poets in the 20th century included Guillaume Apollinaire in France and E.E. Cummings in the United States. In the 20th century, pattern poetry sometimes crossed paths with concrete poetry. A basic distinction between the two types of poetry is the ability of pattern poetry to hold its meaning apart from its typography (i.e., it can be read aloud and still retain its meaning).

PHYSICAL POETRY

Physical poetry (exemplified by Imagist poetry) is primarily concerned with the projection of a descriptive image of material things. An example is the poem "Sea Poppies" (1916) by Hilda Doolittle (H.D.):

> *Amber husk*
> *fluted with gold,*
> *fruit on the sand*
> *marked with a rich grain,*
>
> *treasure*
> *spilled near the shrub-pines*
> *to bleach on the boulders:*
>
> *your stalk has caught root*
> *among wet pebbles*
> *and drift flung by the sea*
> *and grated shells*
> *and split conch-shells.*
>
> *Beautiful, wide-spread,*
> *fire upon leaf,*
> *what meadow yields*
> *so fragrant a leaf*
> *as your bright leaf?*

Pindaric Ode

Pindaric odes are ceremonious poems by or in the manner of Pindar, a Greek professional lyrist of the 5th century BCE. Pindar employed the triadic structure attributed to Stesichorus (7th and 6th centuries BCE), consisting of a strophe (two or more lines repeated as a unit) followed by a metrically harmonious antistrophe, concluding with a summary line (called an epode) in a different metre. These three parts corresponded to the movement of the chorus to one side of the stage, then to the other, and their pause midstage to deliver the epode.

Although fragments of Pindar's poems in all of the Classical choral forms are extant, it is the collection of four books of epinician odes that has influenced poets of the Western world since their publication by Aldus Manutius in 1513. Each of the books is devoted to one of the great series of Greek Classical games: the Olympian, Pythian, Isthmian, and Nemean. Celebrating the victory of a winner with a performance of choral chant and dance, these epinician odes are elaborately complex, rich in metaphor and intensely emotive language. They reveal Pindar's sense of vocation as a poet dedicated to preserving and interpreting great deeds and their divine values. The metaphors, myths, and gnomic sayings that ornament the odes are often difficult to grasp because of the rapid shifts of thought and the sacrifice of syntax to achieving uniform poetic colour. For modern readers, another difficulty is the topicality of the works. They were often composed for particular occasions and made reference to events and personal situations that were well-known to the original audience but not necessarily to later readers.

With the publication of Pierre de Ronsard's four books of French *Odes* (1550), the Pindaric ode was adapted to the vernacular languages. Imitation Pindaric odes were written in England by Thomas Gray in 1757, "The Progress of Poesy" and "The Bard." Abraham Cowley's *Pindarique Odes* (1656) introduced a looser version known as Pindarics. These are irregular rhymed odes in which the length of line and stanza is capriciously varied to suggest, but not reproduce, the style and manner of Pindar. These spurious Pindarics are some of the greatest odes in the English language, including John Dryden's "Alexander's Feast" (1697), William Wordsworth's "Ode: Intimations of Immortality from Recollections of Early Childhood," Percy Bysshe Shelley's "Ode to the West Wind," Alfred, Lord Tennyson's "Ode on the Death of the Duke of Wellington," and John Keats's "Ode on a Grecian Urn."

Poet Laureate

The title of poet laureate was first granted in England in the 17th century for poetic excellence. Its holder is a salaried member of the British royal household, but the post has come to be free of specific poetic duties. In the United States, a similar position was created in 1936. The title of the office stems from a tradition, dating to the earliest Greek and Roman times, of honouring achievement with a crown of laurel, a tree sacred to Apollo, patron of poets.

The British office is remarkable for its continuity. It began with a pension granted to Ben Jonson by James I in 1616, confirmed and increased by Charles I in 1630 (when an annual "butt of Canary wine" was added, to be discontinued at the request of Henry James Pye—made laureate in 1790—who preferred the equivalent in money). Jonson's pension specifically recognized his services to the crown as a poet and envisaged their continuance, but not until 16 months after Jonson's death in 1637 was a similar pension for similar services granted to Sir William Davenant. It was with John Dryden's appointment in 1668, within a week of Davenant's death, that the laureateship was recognized as an established royal office to be filled automatically when vacant.

During the Glorious Revolution (1688–89), Dryden was dismissed for refusing the oath of allegiance, and this gave the appointment a political flavour, which it retained for more than two hundred years. Dryden's successor, Thomas Shadwell, inaugurated the custom of producing New Year and birthday odes; this hardened into a tradition between 1690 and about 1820, becoming the principal mark of the office. The odes were set to music and performed in the sovereign's presence. On his appointment in 1813, Robert Southey sought unsuccessfully to end this custom, but, although it was allowed tacitly to lapse, it was only finally abolished by Queen Victoria. Her appointment of William Wordsworth in 1843 signified that the laureateship had become the reward for eminence in poetry, and the office since then has carried no specific duties. The laureates from Alfred Tennyson onward have written poems for royal and national occasions as the spirit has moved them. Andrew Motion was the first British poet laureate to serve a fixed term, of 10 years (1999–2009). His successor, Carol Ann Duffy, became the first woman appointed to the position.

In the United States, a position similar to that of the British poet laureate—the chair of poetry at the Library of Congress—was established in 1936 by an endowment from the author Archer M. Huntington. In 1985 the U.S. government created a title of poet laureate, to be held by the same person who holds the post of consultant in poetry for the Library of Congress. The American poet laureate receives a modest stipend and is expected to present one major poetic work and to appear at certain national ceremonies. For a table of poets laureate of the United Kingdom and of the United States, see the Appendix.

PRAISE SONG

One of the most widely used poetic forms in Africa is the praise song, a series of laudatory epithets applied to gods, men, animals, plants, and towns that capture the essence of the object being praised. Professional bards, who may be both praise singers to a chief and court historians of their tribe, chant praise songs such as these of the great Zulu chieftain Shaka:

He is Shaka the unshakeable,
Thunderer-while-sitting, son of Menzi.
He is the bird that preys on other birds,
The battle-axe that excels over other
  battle-axes.
He is the long-strided pursuer, son
  of Ndaba,
Who pursued the sun and the moon.
He is the great hubbub like the rocks
  of Nkandla
Where elephants take shelter
When the heavens frown…
                    (trans. by Ezekiel Mphahlele)

Although the praise singer is expected to know all of the traditional phrases handed down by word of mouth in his tribe, the bard is also free to make additions to existing poems. Thus the praise songs of Shango, the Yoruba god of thunder and lightning, might contain a modern comparison of the god to the power and noise of a railway.

Among some Bantu-speaking peoples, the praise song is an important form of oral literature. The Sotho of Lesotho required all boys undergoing initiation to compose praises for themselves that set forth the ideals of action or manhood. Sotho bards also composed traditional praises of chiefs and warriors, and even a boy was allowed to create praises of himself if he had performed feats of great courage.

These praise songs were recited as follows: the reciter stood in an open space, visible to all assembled. He then began reciting in a high voice, punctuating his victories in war by stabbing the ground with his spear, until he had set forth not only his lineage and the battles in which he had fought but his entire life history. Sotho praises are telegraphic, leaving much to the listener's imagination. Their language is poetic, and the sequence of events not necessarily logical. Metaphor is a key device for suggesting worth (a reciter might call himself a ferocious animal), and poetic license is granted for coining new words.

To the subjects used by the Sotho, the Tswana of Botswana add women, tribal groups, domestic (especially cattle) and wild animals, trees, crops, various features of the landscape, and divining bones. Their praise songs consist of a succession of loose stanzas with an irregular number of lines and a balanced metrical form. Experiences such as going abroad to work for Europeans have become a subject of recent praise poems, and recitation has been extended from tribal meetings and ritual occasions such as weddings to the beer hall and labour camp.

In western Africa, also, praise songs have been adapted to the times, and a modern praise singer often serves as an entertainer hired to flatter the rich and socially prominent or to act as a master of ceremonies for paramount chiefs at state functions—e.g., among the Hausa and Malinke peoples. Thus praise-song poems, though still embodying and preserving a tribe's history, have also been adapted to an increasingly urbanized and Westernized African society.

PROSE POEM

A work in prose that has some of the technical or literary qualities of a poem (such as regular rhythm, definitely patterned structure, or emotional or imaginative heightening), though it is set on a page as prose, is called a prose poem.

The form was introduced into French literature by Louis Bertrand, with his *Gaspard de la nuit* (1842; "Gaspard of the Night"). His poetry attracted little interest at the time, but his influence on the Symbolists at the end of the century was acknowledged by Charles Baudelaire in his *Petits poèmes en prose* (1869; "Little Poems in Prose"), later titled *Le Spleen de Paris*. It was this work that gave the form its name, and the *Divagations* (1897; "Wanderings") of Stéphane Mallarmé and *Illuminations* (1886) of Arthur Rimbaud firmly established prose poetry in France. Other turn-of-the-century writers who composed prose poetry were Paul Valéry, Paul Fort, and Paul Claudel.

Prose poems were written in the early 19th century by the German poets Friedrich Hölderlin and Novalis and at the end of the century by Rainer Maria Rilke. The 20th century saw a renewed interest in the form in such works as Pierre Reverdy's *Poèmes en prose* (1915) and in the works of the French poet Saint-John Perse. Other notable practitioners of the form include Max Jacob, Franz Kafka, James Joyce, Gertrude Stein, Sherwood Anderson, Amy Lowell, Kenneth Patchen, Russell Edson, Charles Simic, Robert Bly, N. Scott Momaday, and Rosmarie Waldrop.

RAINER MARIA RILKE

(b. Dec. 4, 1875, Prague, Bohemia, Austria-Hungary—d. Dec. 29, 1926, Valmont, Switz.)

Rainer Maria Rilke was an Austro-German poet who gained an international reputation with such works as Duino Elegies *and* Sonnets to Orpheus *(both 1923). After an unhappy childhood and an ill-planned preparatory education, Rilke began a life of wandering that took him across Europe. His visits to Russia inspired his first serious work, the long poem cycle* The Book of Hours *(1905). For 12 years beginning in 1902 his geographic centre was Paris, where he researched a book on Auguste Rodin, associated with the great sculptor, and developed a new style of lyrical poetry that attempted to capture the plastic essence of a physical object. The results were* New Poems *(1907–08) and its prose counterpart, the novel* The Notebook of Malte Laurids Brigge *(1910). After 13 years of writing very little because of writer's block and depression, in 1922 he finally completed the 10 poems of the* Duino Elegies, *a profound meditation on the paradoxes of human existence and one of the century's poetic masterpieces. Unexpectedly and with astonishing speed, he then composed* Sonnets to Orpheus, *a superb 55-poem cycle inspired by the death of a young girl, which continues the* Elegies' *meditations on death, transcendence, and poetry. The two works brought him international fame.*

PURE POETRY

Pure poetry is message-free verse that is concerned with exploring the essential musical nature of the language rather than with conveying a narrative or having didactic purpose. The term has been associated particularly with the poems of Edgar Allan Poe. Pure poetry was also written by George Moore (who published *An Anthology of Pure Poetry* in 1924), Charles Baudelaire, and T.S. Eliot. Others who have experimented with the form include Stéphane Mallarmé, Paul Verlaine, Paul Valéry, Juan Ramón Jiménez, and Jorge Guillén.

QASIDA

The *qasida* (Arabic *qaṣīdah*) is a poetic form that was developed in pre-Islamic Arabia and perpetuated throughout Islamic literary history into the present. It is a laudatory, elegiac, or satiric poem that is found in Arabic, Persian, and many related Asian literatures. The classic *qasida* is an elaborately structured ode of 60 to 100 lines, maintaining a single end rhyme that runs through the entire piece. The same rhyme also occurs at the end of the first hemistich (half-line) of the first verse. Virtually any metre is acceptable for the *qasida* except the *rajaz,* which has lines only half the length of those in other metres.

The *qasida* opens with a short prelude, the *nasib,* which is elegiac in mood and is intended to gain the audience's involvement. The *nasib* depicts the poet stopping at an old tribal encampment to reminisce about the happiness he shared there with his beloved and about his sorrow when they parted. Imru' al-Qays is said to have been the first to use this device, and nearly all subsequent authors of *qasida* imitate him. After this conventional beginning follows the *rahil,* which consists of descriptions of the poet's horse or camel or of desert animals and scenes of desert events and Bedouin life and warfare. It may conclude with a piece on *fakhr,* or self-praise. The main theme, the *madih,* or panegyric, often coupled with *hija'* (satire of enemies), is last and is the poet's tribute to himself, his tribe, or his patron.

The *qasida* has always been respected as the highest form of the poetic art and as the special forte of the pre-Islamic poets. While poets with a classical tendency maintained the genre, with its confining rules, the changed circumstances of the Arabs made it an artificial convention. Thus, by the end of the 8th century the *qasida* had begun to decline in popularity. It was successfully restored for a brief period in the 10th century by al-Mutanabbi and has continued to be cultivated by the Bedouin. *Qasida* were also written in Persian, Turkish, and Urdu until the 19th century.

SESTINA

The elaborate verse form known as the sestina was first employed by medieval Provençal and Italian poets, and it is still used by some contemporary poets. In its pure medieval form, the sestina consists of six stanzas of blank verse, each of six lines—hence the name. The final words of the first stanza appear in varied order in the other five, the order used by the

Provençals being: *abcdef, faebdc, cfdabe, ecbfad, deacfb, bdfeca*. Following these was a stanza of three lines, in which the six key words were repeated in the middle and at the end of the lines, summarizing the poem or dedicating it to some person.

The sestina was invented by the Provençal troubadour Arnaut Daniel and was used in Italy by Dante and Petrarch, after which it fell into disuse until revived by the 16th-century group of French writers known as La Pléiade, particularly by Pontus de Tyard. In the 19th century, Ferdinand, comte de Gramont, wrote a large number of sestinas, and Algernon Charles Swinburne's "Complaint of Lisa" is an astonishing tour de force—a double sestina of 12 stanzas of 12 lines each. In the 20th century, Ezra Pound, T.S. Eliot, W.H. Auden, and Elizabeth Bishop wrote noteworthy sestinas.

SONNET

The sonnet is a fixed verse form of Italian origin consisting of 14 lines that are typically five-foot iambics rhyming according to a prescribed scheme. It is unique among poetic forms in Western literature in that it has retained its appeal for major poets for five centuries. The form seems to have originated in the 13th century among the Sicilian school of court poets, who were influenced by the love poetry of Provençal troubadours. From there it spread to Tuscany, where it reached its highest expression in the 14th century in the poems of Petrarch. His *Canzoniere*—a sequence of poems including 317 sonnets, addressed to his idealized beloved, Laura—established and perfected the Petrarchan (or Italian) sonnet, which remains one of the two principal sonnet forms, as well as the one most widely used. The other major form is the English (or Shakespearean) sonnet.

The Petrarchan sonnet characteristically treats its theme in two parts. The first eight lines, the octave, state a problem, ask a question, or express an emotional tension. The last six lines, the sestet, resolve the problem, answer the question, or relieve the tension. The octave is rhymed *abbaabba*. The rhyme scheme of the sestet varies; it may be *cdecde, cdccdc,* or *cdedce.* The Petrarchan sonnet became a major influence on European poetry. It soon became naturalized in Spain, Portugal, and France and was introduced to Poland, whence it spread to other Slavic literatures. In most cases the form was adapted to the staple metre of the language—for example, the alexandrine (12-syllable iambic line) in France and iambic pentameter in English.

The sonnet was introduced to England, along with other Italian verse forms, by Sir Thomas Wyatt and Henry Howard, earl of Surrey, in the 16th century. The new forms precipitated the great Elizabethan flowering of lyric poetry, and the period marks the peak of the sonnet's English popularity. In the course of adapting the Italian form to a language less rich in rhymes, the Elizabethans gradually arrived at the distinctive English sonnet, which is composed of three quatrains, each having an independent rhyme scheme, and is ended with a rhymed couplet.

The rhyme scheme of the English sonnet is *abab cdcd efef gg*. Its greater number of rhymes makes it a less demanding form than the Petrarchan sonnet, but this is offset by the difficulty presented by the couplet, which must summarize the impact of the preceding quatrains with the compressed force of a Greek epigram. An example is Shakespeare's Sonnet 116:

> *Let me not to the marriage of true minds*
> *Admit impediments. Love is not love*
> *Which alters when it alteration finds,*
> *Or bends with the remover to remove:*
> *Oh, no! it is an ever-fixéd mark,*
> *That looks on tempests and is never shaken;*
> *It is the star to every wandering bark,*
> *Whose worth's unknown, although his*
> *   height be taken.*
> *Love's not Time's fool, though rosy lips*
> *   and cheeks*
> *Within his bending sickle's compass come;*
> *Love alters not with his brief hours*
> *   and weeks,*
> *But bears it out even to the edge of doom.*
> *If this be error and upon me proved,*
> *I never writ, nor no man ever loved.*

The typical Elizabethan use of the sonnet was in a sequence of love poems in the manner of Petrarch. Although each sonnet was an independent poem, partly conventional in content and partly self-revelatory, the sequence had the added interest of providing something of a narrative development. Among the notable Elizabethan sequences are Sir Philip Sidney's *Astrophel and Stella* (1591), Samuel Daniel's *Delia* (1592), Michael Drayton's *Idea's Mirrour* (1594), and Edmund Spenser's *Amoretti* (1591). The last-named work uses a common variant of the sonnet (known as Spenserian) that follows the English quatrain and couplet pattern but resembles the Italian in using a linked rhyme scheme: *abab bcbc cdcd ee*. Perhaps the greatest of all sonnet sequences is Shakespeare's, addressed to a young man and a "dark lady." In these sonnets the supposed love story is of less interest than the underlying reflections on time and art, growth and decay, and fame and fortune.

In its subsequent development the sonnet was to depart even further from themes of love. By the time John Donne wrote his religious sonnets (*c.* 1610) and Milton wrote sonnets on political and religious subjects or on personal themes such as his blindness (i.e., "When I consider how my light is spent"), the sonnet had been extended to embrace nearly all the subjects of poetry.

It is the virtue of this short form that it can range from "light conceits of lovers" to considerations of life, time, death, and eternity, without doing injustice to any of them. Even during the Romantic era, in spite of the emphasis on freedom and spontaneity, the sonnet forms continued to challenge major poets. Many English writers—including William Wordsworth, John Keats, and Elizabeth Barrett Browning—continued to write Petrarchan sonnets. One of the best-known examples of this in English is Wordsworth's "The World Is Too Much With Us":

*The world is too much with us; late
  and soon,
Getting and spending, we lay waste
our powers;
Little we see in Nature that is ours;
We have given our hearts away, a
  sordid boon!
This Sea that bares her bosom to the moon,
The winds that will be howling at all hours,
And are up-gathered now like
  sleeping flowers,
For this, for everything, we are out of tune;
It moves us not.—Great God! I'd rather be
A Pagan suckled in a creed outworn;
So might I, standing on this pleasant lea,
Have glimpses that would make me
less forlorn;
Have sight of Proteus rising from the sea;
Or hear old Triton blow his wreathéd horn.*

In the later 19th century the love sonnet sequence was revived by Elizabeth Barrett Browning in *Sonnets from the Portuguese* (1850) and by Dante Gabriel Rossetti in *The House of Life* (1876). Perhaps the most distinguished 20th-century work of the kind is Rainer Maria Rilke's *Sonnets to Orpheus* (1922).

STANZA

A stanza is a division of a poem consisting of two or more lines arranged together as a unit. More specifically, a stanza usually is a group of lines arranged together in a recurring pattern of metrical lengths and a sequence of rhymes.

The structure of a stanza (also called a strophe or stave) is determined by the number of lines, the dominant metre, and the rhyme scheme. Thus, a stanza of four lines of iambic pentameter, rhyming *abab*, could be described as a quatrain.

Some of the most common stanzaic forms are designated by the number of lines in each unit—for example, tercet or terza rima (three lines) and ottava rima (eight lines). Other forms are named for their inventors or best-known practitioners or for the work in which they first were heavily used (e.g., the Spenserian stanza, named for Edmund Spenser, or the In Memoriam stanza, popularized by Alfred, Lord Tennyson in the poem by that title). The term *strophe* is often used interchangeably with *stanza*, although *strophe* is sometimes used specifically to refer to a unit of a poem that does not have a regular metre and rhyme pattern or to a unit of a Pindaric ode.

TERZA RIMA

Terza rima is an Italian verse form consisting of stanzas of three lines (tercets), in which the first and third lines rhyme with one another and the second rhymes with the first and third of the following tercet. The series ends with a line that rhymes with the second line of the last stanza, so that the rhyme scheme is *aba, bcb, cdc, . . . , yzy, z*. The metre is often iambic pentameter.

Dante, in his *Divine Comedy* (written *c.* 1310–14), was the first to use terza rima for a long poem, though a similar form had been previously used by the troubadours. After Dante, terza rima was favoured in 14th-century Italy, especially for allegorical and didactic poetry, by Petrarch and Boccaccio, and in the 16th century for satire and burlesque, notably by Ludovico Ariosto. A demanding form, terza rima has not been widely adopted in languages less rich in rhymes than Italian. It was introduced in England by Sir Thomas Wyatt in the 16th century. Many 19th-century Romantic poets such as Shelley ("Ode to the West Wind"), Byron, Elizabeth and Robert Browning, and Longfellow experimented with it. In the 20th century, W.H. Auden used terza rima for *The Sea and the Mirror*, and Archibald MacLeish in "Conquistador," but with many deviations from the strict form.

TRIOLET

The triolet is a medieval French verse form that consists of eight short lines rhyming *ABaAabAB* (the capital letters indicate lines that are repeated). The name *triolet*, which is a Middle French word meaning "clover leaf," is taken from the three repetitions of the first line. The great art of the triolet consists in using the refrain line with naturalness and ease and in each repetition slightly altering its meaning, or at least its relation to the rest of the poem. The triolet is preserved in many modern European literatures, especially for light and humorous verse.

Probably invented in the 13th century, the triolet was cultivated as a serious form by such medieval French

poets as Adenet le Roi and Jean Froissart. Although its popularity declined in the 15th and 16th centuries, the triolet was revived in the 17th century by Jean de La Fontaine and in the 19th century by Alphonse Daudet and Théodore de Banville. Triolets are innumerable in French literature and are frequently used in newspapers to give a point and brightness to a brief stroke of satire.

The earliest triolets in English are those of a devotional nature composed in 1651 by Patrick Cary, a Benedictine monk, at Douai, France. Reintroduced into English by Robert Bridges in 1873, the triolet has since been cultivated widely in that language, most successfully by Austin Dobson, whose five-part "Rose-Leaves" is a masterpiece of ingenuity and easy grace. The first stanza, entitled "A Kiss," reads as follows:

> *Rose kissed me to-day.*
> *Will she kiss me to-morrow?*
> *Let it be as it may,*
> *Rose kissed me to-day,*
> *But the pleasure gives way*
> *To a savour of sorrow;—*
> *Rose kissed me to-day,—*
> *Will she kiss me to-morrow?*

In Germany, anthologies of triolets were published at Halberstadt in 1795 and at Brunswick in 1796. Frederich Rassmann made collections in 1815 and 1817 in which he distinguished three species of triolet: the legitimate form; the loose triolet, which only approximately abides by the rules as to number of rhymes and lines; and the single-strophe poem, which more or less accidentally approaches the true triolet in character. The true form was employed particularly by German Romantic poets of the early 19th century.

VERS DE SOCIÉTÉ

Vers de société (meaning society verse) is light poetry written with particular wit and polish and intended for a limited, sophisticated audience. It has flourished in cultured societies, particularly in court circles and literary salons, from the 6th century BCE. The tone is flippant or mildly ironic. Trivial subjects are treated in an intimate, subjective manner, and even when social conditions form the theme, the light mood prevails.

The Roman poets Catullus, Martial, and Horace produced much witty vers de société and have often been translated or closely paraphrased. But much strikingly original verse has come from poets or other writers known for their serious works. Jean Froissart, the 14th-century historian of feudal chivalry, wrote some of the most charming examples of the late Middle Ages. The English Cavalier poets Robert Herrick, Thomas Carew, and Richard Lovelace wrote much fine vers along with their elegant lyrics.

The 18th century was rich in examples, both in French and English. Among the best English practitioners were John Gay and Alexander Pope, whose poem *The Rape of the Lock* (1712–14) is a masterpiece of the genre. Voltaire, in addition to his political and philosophical works, produced exquisite gems of occasional verse, epistles, and light satires for the enjoyment of his royal friends and patrons.

Vers de société bloomed again in 19th-century literature after the Romantic movement's decline, with the poetry of William Ernest Henley and the scholarly Austin Dobson.

Later in the 20th century, the American poet Ogden Nash created a new, sophisticated, and urbane vers de société with a theme of self-ironic adult helplessness. In England the tradition was kept alive by the neo-Victorian topical poems of Sir John Betjeman.

VERS LIBRE

Vers libre (meaning "free verse") is a 19th-century poetic innovation that liberated French poetry from its traditional prosodic rules. In vers libre, the basic metrical unit is the phrase rather than a line of a fixed number of syllables, as was traditional in French versification since the Middle Ages. In vers libre, the lengths of lines may vary according to the sense of the poem, the complete sentence replaces the stanza as a unit of meaning, and rhyme is optional.

Vers libre appears to have been the independent invention of several different French poets in the late 1880s. Among its early advocates and theoreticians were

Gustave Kahn, Jules Laforgue, Francis Vielé-Griffin, and Édouard Dujardin. The use of a free prosodic structure in French poetry was not entirely new: it had antecedents in the poems of the Symbolists, the prose poems of Rimbaud, and, much earlier, in the metrical experiments of Victor Hugo. But the widespread adoption of vers libre at the end of the 19th century influenced poetic trends in other countries, so that verse patterned on irregular metrical designs has become a tradition in the modern poetry of all Western nations.

VERSET

A verset is a short verse, especially from a sacred book, such as those found in the biblical Song of Solomon and the Psalms, or a stanza form modeled on such biblical verse. The stanza form is characterized by long lines and powerful, surging rhythms and usually expresses fervent religious or patriotic sentiments. The verset is a flexible form approximating free verse and the prose poem and is open to a wide range of emotional expression. Poetic devices such as repetition, assonance, alliteration, and figures of speech contribute to the overall vigour of the lines. The verset appears mainly in the literature of European Christian countries where it was first used in medieval religious and mystical texts. Friedrich Hölderlin, Charles Péguy, and Paul Claudel have all written poems in this form.

VILLANELLE

The villanelle is a rustic song in Italy, where the term originated (from *villano*, "peasant"). The term was used in France to designate a short poem of popular character favoured by poets in the late 16th century. Joachim du Bellay's "Vanneur de Blé" and Philippe Desportes's "Rozette" are examples of this early type, unrestricted in form. Jean Passerat left several villanelles, one so popular that it set the pattern for later poets and, accidentally, imposed a rigorous and somewhat monotonous form: seven-syllable lines using two rhymes, distributed in (normally) five tercets and a final quatrain with line repetitions.

The villanelle was revived in the 19th century by Philoxène Boyer and J. Boulmier. Leconte de Lisle and, later, Maurice Rollinat also wrote villanelles. In England, the villanelle was cultivated by W.E. Henley, Austin Dobson, Andrew Lang, and Edmund Gosse. Villanelles in English include Henley's "A Dainty Thing's the Villanelle," which itself describes the form, and the Welsh poet Dylan Thomas's "Do Not Go Gentle into That Good Night."

WAKA

The *waka* is a type of Japanese poetry, specifically the court poetry of the 6th to the 14th century, including such forms as the *chōka* and *sedōka*, in contrast to such later forms as *renga, haikai,* and haiku.

The term *waka* also is used, however, as a synonym for *tanka* ("short poem"), which is the basic form of Japanese poetry.

The *chōka*, "long poem," is of indefinite length, formed of alternating lines of five and seven syllables, ending with an extra seven-syllable line. Many *chōka* have been lost. The shortest of those extant are 7 lines long, the longest have 150 lines. They may be followed by one or more envoys (*hanka*). The amplitude of the *chōka* permitted the poets to treat themes impossible within the compass of the *tanka*.

The *sedōka,* or "head-repeated poem," consists of two tercets of five, seven, and seven syllables each. An uncommon form, it was sometimes used for dialogues. Kakinomoto Hitomaro's *sedōka* are noteworthy. *Chōka* and *sedōka* were seldom written after the 8th century.

The *tanka* has existed throughout the history of written poetry, outlasting the *chōka* and preceding the haiku. It consists of 31 syllables in five lines of 5, 7, 5, 7, and 7 syllables each. The envoys to *chōka* were in *tanka* form. As a separate form, *tanka* also served as the progenitor of *renga* and haiku.

Renga, or "linked verse," is a form in which two or more poets supplied alternating sections of a poem. The *Kin'yōshū* (*c.* 1125) was the first imperial anthology to include *renga*, at that time simply *tanka* composed by two poets, one supplying the first three lines and the other the last two. The first poet often gave obscure or contradictory details, challenging the second to complete the poem intelligibly and inventively. These were *tan* ("short") *renga* and generally light in tone. Eventually, "codes" were drawn up. Using these, the form developed fully in the 15th century, when a distinction came to be drawn between *ushin* ("serious") *renga*, which followed the conventions of court poetry, and *haikai* ("comic"), or *mushin* ("unconventional") *renga*, which deliberately broke those conventions in terms of vocabulary and diction. The standard length of a *renga* was one hundred verses, although there were variations. Verses were linked by verbal and thematic associations, while the mood of the poem drifted subtly as successive poets took up one another's thoughts. An outstanding example is the melancholy *Minase sangin hyakuin* (1488; *Minase Sangin Hyakuin: A Poem of One Hundred Links Composed by Three Poets at Minase,* 1956), composed by Sōgi, Shōhaku, and Sōchō. Later the initial verse (*hokku*) of a *renga* developed into the independent haiku form.

Japanese poetry has generally consisted of very small basic units, and its historical development has been one of gradual compression down to the three-line haiku, in which an instantaneous fragment of an emotion or perception takes the place of broader exposition.

YUEFU

The form of Chinese poetry derived from the folk-ballad tradition is called the *yuefu* (*yüeh-fu*). The *yuefu* takes its name

LI BAI

(b. 701, Jiangyou, Sichuan province, China—d. 762, Dangtu, Anhui province)

Li Bai was one of China's greatest poets. He left home at age 24 for a period of wandering, after which he married and lived with his wife's family in Anlu (now in Hubei province). He had already begun to write poetry, some of which he showed to various officials in the vain hope of becoming employed as a secretary. After another nomadic period, in 742 he arrived at Chang'an, the Tang dynasty capital, no doubt hoping to be given a post at court. No official post was forthcoming, but he was accepted into a group of distinguished court poets. In the autumn of 744 he began his wanderings again.

In 756 Li Bai became unofficial poet laureate to the military expedition of Prince Lin, the emperor's 16th son. The prince was soon accused of intending to establish an independent kingdom and was executed. Li Bai was arrested and imprisoned at Jiujiang, and in 758 he was banished to Yelang. Before he arrived there, he benefited from a general amnesty. He returned to eastern China, where he died in a relative's house, though popular legend says that he drowned when, sitting drunk in a boat, he tried to seize the moon's reflection in the water.

Li Bai was a romantic in his view of life and in his verse. One of the most famous wine drinkers in China's long tradition of imbibers, Li Bai frequently celebrated the joy of drinking. He also wrote of friendship, solitude, the passage of time, and the joys of nature with brilliance and great freshness of imagination.

from the Yuefu ("Music Bureau") created in 120 BCE by the emperor Wudi of Han for the purpose of collecting songs and their musical scores for ceremonial occasions at court. The music for these songs was later lost, but the words remained, forming a collection of Han dynasty (206 BCE–220 CE) folk poetry that served as the basis of the *yuefu* form.

These poems were significant because they consisted of lines of varying lengths, some having a regular form of five syllables per line rather than the then-standard four-syllable line. The *yuefu* thus broke ground for the later classic *gushi* ("ancient-style poetry"), with its broader use of rhyme and fewer metrical restrictions. Many later writers, including the great Li Bai (701–762) and Bai Juyi (772–846), continued to create poems derived from the *yuefu* tradition.

CHAPTER 2

PROSODY

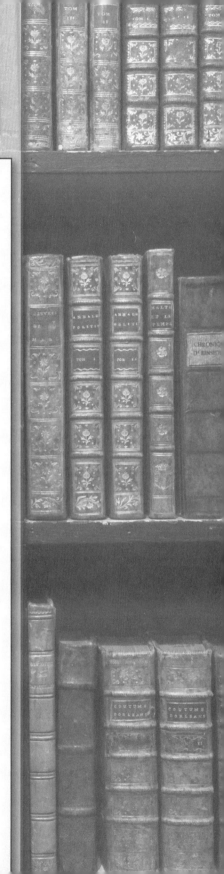

The study of all the elements of language that contribute toward acoustic and rhythmic effects in poetry and prose is called prosody. The term derived from an ancient Greek word that originally meant a song accompanied by music or the particular tone or accent given to an individual syllable. Greek and Latin literary critics generally regarded prosody as part of grammar. It concerned itself with the rules determining the length or shortness of a syllable, with syllabic quantity, and with how the various combinations of short and long syllables formed the metres (i.e., the rhythmic patterns) of Greek and Latin poetry. Prosody was the study of metre and its uses in lyric, epic, and dramatic verse. In sophisticated modern criticism, however, the scope of prosodic study has been expanded until it now concerns itself with what the 20th-century poet Ezra Pound called "the articulation of the total sound of a poem."

Prose as well as verse reveals the use of rhythm and sound effects, but critics do not speak of "the prosody of prose" but of "prose rhythm." The English critic George Saintsbury wrote a definitive three-volume *History of English Prosody from the Twelfth Century to the Present* (1906–10), which treats English poetry from its origins to the end of the 19th century. But he dealt with prose rhythm in an entirely separate work, *A History of English Prose Rhythm* (1912). Many prosodic elements such as the rhythmic repetition of consonants (alliteration) or of vowel sounds (assonance) occur in prose. The repetition of syntactical and grammatical patterns also generates rhythmic effect. Traditional rhetoric, the study of how words work, dealt with acoustic and rhythmic techniques in Classical oratory and literary prose. But although prosody and rhetoric intersected, rhetoric dealt more exactly with verbal meaning than with verbal surface. Rhetoric dealt with grammatical and syntactical manipulations and with figures of speech. It categorized the kinds of metaphor. Twentieth-century critics, especially those who practiced the New Criticism, bore some resemblance to rhetoricians in their detailed concern with such devices as irony, paradox, and ambiguity.

This chapter considers prosody chiefly in terms of the English language. Some examples are given in other languages to illustrate particular points about the development of prosody in those languages. Because these examples are pertinent only for their rhythm and sound, and not at all for their meaning, no translations are given.

ELEMENTS OF PROSODY

As a part of modern literary criticism, prosody is concerned with the study of rhythm and sound effects as they occur in verse and with the various descriptive, historical, and theoretical approaches to the study of these structures. Though many of these elements are inseparable from one another in the effect produced, they are often clearer when discussed discretely.

SCANSION

The various elements of prosody may be examined in the aesthetic structure of prose. The celebrated opening passage of Charles Dickens's novel *Bleak House* (1853) affords a compelling example of prose made vivid through the devices of rhythm and sound:

> *Fog everywhere. Fog up the river, where it flows among green aits and meadows; fog down the river, where it rolls defiled among the tiers of shipping, and the waterside pollutions of a great (and dirty) city. Fog on the Essex Marshes, fog on the Kentish heights. Fog creeping into the cabooses of collier-brigs; fog lying out on the yards, and hovering in the rigging of great ships; fog drooping on the gunwales of barges and small boats. Fog in the eyes and throats of ancient Greenwich pensioners, wheezing by the firesides of their wards; fog in the stem and bowl of the afternoon pipe of the wrathful skipper....*

Two phrases of five syllables each ("Fog everywhere"; "Fog up the river") establish a powerful rhythmic expectation that is clinched in repetition:

> ... *fog down the river* .... *Fog on the Essex* ..., *fog on the Kentish* .... *Fog creeping into* ... ; ... *fog drooping on the* ...

This phrase pattern can be scanned. That is, its structure of stressed and unstressed syllables might be translated into visual symbols:

$$\acute{\text{Fog}} \ \breve{\text{down}} \ \breve{\text{the}} \ \acute{\text{ri}} \ \breve{\text{ver}}.$$

(This scansion notation uses the following symbols: the acute accent [′] marks metrically stressed syllables; the breve [˘] marks metrically weak syllables; a single line [|] marks the divisions between feet [i.e., basic combinations of stressed and unstressed syllables]; a double line [‖] marks the caesura, or pause in the line; and a carat [∧] marks a syllable metrically expected but not actually occurring.) Such a grouping constitutes a rhythmic constant, or cadence, a pattern binding together the separate sentences and sentence fragments into a long surge of feeling. At one point in the passage, the rhythm sharpens into metre. A pattern of stressed and unstressed syllables falls into a regular sequence:

$$\acute{\text{Fog}} \ \breve{\text{on}} \ \breve{\text{the}} | \ \acute{\text{Es}} \ \breve{\text{sex}} \ | \ \acute{\text{mar}} \ \breve{\text{shes}}, \| \ \acute{\text{fog}} \ \breve{\text{on}} \ \breve{\text{the}} |$$
$$\acute{\text{Ken}} \ \breve{\text{tish}} | \ \acute{\text{heights}}.$$

The line is a hexameter (i.e., it comprises six feet), and each foot is either a dactyl (˘ ˘) or a trochee (˘).

The passage from Dickens is strongly characterized by alliteration, the repetition of stressed consonantal sounds:

> *Fog creeping into the cabooses of collier-brigs;*

and by assonance, the patterned repetition of vowel sounds:

> . . . *fog down the river, where it rolls defiled among* ...

Here the vowel sounds are symmetrically distributed: short, long and long, short. Thus, it is clear that Dickens uses loosely structured rhythms, or cadences, an occasional lapse into metre, and both alliteration and assonance.

The rhythm and sound of all prose are subject to analysis. But compared with even the simplest verse, the "prosodic" structure of prose seems haphazard, unconsidered. The poet organizes his structures of sound and rhythm into rhyme, stanzaic form, and, most importantly, metre. Indeed, the largest part of prosodical study is concerned with the varieties of metre, the nature and function of rhyme, and the ways in which lines of verse fall into regular patterns or stanzas. An analysis of "Vertue" by the 17th-century English poet George Herbert reveals how the elements of prosody combine into a complex organism, a life sustained by the technical means available to the poet. When the metre is scanned with the symbols, it can be seen (and heard) how metre in this poem consists of the regular recurrence of feet, how each foot is a pattern of phonetically stressed and unstressed syllables.

˘ ´ ˘ ´ ˘ ´ ˘ ´
1 Sweet day, | so cool, | so calm, | so bright,
˘ ´ ˘ ´ ˘ ´ ˘ ´
2 The bri | dall of | the earth | and skie:
˘ ´ ˘ ´ ˘ ´ ˘ ´
3 The dew | shall weep | thy fall | to-night;
˘ ´ ˘ ´
4   For thou | must die.

˘ ´ ˘ ´ ´ ˘ ˘ ´
5 Sweet rose, | whose hue | an grie | and brave
´ ˘ ˘ ´ ˘ ´ ˘ ´
6 Bids the | rash ga | zer wipe | his eye:
˘ ´ ˘ ´ ˘ ´ ˘ ´
7 Thy root | is ev | er in | its grave,
˘ ´ ˘ ´
8   And thou | must die.

˘ ´ ˘ ´ ˘ ´ ˘ ´ ˘
9 Sweet spring, | full of | sweet dayes | and ro | ses,
˘ ´ ˘ ´ ˘ ´ ˘ ´
10 A box | where sweets | com pac | ted lie;
˘ ´ ˘ ´ ˘ ´ ˘ ´ ˘
11 My mu | sick shows | ye have | your clo | ses,
˘ ´ ˘ ´
12   And all | must die.

´ ˘ ˘ ´ ˘ ´ ˘ ´
13 Onely | a sweet | and ver | tuous soul,
˘ ´ ˘ ´ ˘ ´ ˘ ´
14 Like sea | son'd tim | ber, ne | ver gives;
˘ ´ ˘ ´ ˘ ´ ˘ ´
15 But though | the whole | world turn | to coal,
˘ ´ ˘ ´
16   Then chief | ly lives.

The basic prosodic units are the foot, line, and stanza. The recurrence of similar feet in a line determines the metre. Here there are three lines consisting of four iambic feet (i.e., of four units in which the common pattern is the iamb—an unstressed syllable followed by a stressed syllable), which are followed by a line consisting of two iambic feet. Thus the stanza or recurring set of lines consists of three iambic tetrameters followed by one iambic dimeter. The stanzaic form is clinched by the use of rhyme. In "Vertue" the first and third and second and fourth lines end with the same sequence of vowels and consonants: bright/night, skie/pie, brave/grave, eye/pie, etc. It should be observed that the iambic pattern (˘) is not invariable. The third foot of line 5, the first foot of line 6, the second foot of line 9, and the first foot of line 13 are reversals of the iambic foot or trochees (´). These reversals are called substitutions. They provide tension between metrical pattern and meaning, as they do in these celebrated examples from Shakespeare:

˘ ´ ˘ ´ ˘ ´ ´ ˘ ˘ ´ ˘
To be, | or not | to be, ‖ that is | the ques tion . . . .
(Macbeth)
˘ ´ ˘ ´ ´ ˘ ˘ ´ ˘ ´
His sil | ver skin | *laced with* | his gol | den blood . . .
(Hamlet)

MEANING, PACE, AND SOUND

Scansion reveals the basic metrical pattern of the poem. It does not, however, tell everything about its prosody. The metre combines with other elements, notably propositional sense or meaning, pace or tempo, and such sound effects as alliteration, assonance, and rhyme. In the fifth line of "Vertue," the reversed third foot occurring at *angry* brings that word into particular prominence. The disturbance of the metre combines with semantic reinforcement to generate a powerful surge of feeling. Thus, the metre here is expressive. The pace of the lines is controlled by the length of number of syllables and feet, line 5 obviously takes longer to read or recite. The line contains more long vowel sounds:

Sweet rose, whose hue angrie and brave…

Vowel length is called quantity. In English verse, quantity cannot by itself form metre although a number of English poets have experimented with quantitative verse. Generally speaking, quantity is a rhythmical but not a metrical feature of English poetry. It can be felt, but it cannot be precisely determined. The vowel sounds in "Sweet rose" may be lengthened or shortened at will. No such options are available, however, with the stress patterns of words. The word *angry*, which in English has the emphasis on the first syllable, will not be understood if it is read with the emphasis on the second syllable.

Assonance takes into account the length and distribution of vowel sounds. A variety of vowel sounds can be noted in this line:

Sweet day, so cool, so calm, so bright…

To borrow a term from music, the line modulates from ēē, through ā, ōō, ă,

to ī. Alliteration takes into account the recurrence and distribution of consonants:

so cool, so calm…

Sweet spring…

Rhyme normally occurs at the ends of lines. "Vertue" reveals, however, a notable example of interior rhyme, or rhyme within the line:

My musick shows ye have your closes…

TYPES OF METRE

Metre is the rhythmic pattern of a poetic line. Various principles, based on the natural rhythms of language, have been devised to organize poetic lines into rhythmic units. These have produced distinct kinds of versification, among which the most common are syllable-stress (or accentual-syllabic), strong-stress, syllabic, and quantitative.

SYLLABLE-STRESS METRES

It has been shown that the metre of "Vertue" is determined by a pattern of stressed and unstressed syllables arranged into feet and that a precise number of feet determines the measure of the line. Such verse is called syllable-stress verse and was the norm for English poetry from the beginning of the 16th century to the end of the 19th century. A line of syllable-stress verse is made up of either two-syllable (disyllabic) or three-syllable (trisyllabic) feet. The disyllabic feet are the iamb and the trochee (both can be noted in the scansion of "Vertue"). The trisyllabic feet are the dactyl (′ ˘˘) and anapest (˘˘ ′).

Following are illustrations of the four principal feet found in English verse:

	˘ ′
iambic	be hold
	′ ˘
trochaic	ti ger
	′ ˘ ˘
dactylic	des per ate
	˘ ˘ ′
anapestic	un der stand

Some theorists also admit the spondaic foot (′ ′) and pyrrhic foot (˘ ˘) into their scansions. However, spondees and pyrrhics occur only as substitutions for other feet, never as determinants of a metrical pattern:

When to | the ses | sions of | sweet si | lent thought …

It has been noted that four feet make up a line of tetrameter verse. A line consisting of one foot is called monometer, of two dimeter, of three trimeter, of five pentameter, of six hexameter, and of seven heptameter. Lines containing more than seven feet rarely occur in English poetry.

The following examples illustrate the principal varieties of syllable-stress metres and their scansions:

Iambic (pentameter)

Then say | not Man's | im per | fect,‖ Heaven | in fault;

Say ra | ther,‖ Man's | as per | fect as | he ought:

His know | ledge meas | ured ‖ to | his state | and place,

His time | a mo | ment,‖ and | a point | his space.

(Alexander Pope, *An Essay on Man*, 1733–34)

Trochaic (dimeter)

Could I | catch that

Nim ble | trai tor

Scorn ful | Lau ra,

Swift-foot | Lau ra,

Soon then | would I

Seek a | venge ment.

(Thomas Campion, 1602)

Dactylic (tetrameter)

Af ter the | pangs of a | des per ate | Lover, ∧

When day and | night I have | sigh'd all in | vain, ∧∧

Ah what a | pleas ure it | is to dis | co ver ∧

In her eyes | pi ty, who | cau ses my | pain! ∧∧

(John Dryden, *An Evening's Love*, 1671)

Anapestic (tetrameter)

The As syr | ian came down | like a wolf | on the fold,

And his co | horts were gleam | ing in pur | ple and gold;

And the sheen | of their spears | was like stars | on the sea,

When the blue | wave rolls night | ly on deep | Ga li lee.

(Lord Byron, "The Destruction of Sennacherib", 1815)

Syllable stress became more or less established in the 14th century, in the poetry of Geoffrey Chaucer. In the century that intervened between Chaucer and the early Tudor poets, syllable-stress metres were either ignored or misconstrued. By the end of the 16th century, however, the now-familiar iambic, trochaic, dactylic, and anapestic metres became the traditional prosody for English verse.

STRONG-STRESS METRES

In the middle of the 19th century, with Walt Whitman's free verse and Gerard Manley Hopkins's extensive metrical innovations, the traditional prosody was challenged. Antecedent to the syllable-stress metres was the strong-stress metre of Old English and Middle English poetry. Strong-stress verse is measured by count of stresses alone. The strong stresses are usually constant, but the number of unstressed syllables may vary considerably.

Strong-stress verse survives in nursery rhymes and children's counting songs:

Walt Whitman (shown here five years before his death) challenged the convention of writing poetry in a standard poetic metre, instead by writing in free verse. Library of Congress Prints and Photographs Division

One, two, ‖ buckle my shoe;

Three, four, ‖ knock at the door;

Five, six, ‖ pick up sticks . . .

The systematic employment of strong-stress metre can be observed in the Old English epic poem *Beowulf* (c. 1000) and in William Langland's vision-poem, *Piers Plowman* (A version, c. 1362):

In a somer sesun ‖ whon softe was the sonne,

I schop me in-to a schroud ‖ a scheep as I were;

In habite of an hermite ‖ un-holy of werkes,

Wende I wydene in this world ‖ wondres to here.

These lines illustrate the structural pattern of strong-stress metre. Each line divides sharply at the caesura (‖), or medial pause. On each side of the caesura are two stressed syllables strongly marked by alliteration.

Strong-stress verse is indigenous to the Germanic languages with their wide-ranging levels of stressed syllables and opportunities for alliteration. Strong-stress metre was normative to Old English and Old Germanic heroic poetry, as well as to Old English lyric poetry. With the rising influence of French literature in the 12th and 13th centuries, rhyme replaced alliteration and stanzaic forms replaced the four-stress lines. But the strong-stress rhythm persisted. It can be felt in the anonymous love lyrics of the 14th

T.S. ELIOT

(b. Sept. 26, 1888, St. Louis, Mo., U.S.—
d. Jan. 4, 1965, London, Eng.)

T.S. Eliot, an American-English poet, play-wright, and critic, was a leader of the Modernist movement in poetry. Eliot studied at Harvard University before moving to England in 1914, where he would work as an editor from the early 1920s until his death. His first important poem, and the first modernist masterpiece in English, was the radically experimental "Love Song of J. Alfred Prufrock" (1915). The Waste Land *(1922), which expresses with startling power the disillusionment of the postwar years, made his international reputation. His first critical volume,* The Sacred Wood *(1920), introduced concepts much discussed in later critical theory. He married in 1915. His wife was mentally unstable, and they separated in 1933. (He married again, happily, in 1957.) His conversion to Anglicanism in 1927 shaped all his subsequent works. His last great work was* Four Quartets *(1936–42), four poems on spiritual renewal and the connections of the personal and historical past and present. Influential later essays include "The Idea of a Christian Society" (1939) and "Notes Towards the Definition of Culture" (1948). His play* Murder in the Cathedral *(1935) is a verse treatment of St. Thomas Becket's martyrdom. His other plays, including* The Cocktail Party *(1950), are lesser works. From the 1920s on he was the most influential English-language modernist poet. He won the Nobel Prize for Literature in 1948; from then until his death he achieved public admiration unequaled by any other 20th-century poet.*

century and in the popular ballads of the 15th century.

"Lord Randal" can be comfortably scanned to show a line of mixed iambic and anapestic feet. It clearly reveals, however, a four-stress structure:

'O where ha' you been, ‖ Lord Randal, my son?

And where ha' you been, ‖ my handsome young man?'

'I ha' been at the greenwood; ‖ mother, mak my bed soon,

For I'm wearied wi' huntin', ‖ and fain wad lie down.'

A number of 20th-century poets, including Ezra Pound, T.S. Eliot, and W.H. Auden, revived strong-stress metre. The versification of Pound's *Cantos* and Eliot's *Four Quartets* (1943) shows the vitality of the strong-stress, or, as they are often called, "native," metres.

SYLLABIC METRES

Most of English poetry is carried by the strong-stress and syllable-stress metres. Two other kinds of metres must be mentioned: the purely syllabic metres and the quantitative metres. The count of syllables determines the metres of French, Italian, and Spanish verse. In French poetry the alexandrine, or 12-syllabled line, is a dominant metrical form:

> *O toi, qui vois la honte où je suis descendue,*
> *Implacable Vénus, suis-je assez*
>   *confondue?*
> *Tu ne saurais plus loin pousser ta cruauté.*
> *Ton triomphe est parfait; tous tes traits*
>   *ont porté.*
>
>   (Racine, *Phèdre*, 1677)

Stress and pause in these lines are variable. Only the count of syllables is fixed. English poets have experimented with syllabic metres. Tudor poet Sir Thomas Wyatt's translations from Petrarch's Italian poems of the 14th century attempted to establish a metrical form based on a decasyllabic or 10-syllabled line:

> *The long love that in my thought doth*
> *harbour,*
> *And in my heart doth keep his residence,*
> *Into my face presseth with bold pretense*
> *And there encampeth, spreading his*
> *banner.*
>
> ("The Lover for Shamefastness
> Hideth ...," 1557)

Most ears can detect that these lines waver between syllabic and syllable-stress metre. The second line falls into a pattern of iambic feet. Most ears also discover that the count of syllables alone does not produce any pronounced rhythmic interest. Syllabic metres in English generate a prosody more interesting to the eye than to the ear.

QUANTITATIVE METRES

Quantitative metres determine the prosody of Greek and Latin verse. Renaissance theorists and critics initiated a confused and complicated argument that tried to explain European poetry by the rules of Classical prosody and to draft laws of quantity by which European verse might move in the hexameters of the ancient Roman poets Virgil or Horace. Confusion was compounded because both poets and theorists used the traditional terminology of Greek and Latin prosody to describe the elements of the already existing syllable-stress metres. Iambic, trochaic, dactylic, and anapestic originally named the strictly quantitative feet of Greek and Latin poetry. Poets themselves adapted the metres and stanzas of Classical poetry to their own languages. Whereas it is not possible here to trace the history of Classical metres in European poetry, it is instructive to analyze some attempts to make English and German syllables move to Greek and Latin music. Because neither English nor German has fixed rules of quantity, the poets were forced to revise the formal schemes of the Classical paradigms in accordance with the phonetic structure of their own language.

A metrical paradigm much used by both Greek and Latin poets was the so-called Sapphic stanza. It consisted of three quantitative lines that scanned

- ˘ - - - ˘ ˘ - ˘ - ˘,

followed by a shorter line, called an Adonic,

- ˘ ˘ - - .

"Sapphics" by the 19th-century English poet Algernon Charles Swinburne shows the Sapphic metre and stanza in English:

> *All the night sleep came not upon my*
> *eyelids,*
> *Shed not dew, nor shook nor unclosed a*
> *feather,*
> *Yet with lips shut close and with eyes of iron*

Stood and beheld me . . .
Saw the white implacable Aphrodite,
Saw the hair unbound and the feet
  unsandalled
Shine as fire of sunset on western waters;
Saw the reluctant . . . .

The same metre and stanza in German are found in "Sapphische Ode," by the 19th-century poet Hans Schmidt, which was beautifully set to music by Johannes Brahms (Opus 94, No. 4):

Rosen brach ich nachts mir am
  dunklen Hage;
Süsser hauchten Duft sie, als je am Tage;
Doch verstreuten reich die bewegten Äste
Tau, der mich nässte.
Auch der Küsse Duft mich wie nie berückte,
Die ich nachts vom Strauch deiner Lippen
  pflückte;
Doch auch dir, bewegt im Gemüt
  gleich jenen,
Tauten die Tränen.

Quantitative metres originated in Greek, a language in which the parts of speech appear in a variety of inflected forms (i.e., changes of form to indicate distinctions in case, tense, mood, number, voice, and others). Complicated metrical patterns and long, slow paced lines developed because the language was hospitable to polysyllabic metrical feet and to the alternation of the longer vowels characterizing the root syllables and the shorter vowels characterizing the inflected case-endings. The Classical metres can be more successfully adapted to German than to English because English lost most of its inflected forms in the 15th century, while German is still a highly inflected language. Thus Swinburne's "Sapphics" does not move as gracefully, as "naturally" as Schmidt's. A number of German poets, notably Goethe and Friedrich Hölderlin, both of the early 19th century, made highly successful use of the Classical metres. English poets, however, have never been able to make English syllables move in the ancient metres with any degree of comfort or with any sense of vital rhythmic force.

The American poet Henry Wadsworth Longfellow adapted the Classical hexameter for his *Evangeline* (1847):

This is the | for est pri | me val. The | mur mu ring | pines and
the | hem locks . . .

In Virgil's *Aeneid*, Longfellow's Classical model, the opening line scans:

Ar ma vi rum que ca no, Troj ae qui pri mus ab or is

The rules determining length of syllable in Classical Greek and Latin poetry are numerous and complicated. They were established by precise grammatical and phonetic conventions. No such rules and conventions obtain in English. Robert Bridges, the British poet laureate and an authority on prosody, remarked in his *Poetical Works* (1912) that the difficulty of adapting English syllables to the Greek rules is "very great, and even deterrent." Longfellow's hexameter is in reality

Ezra Pound mastered the traditional metres but also experimented with different cadences. Keystone/Hulton Archive/Getty Images

a syllable-stress line of five dactyls and a final trochee. Syllabic quantity plays no part in determining the metre.

PROSODIC STYLE

The analysis of prosodic style begins with recognizing the metrical form the poet uses. Is he writing syllable-stress, strong-stress, syllabic, or quantitative metre? Or is he using a nonmetrical prosody? Again, some theorists would not allow that poetry can be written without metre. The examples of Whitman and many 20th-century innovators, however, have convinced most critics that a nonmetrical prosody is not a contradiction in terms but an obvious feature of modern poetry. Metre has not disappeared as an important element of prosody. Indeed, some of the greatest poets of the 20th century—William Butler Yeats, T.S. Eliot, Ezra Pound, Wallace Stevens—revealed themselves as masters of the traditional metres. They also experimented with newer prosodies based on prose cadences, on expansions of the blank-verse line, and revivals of old forms— such as strong-stress and ballad metres. Also noteworthy are the "visual" prosodies fostered by the poets of the Imagist

E.E. CUMMINGS

(b. Oct. 14, 1894, Cambridge, Mass., U.S.—
d. Sept. 3, 1962, North Conway, N.H.)

The American poet and painter E.E. Cummings first attracted attention, in an age of literary experimentation, for his eccentric punctuation and phrasing. The spirit of New England dissent and of Emersonian "Self-Reliance" underlies the urbanized Yankee colloquialism of Cummings's verse. Cummings's name is often styled "e.e. cummings" in the mistaken belief that the poet legally changed his name to lowercase letters only. Cummings used capital letters only irregularly in his verse and did not object when publishers began lowercasing his name, but he himself capitalized his name in his signature and the title pages of original editions of his books. Cummings attended Harvard University. His experience in World War I of being held in a detention camp because of a censor's error gave rise to his first prose book, The Enormous Room *(1922). His first book of poems,* Tulips and Chimneys *(1923), was followed by 11 more. Cummings's poetry often exhibited a childlike playfulness, which won it a wide readership. His Norton lectures at Harvard were published as* i: six nonlectures *(1953).*

movement and by such experimenters as E.E. Cummings. Cummings revived the practice of certain 17th-century poets (notably George Herbert) of "shaping" the poem by typographic arrangements.

The prosodic practice of poets has varied enormously with the historical period, the poetic genre, and the poet's individual style. In English poetry, for example, during the Old English period (to 1100), the strong-stress metres carried both lyric and narrative verse. In the Middle English period (from c. 1100 to c. 1500), stanzaic forms developed for both lyric and narrative verse. The influence of French syllable counting pushed the older stress lines into newer rhythms. Chaucer developed for *The Canterbury Tales* a line of 10 syllables with alternating accent and regular end rhyme—an ancestor of the heroic couplet. The period of the English Renaissance (from c. 1500 to 1660) marks the fixing of syllable-stress metre as normative for English poetry. Iambic metre carried three major prosodic forms: the sonnet, the rhyming couplet, and blank verse. The sonnet was the most important of the fixed stanzaic forms. The iambic pentameter rhyming couplet (later known as the heroic couplet) was used by Christopher Marlowe for his narrative poem *Hero and Leander* (1598) and by John Donne in the early 17th century for his satires, elegies, and longer meditative poems. Blank verse (unrhymed iambic pentameter), first introduced into English in a translation by Henry Howard, earl of Surrey, published in 1557, became the metrical norm for Elizabethan drama. The period of the Renaissance also saw the refinement of a host of lyric and song forms; the rapid development of English music during the second half of the 16th century had a salutary effect on the expressive capabilities of poetic rhythms.

THE PERSONAL ELEMENT

A poet's choice of a prosody obviously depends on what his language and tradition afford. These are primary considerations. The anonymous author of the Old English poem *Deor* used the conventional four-stress metric available to him, but he punctuated groups of lines with a refrain:

> *Þæs ofereode, þisses swa mæg!*
> *(that passed away: this also may!)*

The refrain adds something to the prosodic conventions of regulated stress, alliteration, and medial pause: a sense of a smaller and sharper rhythmic unit within the larger rhythms of the given metre. While the poet accepts from history his language and from poetic convention the structure of his metre, he shapes his own style through individual modifications of the carrying rhythms. When critics speak of a poet's "voice," his personal tone, they are also speaking of his prosodic style.

Prosodic style must be achieved through a sense of tension. It is no accident that the great masters of poetic rhythm work against the discipline of a given metrical form. In his sonnets, Shakespeare may proceed in solemn iambic regularity, creating an effect of measured progression through time and its legacy of suffering and despair:

> *No longer mourn for me when I am dead*
> *Than you shall hear the surly sullen bell*
> *Give warning to the world that I am fled....*
> "Sonnet 71"

Or he may wrench the metre and allow the reader to feel the sudden violence of his feelings, the power of a conviction raised to a command:

Let me | not to | the mar | riage of | true minds
Ad mit | im pe | di ments. | Love is | not love ....
("Sonnet 116")

The first two feet of the first line are trochaic reversals. The last two feet comprise a characteristic pyrrhic-spondaic formation. A trochaic substitution is quite normal in the first foot of an iambic pentameter line. A trochaic substitution in the second foot, however, creates a marked disturbance in the rhythm. There is only one "normal" iambic foot in the first line. This line runs over (or is enjambed) to the second line with its three consecutive iambic feet followed by a strong caesura and reversed fourth foot. These lines are, in Gerard Manley Hopkins's terms, metrically "counter-pointed." Trochees, spondees, and pyrrhics are heard against a ground rhythm of regular iambics. Without the ground rhythm, Shakespeare's expressive departures would not be possible.

A poet's prosodic style may show all of the earmarks of revolt against prevailing metrical practice. Whitman's celebrated "free verse" marks a dramatic break with the syllable-stress tradition. He normally does not count syllables, stresses, or feet in his long sweeping lines. Much of his prosody is rhetorical; that is, Whitman urges his language into rhythm by such means as anaphora (i.e., repetition at the beginning of successive verses) and the repetition of syntactical units. He derives many of his techniques from the example of biblical verses, with their line of various types of parallelism. But he often moves toward traditional rhythms; lines fall into conventional parameters:

> *O past! O happy life! O songs of joy!*
> ("Out of the Cradle Endlessly Rocking," 1859)

Or they fall more often into disyllabic hexameters:

> *Borne through the smoke of the battles and pierc'd*
> *with missiles I saw them . . . .*
> ("When Lilacs Last in the Dooryard Bloom'd," 1865–66)

Despite the frequent appearance of regular metrical sequences, Whitman's lines cannot be scanned by the usual graphic method of marking syllables and feet. His prosody, however, is fully available to analysis. The shape on the page of the following lines (they comprise a single strophe or verse unit) should be noted, specifically the gradual elongation and sudden diminution of line length. Equally noteworthy are the repetition of the key word *carols*, the alliteration of the *s* sounds, and the use of words in falling (trochaic) rhythm, *lagging, yellow, waning*:

> *Shake out carols!*
> *Solitary here, the night's carols!*
> *Carols of lonesome love! death's carols!*
> *Carols under that lagging, yellow, waning moon!*

> *O under that moon where she droops almost down into the sea!*
> *O reckless despairing carols.*
> ("Out of the Cradle")

No regular metre moves these lines. But a clearly articulated rhythm—produced by shape, thematic repetitions, sound effects, and patterns of stress and pause—defines a prosody.

Whitman's prosody marks a clear break with previous metrical practices. Often a new prosody modifies an existing metrical form or revives an obsolete one. In "Gerontion" (1920), T.S. Eliot adjusted the blank-verse line to the emotionally charged, prophetic utterance of his persona, a spiritually arid old man:

> *After such knowledge, what forgiveness?*
> *Think now*
> *History has many cunning passages,*
> *contrived corridors*
> *And issues, deceives with whispering ambitions,*
> *Guides us by vanities. Think now . . .*
> (From T.S. Eliot, *Collected Poems 1909–1962*, Harcourt Brace Jovanovich, Inc.)

The first three lines expand the pentameter line beyond its normal complement of stressed and unstressed syllables. The fourth line contracts, intensifying the arc of feeling. Both Pound and Eliot used stress prosodies. Pound counted out four strong beats and used alliteration in his brilliant adaptation of the old English poem "The Seafarer" (1912):

Chill its chains are; chafing sighs
Hew my heart round and hunger begot
Mere-weary mood. Lest man known not
That he on dry land loveliest liveth . . .
(From Ezra Pound, *Personae*, Copyright 1926
by Ezra Pound. Reprinted by permission of
New Directions Publishing Corporation.)

He uses a similar metric for the energetic opening of his "Canto I." Eliot mutes the obvious elements of the form in the celebrated opening of *The Waste Land* (1922):

April is the cruellest month, breeding
Lilacs out of the dead land, mixing
Memory and desire, stirring
Dull roots with spring rain.
(From T.S. Eliot, *Collected Poems 1909-*
1962, Harcourt Brace Jovanovich, Inc.)

Here is the "native metre" with its falling rhythm, elegiac tone, strong pauses, and variably placed stresses. If this is free verse, its freedoms are most carefully controlled. "No verse is free," said Eliot, "for the man who wants to do a good job."

The prosodic styles of Whitman, Pound, and Eliot—though clearly linked to various historical antecedents—are innovative expressions of their individual talents. In a sense, the prosody of every poet of genius is unique. Rhythm is perhaps the most personal element of the poet's expressive equipment. Alfred, Lord Tennyson and Robert Browning, English poets who shared the intellectual and spiritual concerns of the Victorian age, are miles apart in their prosodies.

Both used blank verse for their dramatic lyrics, poems that purport to render the accents of real men speaking. The blank verse of Tennyson's "Ulysses" (1842) offers smoothly modulated vowel music, carefully spaced spondaic substitutions, and unambiguous pentameter regularity:

The long day wanes; the slow moon
climbs; the deep
Moans round with many voices. Come,
my friends,
'Tis not too late to seek a newer world.

Browning's blank verse aims at colloquial vigour. Its "irregularity" is a function not of any gross metrical violation—it always obeys the letter of the metrical law—but of the adjustment of abstract metrical pattern to the rhythms of dramatic speech. If Tennyson's ultimate model is Milton's Baroque prosody with its oratorical rhythms, Browning's model was the quick and nervous blank verse of the later Elizabethan dramatists. Characteristic of Browning's blank verse are the strong accents, involuted syntax, pregnant caesuras, and headlong energy in "The Bishop Orders His Tomb at St. Praxed's Church" (1845):

Vanity, saith the preacher, vanity!
Draw round my bed: is Anselm
keeping back?
Nephews—sons mine . . . ah God, I know
not! Well—
She, men would have to be your
mother once,
Old Gandolf envied me, so fair she was!

INFLUENCE OF PERIOD AND GENRE

In the lyric genres, the rhythms of the individual poet—or, in the words of the 20th-century American poet Robert Lowell, "the person himself"—can be heard in the prosody. In the long poem, the dramatic, narrative, and didactic genres, a period style is more likely to be heard in prosody. The blank-verse tragedy of the Elizabethan and Jacobean dramatists, the blank verse of Milton's *Paradise Lost* (1667) and its imitators in the 18th century (James Thomson and William Cowper), and the heroic couplet of Neoclassical satiric and didactic verse, each, in different ways, defines the age in which these prosodies flourished. The flexibility and energy of the dramatic verse of Marlowe, Shakespeare, and John Webster reflect the later Renaissance with its nervous open-mindedness, its obsessions with power and domination, and its lapses into despair. Miltonic blank verse, based on Latin syntax and adaptations of the rules of Latin prosody, moved away from the looseness of the Elizabethans and Jacobeans toward a more ceremonial style. It is a Baroque style in that it exploits the musical qualities of sounds for their ornamental values. The heroic couplet, dominating the poetry of the entire 18th century, was unequivocally a prosodic period style. Its elegance and epigrammatic precision entirely suited an age that valued critical judgment, satiric wit, and the powers of rationality.

It is in dramatic verse, perhaps, that a prosody shows its greatest vitality and clarity. Dramatic verse must make a direct impression not on an individual reader able to reconsider and meditate on what he has read but on an audience that must immediately respond to a declaiming actor or a singing chorus. The ancient Greek dramatists developed two distinct kinds of metres: "stichic" forms (i.e., consisting of "stichs," or lines, as metrical units) such as the iambic trimeter for the spoken dialogues; and lyric, or strophic, forms (i.e., consisting of stanzas), of great metrical intricacy, for the singing and chanting of choruses. Certain of the Greek metres developed a particular ethos. Characters of low social standing never were assigned metres of the lyric variety. Similar distinctions obtained in Elizabethan drama. Shakespeare's kings and noblemen speak blank verse; comic characters, servants, and country bumpkins discourse in prose; clowns, romantic heroines, and supernatural creatures sing songs. In the early tragedy *Romeo and Juliet,* the chorus speaks in "excellent conceited" sonnets: in what was one of the most popular and easily recognized lyric forms of the period.

The metrical forms used by ancient and Renaissance dramatists were determined by principles of decorum. The use or non-use of a metrical form (or the use of prose) was a matter of propriety. It was important that the metre be suitable to the social status and ethos of the individual character as well as be suitable to the emotional intensity of the particular situation. Decorum, in turn, was a function of the dominant Classical and Neoclassical theories of imitation.

THEORIES OF PROSODY

Ancient critics such as Aristotle and Horace insisted that certain metres were natural to the specific poetic genres. Thus, Aristotle (in the *Poetics*) noted that "Nature herself, as we have said, teaches the choice of the proper measure." In epic verse the poet should use the heroic measure (dactylic hexameter) because this metre most effectively represents or imitates such qualities as grandeur, dignity, and high passion. Horace narrowed the theory of metrical decorum, making the choice of metre prescriptive. Only an ill-bred and ignorant poet would treat comic material in metres appropriate to tragedy. Horace prepared the way for the legalisms of the Renaissance theorists who were quite willing to inform practicing poets that they used "feete without joyntes," in the words of Roger Ascham, Queen Elizabeth's tutor, and should use the quantitative metres of Classical prosody.

THE MIDDLE AGES

During the Middle Ages little of importance was added to actual prosodic theory. In poetic practice, however, crucial developments were to have important ramifications for later theorists. From about the second half of the 6th century to the end of the 8th century, Latin verse was written that no longer observed the rules of quantity but was clearly structured on accentual and syllabic bases. This change was aided by the invention of the musical sequence. It became necessary to fit a musical phrase to a fixed number of syllables, and the older, highly complex system of quantitative prosody could not be adapted to simple melodies that must be sung in sequential patterns. In the musical sequence lies the origin of the modern lyric form.

The 9th-century hymn "Ave maris stella" is a striking instance of the change from quantitative to accentual syllabic prosody. Each line contains three trochaic feet determined not by length of syllable but by syllabic intensity or stress:

> *Ave maris stella*
> *Dei Mater alma*
> *atque semper Virgo,*
> *felix caeli porta.*
> *Sumens illud* Ave
> *Gabrielis ore,*
> *funda nos in pace,*
> *mutans Hevae nomen.*

The rules of quantity have been disregarded or forgotten. Rhyme and stanza and a strongly felt stress rhythm have taken their place. In the subsequent emergence of the European vernacular literatures, poetic forms follow the example of the later Latin hymns. The earliest art lyrics, those of the Provençal troubadours of the 12th and 13th centuries, show the most intricate and ingenious stanzaic forms. Similarly, the Goliardic songs of the *Carmina Burana* (13th century) reveal a rich variety of prosodic techniques. This "Spring-song" embodies varying lines of trochees and iambs and an *ababcdccd* rhyme scheme:

Ver redit optatum
Cum gaudio,
Flore decoratum
Purpureo;
Aves edunt cantus
Quam dulciter!
Revirescit nemus,
Cantus est amoenus
Totaliter.

THE RENAISSANCE

Renaissance prosodic theory had to face the fact of an accomplished poetry in the vernacular that was not written in metres determined by "rules" handed down from the practice of Homer and Virgil. Nevertheless, the classicizing theorists of the 16th century made a determined attempt to explain existing poetry by the rules of short and long and to draft "laws" by which modern verse might move in Classical metres. Roger Ascham, in *The Scholemaster* (1570), attacked "the Gothic . . . barbarous and rude Ryming" of the early Tudor poets. He admitted that Henry Howard, earl of Surrey, did passably well as a poet but complained that Surrey did not understand "perfite and trewe versifying." That is, Surrey did not compose his English verses according to the principles of Latin and Greek quantitative prosody.

Ascham instigated a lengthy argument, continued by succeeding theorists and poets, on the nature of English prosody. Sir Philip Sidney, Gabriel Harvey, Edmund Spenser, and Thomas Campion all (to use Saintsbury's phrase) committed whoredom with the enchantress of quantitative metric. While this hanky-panky had no adverse effect on poetry itself (English poets went on writing verses in syllable-stress, the prosody most suitable to the language), it produced misbegotten twins of confusion and discord, whose heirs, however named, are still apparent today. Thus, those who still talk about "long and short" (instead of stressed and unstressed), those who perpetuate a punitive prosodic legalism, and those who regard prosody as an account of what poets should have done and did not, trace their ancestry back to Elizabethan dalliance and illicit classicizing.

Although Renaissance prosodic theory produced scarcely anything of value to either literary criticism or poetic technique—indeed, it did not even develop a rational scheme for scanning existing poetry—it raised a number of important questions. What were the structural principles animating the metres of English verse? What were the aesthetic nature of prosody and the functions of metre? What were the connections between poetry and music? Was poetry an art of imitation (as Aristotle and all of the Neoclassical theorists had maintained), and was its sister art painting? Or was poetry (as Romantic theory maintained) an art of expression, and prosody the element that produced (in Coleridge's words) the sense of musical delight originating (in T.S. Eliot's words) in the auditory imagination?

THE 18TH CENTURY

Early in the 18th century, Pope affirmed, in his *Essay on Criticism* (1711), the classic doctrine of imitation. Prosody was to be more nearly onomatopoetic. The movement of sound and metre should represent the actions they carry:

> *'Tis not enough no harshness gives offence,*
> *The sound must seem an Echo to the sense:*
> *Soft is the strain when Zephyr gently blows,*
> *And the smooth stream in smoother numbers flows;*
> *But when loud surges lash the sounding shoar,*
> *The hoarse, rough verse should like the torrent roar.*
> *When Ajax strives some rock's vast weight to throw,*
> *The line too labours, and the words move slow;*
> *Not so, when swift Camilla scours the plain,*
> *Flies o'er th' unbending corn, and skims along the main.*

In 18th-century theory the doctrine of imitation was joined to numerous strictures on "smoothness," or metrical regularity. Theorists advocated a rigid regularity, and minor poets composed in a strictly regular syllable-stress verse devoid of expressive variations. This regularity itself expressed the rationalism of the period. The prevailing dogmas on regularity made it impossible for Samuel Johnson to hear the beauties of Milton's versification, and he characterized the metrically subtle lines of "Lycidas" as "harsh" and without concern for "numbers." Certain crosscurrents of metrical opinion in the 18th century, however, moved toward new theoretical stances. Joshua Steele's *Prosodia Rationalis* (1779) is an early attempt to scan English verse by means of musical notation. (A later attempt was made by the American poet Sidney Lanier in his *Science of English Verse*, 1880.) Steele's method is highly personal, depending on an idiosyncratic assigning of such musical qualities as pitch and duration to syllabic values. But he recognized that a prosodic theory must take into account not merely metre but "all properties or accidents belonging to language." His work foreshadows the current concerns of the structural linguists who attempt an analysis of the entire range of acoustic elements contributing to prosodic effect. Steele is also the first "timer" among metrists. That is, he bases his scansions on musical pulse and claims that English verse moves in either common or triple time. Twentieth-century critics of musical scanners pointed out that musical scansion constitutes a performance, not an analysis of the metre, that it allows arbitrary readings, and that it levels out distinctions between poets and schools of poetry.

THE 19TH CENTURY

With the Romantic movement and its revolutionary shift in literary sensibility, prosodic theory became deeply influenced by early 19th-century speculation on the nature of imagination, on poetry as expression—"the spontane- ous overflow of powerful feelings," in Wordsworth's famous phrase—and on the concept of the poem as organic form. The discussion between Wordsworth and Coleridge on the nature and func- tion of metre illuminates the crucial transition from Neoclassical to modern theories. Wordsworth (in his "Preface" to the *Lyrical Ballads*, 1800) followed 18th-century theory and saw metre as "superadded" to poetry. Its function is more nearly ornamental, a grace of style and not an essential quality. Coleridge saw metre as being organic. It functions together with all of the other parts of a poem and is not merely an echo to the sense or an artifice of style. Coleridge also examined the psychological effects of metre, the way it sets up patterns of expectation that are either fulfilled or disappointed:

> As far as metre acts in and for itself, it tends to increase the vivac- ity and susceptibility both of the general feelings and of the atten- tion. This effect it produces by the continued excitement of surprize, and by the quick reciprocations of curiosity still gratified and still re-excited, which are too slight indeed to be at any one moment objects of distinct conscious- ness, yet become considerable in their aggregate influence. As a medicated atmosphere, or as wine during animated conversa- tion; they act powerfully, though

themselves unnoticed. Where, therefore, correspondent food and appropriate matter are not provided for the attention and feelings thus roused, there must needs be a disappointment felt; like that of leaping in the dark from the last step of a staircase, when we had prepared our mus- cles for a leap of three or four.
> (*Biographia Literaria*, XVIII, 1817)

Romantic literary theory, although vastly influential in poetic practice, had little to say about actual metrical struc- ture. Coleridge described the subtle relationships between metre and mean- ing and the effects of metre on the reader's unconscious mind, but he devoted little attention to metrical analy- sis. Two developments in 19th-century poetic techniques, however, had greater effect than any prosodic theory formu- lated during the period. Walt Whitman's nonmetrical prosody and Gerard Manley Hopkins's far-ranging metrical experiments mounted an assault on the traditional syllable-stress metric. Both Whitman and Hopkins were at first bit- terly denounced, but, as is often the case, the heresies of a previous age become the orthodoxies of the next. Hopkins's "sprung rhythm"—a rhythm imitating nat- ural speech, using mixed types of feet and counterpointed verse—emerged as viable techniques in the poetry of Dylan Thomas and W.H. Auden. It is virtually impossible to assess Whitman's influence on the various prosodies of modern poetry. Such

American poets as Hart Crane, William Carlos Williams, and Theodore Roethke all used Whitman's long line, extended rhythms, and "shaped" strophes.

THE 20TH CENTURY AND BEYOND

Since 1900 the study of prosody has emerged as an important and respectable part of literary study. George Saintsbury published his great *History of English Prosody* during the years 1906–10. Sometime later, a number of linguists and aestheticians turned their attention to prosodic structure and the nature of poetic rhythm. Graphic prosody (the traditional syllable and foot scansion of syllable-stress metre) was placed on a securer theoretical footing. A number of prosodists, taking their lead from the work of Joshua Steele and Sidney Lanier, attempted to use musical notation to scan English verse. For the convenience of synoptic discussion, prosodic theorists are sometimes divided into four groups: the linguists who examine verse rhythm as a function of phonetic structures; the aestheticians who examine the psychological effects, the formal properties, and the phenomenology of rhythm; the musical scanners, or "timers," who try to adapt the procedures of musical notation to metrical analysis; and the traditionalists who rely on the graphic description of syllable and stress to uncover metrical paradigms. It is necessary to point out that only the traditionalists concern themselves specifically with metrical form. Aestheticians, linguists, and timers all examine prosody in its larger dimensions.

Structural linguistics placed the study of language on a solid scientific basis. Linguists measured the varied intensities of syllabic stress and pitch and the durations of junctures or the pauses between syllables. These techniques of objective measurement were applied to prosodic study. The Danish philologist Otto Jespersen's early essay "Notes on Metre" (1900) made a number of significant discoveries. He established the principles of English metre on a demonstrably accurate structural basis. He recognized metre as a gestalt phenomenon (i.e., with emphasis on the configurational whole). Additionally, he saw metrics as descriptive science rather than proscriptive regulation. Jespersen's essay was written before the burgeoning interest in linguistics, but after World War II numerous attempts were made to formulate a descriptive science of metrics.

It has been noted that Coleridge defined metrical form as a pattern of expectation, fulfillment, and surprise. Taking his cue from Coleridge, the British aesthetician I.A. Richards in *Principles of Literary Criticism* (1924) developed a closely reasoned theory of the mind's response to rhythm and metre. His theory is organic and contextual. The sound effects of prosody have little psychologic effect by themselves. It is prosody in conjunction with "its contemporaneous other effects"—chiefly meaning or propositional sense—that produces its characteristic impact on our neural structures. Richards insisted that everything that happens in a poem depends on the organic environment. In his *Practical Criticism* (1929) he constructed a celebrated "metrical dummy" to "support [an] argument against anyone who affirms that the mere sound of verse has *independently* any considerable aesthetic virtue." For Richards the most important function of metre was to provide aesthetic framing and control. Metre makes possible, by its stimulation and release of tensions, "the most difficult and delicate utterances."

Other critics, following the Neo-Kantian theories of the philosophers Ernst Cassirer and Susanne Langer, have suggested that rhythmic structure is a species of symbolic form. Harvey Gross in *Sound and Form in Modern Poetry* (1964) saw rhythmic structure as a symbolic form, signifying ways of experiencing organic processes and the phenomena of nature. The function of prosody, in his view, is to image life in a rich and complex way. Gross's theory is also expressive. Prosody articulates the movement of feeling in a poem. The unproved assumption behind Gross's expressive and symbolic theory is that rhythm is in some way iconic to human feeling: that a particular rhythm or metre symbolizes, as a map locates the features of an actual terrain, a particular kind of feeling.

The most sophisticated argument for musical scansion was given by Northrop Frye in his influential *Anatomy of Criticism* (1957). He differentiates between verse that shows unmistakable musical quality and verse written according to the imitative doctrines current in the Renaissance and Neoclassic periods. All of the poetry written in the older strong-stress metric, or poetry showing its basic structure, is musical poetry, and its structure resembles the music contemporary with it.

The most convincing case for traditional "graphic prosody" was made by the American critics W.K. Wimsatt and Monroe C. Beardsley. Their essay "The Concept of Meter" (1965) argues that both the linguists and musical scanners do not analyze the abstract metrical pattern of poems but only interpret an individual performance of the poem. Poetic metre is not generated by any combination of stresses and pauses capable of precise scientific measurement. Rather, metre is generated by an abstract pattern of syllables standing in positions of relative stress to each other. In a line of iambic pentameter

> *Preserved in Milton's or in Shakespeare's name ...*

the *or* of the third foot is only slightly stronger than the preceding syllable *-ton's*, but this minor difference makes the line recognizable as iambic metre. Wimsatt and Beardsley underlined the paradigmatic nature of metre. As an element in poetic structure, it is capable of exact abstraction.

ASIAN THEORIES

The metres of the verse of ancient India were constructed on a quantitative basis. A system of long and short syllables, as in Greek, determined the variety of

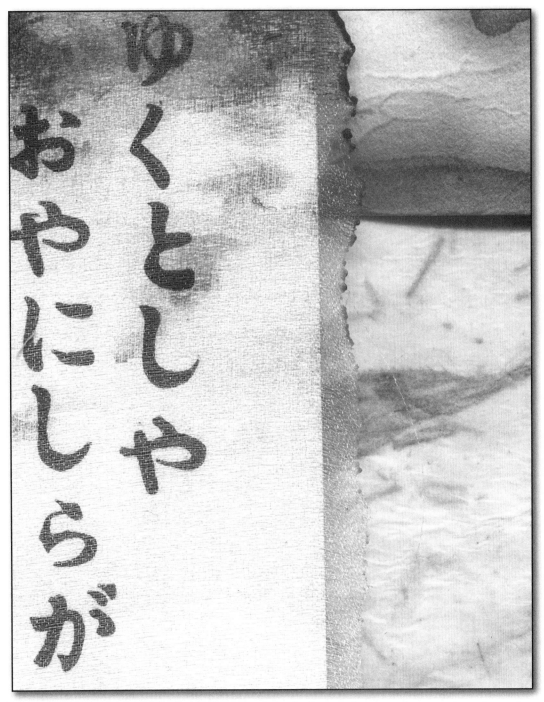

Haikus like this are deceptively simple. Part of the challenge of writing them consists of creating a 17-syllable verse with alternating lines of 5, 7, and 5 syllables. istockPhoto/Thinkstock

complicated metrical forms that are found in poetry of post-Vedic times—that is, after the 5th century BCE.

Chinese prosody is based on the intricate tonal system of Chinese languages. In the Tang dynasty (618–907 CE) the metrical system for classical verse was fixed. The various tones of the language were subsumed under two large groups, even tones and oblique tones. Patterned arrangements of tones and the use of pauses, or caesuras, along with rhyme determine the Chinese prosodic forms.

Japanese poetry is without rhyme or marked metrical structure; it is purely syllabic. The two main forms of syllabic verses are the *tanka* and the haiku. *Tanka* is written in a stanza of 31 syllables that are divided into alternating lines of five and seven syllables. Haiku is an extremely concentrated form of only 17 syllables. Longer poems of 40 to 50 lines are also written; however, alternate lines must contain either five or seven syllables. The haiku form has been adapted to English verse and is a popular form. Other experimenters in English syllabic verse show the influence of Japanese prosody. Syllabic metre in English, however, is limited in its rhythmic effects. It is incapable of expressing the range of feeling that is available in the traditional stress and syllable-stress metres.

PROSODY: TERMS AND CONCEPTS

Among terms a reader may encounter when examining aspects of prosody are those that define verse forms. Others include elements of sound production, types of metrical feet, and categories of stanza. The brief descriptions that follow provide a representative selection.

ALCAIC

An alcaic is a classical Greek poetic stanza composed of four lines of varied metrical feet, with five long syllables in the first two lines, four in the third and fourth lines, and an unaccented syllable at the beginning of the first three lines (anacrusis). Named for and perhaps invented by Alcaeus, a poet of the late 7th and early 6th centuries BCE, the alcaic became an important Latin verse form, especially in the *Odes* of Horace. Variations on the traditional alcaic include the use of a long initial syllable and of a spondee (— —) in the first complete foot of the first three lines. Alcaics were adapted to English and French verse during the Renaissance and later appeared in works such as "Milton" by Alfred, Lord Tennyson.

ALEXANDRINE

The alexandrine verse form is the leading measure in French poetry. It consists of a line of 12 syllables with major stresses on the 6th syllable (which precedes the medial caesura [pause]) and on the last syllable, and one secondary accent in each half line. Because six syllables is a normal breath group and the secondary stresses can be on any other syllables in the line, the alexandrine is a flexible form, adaptable to a wide range of subjects. Its structural metrical principle is stress according to sense. The form thus lends itself to the expression of simple or complex emotions, narrative description, or grandiose patriotic sentiment (it is known as the heroic line in French poetry).

The name *alexandrine* is probably derived from the early use of the verse in the French *Roman d'Alexandre,* a collection of romances that was compiled in the 12th century about the adventures of Alexander the Great. Revived in the 16th century by the poets of La Pléiade, especially Pierre de Ronsard, the alexandrine became, in the following century, the preeminent French verse form for dramatic and narrative poetry and reached its highest development in the classical tragedies of Pierre Corneille and Jean Racine. In the late 19th century, a loosening of structure occurred, notable in the work of Paul Verlaine. Poets frequently wrote a modified alexandrine, a three-part line known as *vers romantique,* or *trimètre.* Vers libre ("free verse") soon replaced the alexandrine as the leading verse form of French poetry.

In English versification, the alexandrine, also called iambic hexameter, contains six primary accents rather than the two major and two secondary accents of the French. Though it was introduced to England in the 16th century and was adapted to German and Dutch poetry in the 17th century, its success outside France has been limited.

ALLITERATION

Alliteration is the repetition of consonant sounds at the beginning of words or stressed syllables. Sometimes the repetition of initial vowel sounds (head rhyme) is also referred to as alliteration. As a poetic device, it is often discussed with assonance and consonance. In languages (such as Chinese) that emphasize tonality, the use of alliteration is rare or absent.

Alliteration is found in many common phrases, such as "pretty as a picture" and "dead as a doornail," and is a common poetic device in almost all languages. In its simplest form, it reinforces one or two consonantal sounds, as in William Shakespeare's line:

> *When I do count the clock that tells the time*
>
> (Sonnet 12)

A more complex pattern of alliteration is created when consonants both at the beginning of words and at the beginning of stressed syllables within words are repeated, as in Percy Bysshe Shelley's line:

> *The City's voice itself is soft like Solitude's*
>
> ("Stanzas Written in Dejection Near Naples")

Though alliteration is now a subsidiary embellishment in both prose and poetry, it was a formal structural principle in ancient Germanic verse.

ANAPEST

The metrical foot that consists of two short or unstressed syllables followed by one long or stressed syllable is called an anapest. First found in early Spartan marching songs, anapestic metres were widely used in Greek and Latin dramatic verse, especially for the entrance and exit of the chorus. Lines composed primarily of anapestic feet, often with an additional unstressed syllable at the end of the first line, are much rarer in English verse. Because of its jog-trot rhythm, pure anapestic metre was originally used only in light or popular English verse, but after the 18th century it appeared in serious poetry. Byron used it effectively to convey a sense of excitement and galloping in "The Destruction of Sennacherib:"

The Assyr | ian came down | like a wolf | on the fold.
And his co | horts were gleam | ing in pur | ple and gold.

In Swinburne's "By the North Sea," however, anapestic trimeter conveys a more subdued effect:

And his hand | is not wea | ry of giv | ing.
And the thirst | of her heart | is not fed.

ASSONANCE

Assonance is the repetition of stressed vowel sounds within words with different end consonants, as in the phrase "quite like." It is unlike rhyme, in which initial consonants differ but both vowel and end-consonant sounds are identical, as in the phrase "quite right." Many common phrases, such as "mad as a hatter," "free as a breeze," or "high as a kite," owe their appeal to assonance. As a poetic device, internal assonance is usually combined with alliteration (repetition of initial consonant sounds) and consonance (repetition of end or medial consonant sounds) to enrich the texture of the poetic line. Sometimes a single vowel sound is repeated, as in the opening line of Thomas Hood's "Autumn":

I saw old Autumn in the misty morn

Sometimes two or more vowel sounds are repeated, as in the opening lines of Shelley's "The Indian Serenade," which creates a musical counterpoint with long *i* and long *e* sounds:

I arise from dreams of thee
In the first sweet sleep of night

Assonance at the end of a line, producing an impure, or off, rhyme, is found in *La Chanson de Roland* and most French verses composed before the introduction of pure rhyme into French verse in the 12th century. It remains a feature of Spanish and Portuguese poetry. In English verse, assonance is frequently found in the traditional ballads, where its use may have been careless or unavoidable. The last verse of "Sir Patrick Spens" is an example:

Haf owre, haf owre to Aberdour,
It's fiftie fadom deip:
And thair lies guid Sir Patrick
Spence,
Wi' the Scots lords at his feit.

Otherwise, it was rarely used in English as a deliberate technique until the late 19th and 20th centuries, when it was discerned in the works of Gerard Manley Hopkins and Wilfred Owen. Their use of assonance instead of end rhyme was often adopted by such poets as W.H. Auden, Stephen Spender, and Dylan Thomas.

CAESURA

A pause within a poetic line that breaks the regularity of the metrical pattern is called a caesura (cesura). It is represented in scansion by the sign ‖. The caesura sometimes is used to emphasize the formal metrical construction of a line, but it more often introduces the cadence of natural speech patterns and habits of phrasing into the metrical scheme. The caesura may coincide with conventional punctuation marks, as in the following Shakespearean line, in which a strong pause is demanded after each comma for rhetorical expression:

This blessed plot, ‖ this earth,
‖ this realm,
‖ this England, ...

The caesura is not necessarily set off by punctuation, however, as in this line from John Keats:

Thou foster-child of silence ‖ and
slow time,

In Germanic and Old English alliterative poetry, the caesura was a formal device dividing each line centrally into two half lines, as in this example from "The Battle of Maldon:"

Hige sceal þe heardra,
hearte þe cenre,
mod sceal þe mare,
þe ure mægen lytlaþ
(Mind must be firmer, ‖ heart the
more fierce,
Courage the greater, ‖ as our strength
diminishes.)

In formal, Romance, and Neoclassical verse, the caesura occurs most frequently in the middle of the line (medial caesura). In modern verse its place is flexible. It may occur near the beginning of one line (an initial caesura) and near the end of the next (terminal caesura). There may be several caesuras within a single line or none at all. Thus, it has the effect of interposing the informal and irregular patterns of speech as a subtle counterpoint to the poem's regular rhythm. It prevents metrical monotony and emphasizes the meaning of lines.

Types of caesura that are differentiated in modern prosody are the *masculine caesura*, a caesura that follows a stressed or long syllable, and the *feminine caesura*, which follows an unstressed or short syllable. The feminine caesura is further divided into the epic caesura and the lyric caesura. An *epic caesura* is a feminine caesura that follows an extra unstressed syllable that has been inserted in accentual iambic metre. An epic caesura occurs in these lines from Shakespeare's *Macbeth*: "but how of Cawdor? / The Thane of Cawdor lives." The *lyric caesura* is a feminine caesura that follows an unstressed syllable normally required by the metre. It can be seen in A.E. Houseman's "they cease not fighting / east and west."

CONSONANCE

Consonance is the recurrence or repetition of identical or similar consonants; specifically the correspondence of end or intermediate consonants unaccompanied by like correspondence of vowels at the end of two or more syllables, words, or other units of composition.

As a poetic device, it is often combined with assonance (the repetition of stressed vowel sounds within words with different end consonants) and alliteration (the repetition of initial consonant sounds). Consonance is also occasionally used as an off-rhyme, but it is most commonly found as an internal sound effect, as in Shakespeare's song, "The ousel co*ck* so bla*ck* of hue," or "The curfew to*lls* the kne*ll* of parting day," from Thomas Gray's "Elegy Written in a Country Church Yard."

DACTYL

The metrical foot consisting of one long (classical verse) or stressed (English verse) syllable followed by two short, or unstressed, syllables is known as a dactyl. Probably the oldest and most common metre in classical verse is the dactylic hexameter, the metre of Homer's *Iliad* and *Odyssey* and of other ancient epics. Dactylic metres are fairly rare in English verse, one difficulty being that the prolonged use of the dactyl tends to distort normal word accent, giving the lines a jerky movement. They appeared with regularity only after poets like Robert Browning and Algernon Charles Swinburne successfully used the form in the 19th century. Dactylic rhythm produces a lilting movement as in the following example from Byron's *Bride of Abydos*:

This line contains the common variation of omitting an unstressed syllable at the end of a line.

DIAERESIS

Diaeresis is the resolution of one syllable into two, especially by separating the vowel elements of a diphthong and, by extension, two adjacent vowels, as in the word cooperation. It is also the mark placed over a vowel to indicate that it is pronounced as a separate syllable. In classical prosody, diaeresis refers to the end of a word coinciding with the completion of the metrical foot, in contrast to caesura, which refers to a word ending within a metrical foot.

ELISION

The slurring or omission of a final unstressed vowel that precedes either another vowel or a weak consonant sound, as in the word *heav'n*, is called elision. It may also be the dropping of a consonant between vowels, as in the word *o'er* for *over*. Elision is used to fit words into a metrical scheme, to smooth the rhythm of a poem, or to ease the pronunciation of words. In classical Greek poetry, an apostrophe (') is substituted for an elided letter, as is frequently the case in English verse. In Latin, however, the elided vowel or consonant remains, but it is ignored in scanning the line.

FOOT

The smallest metrical unit of measurement is the foot. The prevailing kind and number of feet, revealed by scansion, determines the metre of a poem. In classical (or quantitative) verse, a foot, or metron, is a combination of two or more long and short syllables. A short syllable is known as an arsis, a long syllable as a thesis. There are 28 different feet in classical verse, ranging from the pyrrhic (two short syllables) to the dispondee (four long syllables). The adaptation of classical metrics to the strongly accented Germanic languages, such as English, does not provide an entirely reliable standard of measurement. The terminology persists, however, a foot usually being defined as a group of one stressed (´) and one or two unstressed (˘)

syllables. An exception is the spondee, which consists of two stressed syllables. In English verse, this is usually two monosyllables, such as the phrase "He who." The commonest feet in English verse are the iamb, an unstressed followed by a stressed syllable, as in the word ˘re| ´port; the trochee, a stressed followed by an unstressed syllable, as in the word ´dai|˘ly; the anapest, two unstressed syllables followed by a stressed syllable, as in ˘ser|e˘| ´nade; and the dactyl, a stressed syllable followed by two unstressed syllables, as in ´mer|˘ri|˘ly.

If a single line of the poem contains only one foot, it is called monometer; two feet, dimeter; three feet, trimeter; four feet, tetrameter; five feet, pentameter; six feet, hexameter; seven feet, heptameter; eight feet, octameter. More than six, however, is rare. The metre of a poem (e.g., iambic pentameter, dactylic hexameter) is the kind plus the number of feet in each line.

HEXAMETER

A line of verse containing six feet, usually dactyls (´ ˘ ˘). Dactylic hexameter is the oldest known form of Greek poetry and is the preeminent metre of narrative and didactic poetry in Greek and Latin, in which its position is comparable to that of iambic pentameter in English versification. The epics of Homer and of Virgil are composed in dactylic hexameter. Although the hexameter has been used in English verse by such 19th-century poets as Henry Wadsworth Longfellow (notably in *Evangeline*), its rhythms are not readily adapted to the language, and it has never been a popular form.

HIATUS

A break in sound between two vowels that occur together without an intervening consonant, both vowels being clearly enunciated is termed a hiatus. The two vowels may be either within one word, as in the words V*ie*nna and n*ai*ve, or the final and initial vowels of two successive words, as in the phrases "see *it*" and "go *in*." Hiatus is the opposite of elision, the dropping or blurring of the second vowel. It is also distinct from diphthongization, in which the vowels blend to form one sound.

IAMB

An iamb is a metrical foot consisting of one short syllable (as in classical verse) or one unstressed syllable (as in English verse) followed by one long or stressed syllable, as in the word ˘be|cause´. Considered by the ancient Greeks to approximate the natural rhythm of speech, iambic metres were used extensively for dramatic dialogue, invective, satire, and fables. Also suited to the cadence of the English language, iambic rhythms, especially iambic tetrameter and pentameter, are the preeminent metres of English verse. Substitution of other types of feet

to add variety is common in basically iambic verse. An example of iambic metre is the English ballad, composed of quatrains written in alternating lines of iambic tetrameter and iambic trimeter. For example:

$$\text{There lived} \mid \text{a wife} \mid \text{at Ush} \mid \text{er's Well,}$$
$$\text{And a weal} \mid \text{thy wife} \mid \text{was she:}$$
$$\text{She had} \mid \text{three stout} \mid \text{and stal} \mid \text{wart sons,}$$
$$\text{And sent} \mid \text{them o'er} \mid \text{the sea.}$$

PENTAMETER

A line of verse containing five metrical feet is known as pentameter. In English verse, in which pentameter has been the predominant metre since the 16th century, the preferred foot is the iamb—that is, an unstressed syllable followed by a stressed one, represented in scansion as ˘ ´.

Geoffrey Chaucer employed iambic pentameter in *The Canterbury Tales* as early as the 14th century, although without the regularity that is found later in the heroic couplets of John Dryden and Alexander Pope. Most English sonnets have been written in iambic pentameter, as in this example from Shakespeare:

$$\text{So long} \mid \text{as men} \mid \text{can breathe} \mid \text{or eyes} \mid \text{can see,}$$
$$\text{So long} \mid \text{lives this} \mid \text{and this} \mid \text{gives life} \mid \text{to thee.}$$
(Sonnet 18)

Shakespeare also used pentameter in his blank-verse tragedies.

REFRAIN

A refrain is a phrase, line, or group of lines repeated at intervals throughout a poem, generally at the end of the stanza. Refrains are found in the ancient Egyptian *Book of the Dead* and are common in primitive tribal chants. They appear in literature as varied as ancient Hebrew, Greek, and Latin verse, popular ballads, and Renaissance and Romantic lyrics. Three common refrains are the chorus, recited by more than one person; the burden, in which a whole stanza is repeated; and the repetend, in which the words are repeated erratically throughout the poem. A refrain may be an exact repetition, or it may exhibit slight variations in meaning or form as in the following excerpt from "Jesse James":

> *Jesse had a wife to mourn him all her life,*
> *The children they are brave.*
> *'Twas a dirty little coward shot Mister*
>   *Howard,*
> *And laid Jesse James in his grave.*
> … … . .
> *It was Robert Ford, the dirty little coward,*
> *I wonder how he does feel,*
> *For he ate of Jesse's bread and he slept*
>   *in Jesse's bed,*
> *Then he laid Jesse James in his grave.*
> (Anonymous)

RHYME ROYAL

Rhyme (or rime) royal is a seven-line iambic pentameter stanza rhyming *ababbcc*.

The rhyme royal was first used in English verse in the 14th century by Geoffrey Chaucer in *Troilus and Criseyde* and *The Parlement of Foules*. Traditionally, the name *rhyme royal* is said to derive from *The Kingis Quair* ("The King's Book"), attributed to James I of Scotland (1394–1437), but some critics trace the name to the French chant royal. Chaucer probably borrowed it from the French poet and musician Guillaume de Machaut (c. 1300–77), who may have invented it or derived it from earlier French and Provençal poets.

Rhyme royal became the favourite form for long narrative poems during the 15th and early 16th centuries. Shakespeare's *Rape of Lucrece* (1594) was the last important poem of the period in rhyme royal. Later, Milton experimented with the form, and it was successfully used by William Morris in the 19th century and by John Masefield in the 20th.

RHYTHM

Rhythm is the patterned recurrence, within a certain range of regularity, of specific language features, usually features of sound. Although difficult to define, rhythm is readily discriminated by the ear and the mind, having as it does a physiological basis. It is universally agreed to involve qualities of movement, repetition, and pattern and to arise from the poem's nature as a temporal structure. Rhythm, by any definition, is essential to poetry. Prose may be said to exhibit rhythm but in a much less highly organized sense. The presence of rhythmic patterns heightens emotional response and often affords the reader a sense of balance.

Metre, although often equated with rhythm, is perhaps more accurately described as one method of organizing a poem's rhythm. Unlike rhythm, metre is not a requisite of poetry. It is, rather, an abstract organization of elements of stress, duration, or number of syllables per line into a specific formal pattern. The inter-action of a given metrical pattern with any other aspect of sound in a poem produces a tension, or counterpoint, that creates the rhythm of metrically based poetry.

Compared with the wide variety of metrical schemes, the types of metrically related rhythms are few. Duple rhythm occurs in lines composed in two-syllable feet, as in Shakespeare's line,

ˊ ᵕ ᵕ ᵕ ᵕ ˊ ᵕ ˊ ᵕ ˊ
Tired with| all these,| for rest | ful death | I cry

In metrical schemes based on three-syllable feet, the rhythm is triple:

ᵕ ᵕ ˊ ᵕ ᵕ ˊ ᵕ ᵕ ˊ
For the strength | of the Pack | is the Wolf, |

ᵕ ᵕ ˊ ᵕ ᵕ ˊ ᵕ ᵕ ˊ
and the strength | of the Wolf | is the Pack
(Kipling)

Rising rhythm results when the stress falls on the last syllable of each foot in a line:

ᵕ ˊ ᵕ ˊ ᵕ ˊ ᵕ ˊ ᵕ ˊ
When I | consid |er how |my light | is spent
(Milton)

The reverse of this is falling rhythm:

ˊ ᵕ ˊ ᵕ ˊ ᵕ ˊ ᵕ
Bacchus' | blessings | are a | treasure
(Dryden)

Running, or common, rhythm occurs in metres in which stressed and unstressed syllables alternate (duple rhythm, rising or falling). Gerard Manley Hopkins, in reaction against traditional metres, coined the term sprung rhythm to apply to verse wherein the line is mea-sured by the number of speech-stressed syllables, the number of unstressed syl-lables being indeterminate.

The rhythms of free verse derive from the systematic repetition of lan-guage elements other than metrical stress patterns. Differentiation between the rhythmical basis of free verse and that of metrical verse involves a rela-tive, rather than an absolute, distinction regarding the range of language fea-tures considered and the extent to which they are patterned. Because metrical verse is principally concerned with the distribution of relative stress values, it does not account for the significance of other linguistic features that may con-tribute to rhythmic effect. In free verse, rhythm most commonly arises from the arrangement of linguistic elements into patterns that more nearly approximate the natural cadence of speech and that give symmetry to the verse. The rhyth-mical resources available to free verse include syntactical patterning; system-atic repetition of sound, words, phrases, and lines; and the relative value of temporal junctures occasioned by caesura (a marked pause in the middle of a line), line length, and other determinants of pace. Some authorities recognize in the highly organized patterning of imagery a further source of poetic rhythm. The following lines from Walt Whitman's "Song of Myself" illustrate many of these rhythmical devices:

> Twenty-eight young men bathe by
>   the shore,
> Twenty-eight young men and all so
>   friendly;
> Twenty-eight years of womanly life and
>   all so lonesome.
> She owns the fine house by the rise of
>   the bank,
> She hides, handsome and richly drest
>   aft the blinds of the window.

The rhythms that are characteristic of particular poets are sometimes ascribed to units of breath, as in the essay "Projective Verse" (1950) by the poet and critic Charles Olson: "And the line comes (I swear it) from the breath, from the breathing of the man who writes, at the moment that he writes . . . ."

SPENSERIAN STANZA

The Spenserian stanza is a verse form that consists of eight iambic pentameter lines followed by a ninth line of six iambic feet (an alexandrine). The rhyme scheme is *ababbcbcc*. The first eight lines produce an effect of formal unity, while the hexameter completes the thought of the stanza. Invented by Edmund Spenser for his poem *The Faerie Queene* (1590–1609), the Spenserian stanza has origins in the Old French ballade (eight-line stanzas, rhyming *ababbcbc*), the Italian ottava rima (eight iambic pentameter lines with a rhyme scheme of *abababcc*), and the stanza form used by Chaucer in his "Monk's Tale" (eight lines rhyming *ababbcbc*). A revolutionary innovation in its day, the Spenserian stanza fell into general disuse during the 17th and 18th centuries. It was revived in the 19th century by the Romantic poets (e.g., Byron in *Childe Harold's Pilgrimage*, Keats in "The Eve of St. Agnes," and Shelley in "Adonais").

SPONDEE

The metrical foot consisting of two long (as in classical verse) or stressed (as in English verse) syllables occurring together is called a spondee. The term was derived from a Greek word describing the two long musical notes that accompanied the pouring of a libation. Spondaic metre occurred occasionally in classical verse. It does not, however, form the basis for any English verse, as there are virtually no English words in which syllables receive equal stress. An approximation of a spondaic foot is sometimes achieved with such compounds as *heyday* or *childhood*, but even these words

Edmund Spenser created his own form, now known as the Spenserian stanza, specifically for his poem The Faerie Queene *(1590–1609).* Archive Photos/Getty Images

can be seen as examples of primary and secondary stress rather than equal stress. In English verse, the spondaic foot is usually composed of two monosyllables.

SPRUNG RHYTHM

Sprung rhythm is the irregular system of prosody developed by the 19th-century English poet Gerard Manley Hopkins. It is based on the number of stressed syllables in a line and permits an indeterminate number of unstressed syllables. In sprung rhythm, a foot may be composed of from one to four syllables. (In regular English metres, a foot consists of two or three syllables.) Because stressed syllables often occur sequentially in this patterning rather than in alternation with unstressed syllables, the rhythm is said to be "sprung." Hopkins claimed to be only the theoretician, not the inventor, of sprung rhythm. He saw it as the rhythm of common English speech and the basis of such early English poems as Langland's *Piers Plowman* and nursery rhymes such as

> Ding, dong, bell;
>
> Pussy's in the well.

Sprung rhythm is a bridge between regular metre and free verse. An example of Hopkins's use of it can be found in "Spring and Fall to a Young Child":

> Margaret are you grieving
>
> Over Goldengrove unleaving?

GERARD MANLEY HOPKINS

(b. July 28, 1844, Stratford, Essex, Eng.— d. June 8, 1889, Dublin, Ire.)

The English poet and Jesuit priest Gerard Manley Hopkins was one of the most individual of Victorian writers. His work was not published in collected form until 1918, but it influenced many leading 20th-century poets. After studies at Oxford, Hopkins converted to Roman Catholicism and eventually became a priest. He burned his youthful verses as inappropriate to his profession, but, moved by the death of five Franciscan nuns in a shipwreck in 1875, he broke his silence to write the long poem "The Wreck of the Deutschland." His poem was rejected, however, by the Jesuit magazine The Month. *He also wrote a series of sonnets strikingly original in their richness of language and use of rhythm, including the remarkable "The Windhover," one of the most frequently analyzed poems in the language. He was ordained and worked at a variety of posts in Jesuit churches and institutions. From 1885 he wrote another series of sonnets, beginning with "Carrion Comfort." They show a sense of desolation produced partly by a sense of spiritual aridity and partly by a feeling of artistic frustration. These poems, known as the "terrible sonnets," reveal strong tensions between his delight in the sensuous world and his urge to express it and his equally powerful sense of religious vocation. Hopkins is noted for intense language, compressed syntax, and innovations in prosody, including sprung rhythm. In addition to the works mentioned above, his best-known poems include "Pied Beauty" and "God's Grandeur." He died of typhoid at age 44.*

TETRAMETER

A line of poetic verse that consists of four metrical feet is called tetrameter. In English versification, the feet are usually iambs (an unstressed syllable followed by a stressed one, as in the word ˘be|cause´), trochees (a stressed syllable followed by an unstressed one, as in the word ti´|ger),˘ or a combination of the two. Iambic tetrameter is, next to iambic pentameter, the most common metre in English poetry. It is used in the English and Scottish traditional ballads, which are usually composed of four-line stanzas of alternating iambic tetrameter and trimeter.

TROCHEE

The metrical foot consisting of one long syllable (as in classical verse) or stressed syllable (as in English verse) followed by one short or unstressed syllable, as in the word hap´|˘py is called a trochee. Trochaic metres were extensively used in ancient Greek and Latin tragedy and comedy in a form, particularly favoured by Plautus and Terence, called trochaic catalectic tetrameter. Trochaic metres are not easily adapted to English verse. In long poems, such as Henry Wadsworth Longfellow's *Song of Hiawatha,* their overall effect is monotony. But they have been used with great effect in shorter poems, particularly by William Blake, as in his best-known poem, "The Tyger":

´ ˘ ´ ˘   ´ ˘ ´
Tyger | Tyger | burning | bright
´ ˘ ´ ˘   ´ ˘ ´
In the | forests | of the | night

CHAPTER 3

EPIC

An epic is a long narrative poem recounting heroic deeds, although the term has also been loosely used to describe novels, such as Leo Tolstoy's *War and Peace*, and motion pictures, such as Sergey Eisenstein's *Ivan the Terrible*. In literary usage, the term encompasses both oral and written compositions. The prime examples of the oral epic are Homer's *Iliad* and *Odyssey*. Outstanding examples of the written epic include Virgil's *Aeneid* and Lucan's *Pharsalia* in Latin, *Chanson de Roland* in medieval French, Ludovico Ariosto's *Orlando furioso* and Torquato Tasso's *Gerusalemme liberata* in Italian, *Cantar de mio Cid* in Spanish, and John Milton's *Paradise Lost* and Edmund Spenser's *Faerie Queene* in English. There are also seriocomic epics, such as the *Morgante* of a 15th-century Italian poet, Luigi Pulci, and the pseudo-Homeric *Battle of the Frogs and Mice*. Another distinct group is made up of the so-called beast epics—narrative poems written in Latin in the Middle Ages and dealing with the struggle between a cunning fox and a cruel and stupid wolf. Underlying all of the written forms is some trace of an oral character, partly because of the monumental persuasiveness of Homer's example but more largely because the epic was, in fact, born of an oral tradition. It is on the oral tradition of the epic form that this chapter focuses.

GENERAL CHARACTERISTICS

An epic may deal with such various subjects as myths, heroic legends, histories, edifying religious tales, animal stories,

In Book 6 of the renowned epic Paradise Lost, *John Milton portrays the struggle between good and evil angels.* Hulton Archive/Getty Images

or philosophical or moral theories. Epic poetry has been and continues to be used by peoples all over the world to transmit their traditions from one generation to another, without the aid of writing. These traditions frequently consist of legendary narratives about the glorious deeds of their national heroes. Thus, scholars have often identified "epic" with a certain kind of heroic oral poetry, which comes into existence in so-called heroic ages. Such ages have been experienced by many nations, usually at a stage of development in which they have had to struggle for a national identity. This effort, combined with such other conditions as an adequate material culture and a sufficiently productive economy, tend to produce a society dominated by a powerful and warlike nobility, constantly occupied with martial activities, whose individual members seek, above all, everlasting fame for themselves and for their lineages.

Uses of the Epic

The main function of poetry in heroic-age society appears to be to stir the spirit of the warriors to heroic actions by praising their exploits and those of their illustrious ancestors, by assuring a long and glorious recollection of their fame, and by supplying them with models of ideal heroic behaviour. One of the favourite pastimes of the nobility in heroic ages in different times and places has been to gather in banquet halls to hear heroic songs, in praise of famous deeds sung by professional singers as well as by the warriors themselves. Heroic songs also were often sung before a battle, and such recitations had tremendous effect on the morale of the combatants. Among the Fulani (Fulbe) people in the Sudan, for instance, whose epic poetry has been recorded, a nobleman customarily set out in quest of adventures accompanied by a singer (*mabo*), who also served as his shield bearer. The singer was thus the witness of the heroic deeds of his lord, which he celebrated in an epic poem called *baudi*.

The aristocratic warriors of the heroic ages were thus members of an illustrious family, a link in a long chain of glorious heroes. And the chain could snap if the warrior failed to preserve the honour of the family, whereas, by earning fame through his own heroism, he could give it new lustre. Epic traditions were to a large extent the traditions of the aristocratic families: the Old French word *geste*, used for a form of epic that flourished in the Middle Ages, means not only a story of famous deeds but also a genealogy.

The passing of a heroic age does not necessarily mean the end of its heroic oral poetry. An oral epic tradition usually continues for as long as the nation remains largely illiterate. Narratives about legendary heroes usually are not fully elaborated until the heroic age has passed. Even when the nobility that originally created the heroic epic perishes or loses interest, the old songs can persist as entertainments among the people. Court singers, then, are replaced by popular singers, who recite at public gatherings. This popular tradition, however, must be distinguished from a tradition that still forms an integral part of the culture of a nobility. For when a heroic epic loses its contact with the banquet halls of the princes and noblemen, it cannot preserve its power of renewal for long. Soon it enters what has been called the reproductive stage in the life cycle of an oral tradition, in which the bards become noncreative reproducers of songs learned from older singers. Popular oral singers, like the *guslari* of the Balkans, no doubt vary their songs to a certain extent each time they recite them, but they do so mainly by transposing language and minor episodes from one acquired song to another. Such variations must not be confounded with the real enrichment of the tradition by succeeding generations of genuine oral poets of the creative stage. The spread of literacy, which has a disastrous effect on the oral singer, brings about a quick corruption of the tradition. At this degenerate stage, the oral epic soon dies out if it is not written down or recorded.

The ancient Greek epic exemplifies the cycle of an oral tradition. Originating in the late Mycenaean period, the Greek epic outlasted the downfall of the typically heroic-age culture (c. 1100 BCE) and maintained itself through the "Dark Age" to reach a climax in the Homeric poems by the close of the Geometric period (900–750 BCE). After Homer, the activity of the *aoidoi*, who sang their own epic songs at the courts of the nobility, slowly declined. During the first half of the 7th century, the *aoidoi* produced such new poems as those of Hesiod and some of the earlier poems of what was to become known as the Epic Cycle. Between 625 and 575 BCE, the *aoidoi* gave way to oral reciters of a new type, called rhapsodes or "stitchers of songs," who declaimed for large audiences the already famous works of Homer while holding in their hand a staff (*rhabdos*), which they used to give emphasis to their words. Rhapsodes, who played a crucial role in the transmission of the Homeric epic, likely used some sort of written aids to memory before Homeric recitations were adopted in 6th-century Athens as part of the Panathenaic festivals held each year in honour of the goddess Athena.

VERBAL FORMULAS

To compose and memorize long narrative poems like the *Iliad* and the *Odyssey*, oral poets used a highly elaborate technical language with a large store of traditional verbal formulas, which could describe recurring ideas and situations in ways that suited the requirements of metre. So long as an oral epic tradition remains in its creative period, its language will be continually refined by each generation of poets in opposite directions, refinements that are called scope and economy. Scope is the addition of new phrases to express a larger number of recurrent concepts in varying metrical values fitting the possible positions in a verse. Economy is the elimination of redundancies that arise as gifted poets invent new set phrases that duplicate, both in a general sense and in metrical value, the formulas that already exist in the traditional stock.

Nowhere has this refinement proceeded any nearer to perfection than in the language of the Homeric epic. As has been shown by statistical analysis, it exhibits a remarkable efficiency, both in the rareness of unnecessarily duplicative variants and in the coverage of each common concept by the metrical alternatives useful in the composition of the six-foot metric line the Greeks used for epic poetry.

Thus, for example, if the idea of a ship has to be expressed at the end of a line of verse, the ship may be described as "well-trimmed" (*nēos eisēs*), "curved" (*nēos amphielissa*), or "dark-prowed" (*nēos kyanoprōiros*), depending entirely on the number of feet that remain to be filled by the phrase in the hexameter. If the phrase must cover the two final feet of the verse and the words must be put in the dative case, the formula "of a well-trimmed ship" will be replaced by "to a black ship" (*nēi melainē*). The sole occurrence of "Zeus who gathers lightning" (*steropēgereta Zeus*), which is an exact metrical equivalent of the more common "Zeus who delights in thunder" (*Zeus terpikeraunos*), constitutes one of the very few actual duplications of such formulas found in Homer.

Finally, some typical scenes in the heroic life, such as the preparation of a meal or sacrifice or the launching or beaching of a ship, contain set descriptions comprising several lines that are

HOMER

(fl. 9th or 8th century BCE, Ionia?)

The Greek poet Homer was one of the greatest and most influential writers of all time. Though almost nothing is known of his life, tradition holds that he was blind. The ancient Greeks attributed to him the great epic poems the Iliad *and the* Odyssey. *Modern scholars generally agree that he composed (but probably did not literally write) the* Iliad, *most likely relying on oral traditions, and at least inspired the composition of the* Odyssey. *The* Iliad, *set during the Trojan War, tells the story of the wrath of Achilles; the* Odyssey *tells the story of Odysseus as he travels home from the war. The two epics provided the basis of Greek education and culture in the Classical age, and they have remained among the most significant poems of the European tradition.*

used by rote each time the events are narrated.

This highly formalized language was elaborated by generations of oral poets to minimize the conscious effort needed to compose new poems and memorize existing ones. Because of it, an exceptionally gifted *aoidos*, working just prior to the corruption of the genre, could orally create long and finely structured poems like the *Iliad* and the *Odyssey*, and those poems could then be transmitted accurately by the following generations of rhapsodes until complete written texts were produced.

BASES

Oral heroic poetry, at its origin, usually deals with outstanding deeds of kings and warriors who lived in the heroic age of the nation. Because the primary function of this poetry is to educate rather than to record, however, the personages are necessarily transformed into ideal heroes and their acts into ideal heroic deeds that conform to mythological or ideological patterns. Some patterns are archetypes found all over the world, while others are peculiar to a specific nation or culture. Thus, in many epic traditions, heroes are born as a result of the union of a maiden with a divine or supernatural being. Because these unions occur outside the usual social norms, the heroes are exposed at birth, fed by an animal, and brought up by humble foster parents in a rustic milieu. They grow up with marvellous speed, fight a dragon—in their first combat—to rescue a maiden whom they marry, and die young in circumstances as fabulous as those that surrounded their birth.

Aeneas and Sibyl in the Underworld, Jan Brueghel the Elder. *In many epic tales, the hero rescues and subsequently marries a maiden.* The Bridgeman Art Library/Getty Images

In the traditions of Indo-European peoples, a hero is often a twin who acquires soon after his supernatural birth an invulnerability that has one defect, generally of his heel or of some other part of his foot, which ultimately causes his death. He is educated by a blacksmith, disguises himself as a woman at some time in his youth, and conquers a three-headed dragon, or some other kind of triple opponent, in his first battle. He then begets, by a foreign or supernatural woman, a child who, reared by his mother in her country, becomes a warrior as brave as his father. When this child meets his unknown father, the latter fails to recognize him, so that the father kills his own child after a long and fierce single combat. The hero himself usually dies after committing the third of three sins.

In Japan, to take another example, renowned members of the warrior aristocracy of the past, who have acquired the status of popular heroes, are in many cases supplied in their legend with four exceptionally brave and faithful retainers called their *shi-tennō* ("guardian kings"), who guard the four cardinal points; these form the closest entourage of their lord—who is usually depicted as excelling in command but not in physical strength—and defend him from dangers. The retainers reflect a mythological model, taken from Buddhism, of four *deva* kings, who guard the teaching of the Buddha against the attack of the devils.

A striking pattern for a number of epic traditions has been found in a so-called tripartite ideology or "trifunctional system" of the Indo-Europeans. The concept was based on the discovery of the remarkable philosophy of a prehistoric nation that survived as a system of thought in the historic Indo-European civilizations and even in the subconsciousness of the modern speakers of Indo-European tongues.

This philosophy sees in the universe three basic principles that are realized by three categories of people: priests, warriors, and producers of riches. In conformity with this philosophy, most Indo-European epics have as their central themes interaction among these three principles or functions: (1) religion and kingship; (2) physical strength; and (3) fecundity, health, riches, beauty, and so forth. In the long Indian epic the *Mahabharata*, for example, the central figures, the Pandava brothers, together with their father, Pandu, their two uncles, Dhritarashtra and Vidura, and their common wife, Draupadi, correspond to traditional deities presiding over the three functions of the Indo-European ideology.

During the first part of their earthly career, the Pandavas suffer constantly from the persistent enmity and jealousy of their cousins, Duryodhana and his 99 brothers, who, in reality, are incarnations of the demons Kali and the Paulastya. The demons at first succeeded in snatching the kingdom from the Pandavas and in exiling them. The conflict ends in a devastating war, in which all the renowned heroes of the time take part. The Pandavas survive the massacre, and establish on earth a peaceful and prosperous reign, in which Dhritarashtra and Vidura also participate.

This whole story, it has been shown, is a transposition to the heroic level of an Indo-European myth about the incessant struggle between the gods and the demons since the beginning of the world. Eventually, it results in a bloody eschatological battle, in which the gods and the devils exterminate each other. The destruction of the former world order, however, prepares for a new and better world, exempt from evil influences, over which reign a few divine survivors of the catastrophe.

THE DEVELOPMENT OF THE EPIC

The earliest known epic poetry is that of the Sumerians. Its origin has been traced to a preliterate heroic age, not later than 3000 BCE, when the Sumerians had to fight, under the direction of a warlike aristocracy, for possession of this fertile Mesopotamian land. Among the existing literature of this highly gifted people are fragments of narrative poems recounting the heroic deeds of their early kings: Enmerkar, Lugalbanda, and Gilgamesh.

By far the most important in the development of Mesopotamian literature are the five poems of the *Epic of Gilgamesh*. This cycle tells the odyssey of a king, Gilgamesh, part human and part divine, who seeks immortality. A god who dislikes his rule, fashions a wild man, Enkidu, to challenge him. Enkidu first lives among wild animals, then goes

to the capital and engages in a trial of strength with Gilgamesh, who emerges victorious. The two, now friends, set out on various adventures, in one of which they kill a wild bull that the goddess of love had sent to destroy Gilgamesh because he spurned her marriage proposal. Enkidu dreams the gods have decided he must die for the death of the bull, and, upon awakening, he does fall ill and die. Gilgamesh searches for a survivor of the Babylonian flood to learn how to escape death. The survivor shows him where to find a plant that renews youth, but after Gilgamesh gets the plant it is snatched away by a serpent. Gilgamesh returns, saddened, to his capital.

The legend of Gilgamesh was taken over by the Babylonians. They developed it into a long and beautiful poem, one of the masterpieces of humankind.

Another Babylonian epic, composed about 2000 BCE, is called in Akkadian *Enuma elish*, after its opening words, meaning "When on high." Its subject is not heroic but mythological. It recounts events from the beginning of the world to the establishment of the power of Marduk, the great god of Babylon. The outline of a Babylonian poem narrating the adventure of a hero named Adapa ("Man") can be reconstructed from four fragmentary accounts. It shares with the *Epic of Gilgamesh* the theme of a human potential for and loss of immortality.

Among clay tablets of the 14th century BCE, covered with inscriptions in an old Phoenician cuneiform alphabet, from Ras Shamra (the site of ancient Ugarit),

The Flood Tablet, 11th cuneiform slab in a series relating the Gilgamesh epic, from Nineveh, 7th century BCE; in the British Museum, London. © Photos.com/Jupiterimages

in northern Syria, there are important fragments of three narrative poems. One of these is mythological and recounts the career of the god Baal, which seems to coincide with the yearly cycle of vegetation on earth. As was usual with the death of gods in the ancient Mediterranean world, Baal's end brings about a drought that ceases only with his resurrection. Another fragment, about a hero named Aqhat, is perhaps a transposition of this myth of Baal to the human level. Just as the death of Baal is avenged on his slayer by Baal's sister Anath, so is the murder of Aqhat, which also causes a drought, revenged by his sister Paghat. Because the end of the poem is missing, however, we do not know if Paghat, like Anath, succeeds in bringing her brother back to life.

The third fragment, the Ugaritic epic of Keret, has been interpreted as a Phoenician version of the Indo-European theme of the siege of an enemy city for the recovery of an abducted woman. This theme is also the subject of the Greek legend of the Trojan War and of the Indian epic *Ramayana*. The fragmentary text does not reveal, however, whether the expedition of Keret, like that of the Achaean army against Troy, was meant to regain the hero's wife or to acquire for him a new bride.

THE GREEK EPIC

Especially in its originative stage, the Greek epic may have been strongly influenced by these Asian traditions. The Greek world in the late Bronze Age was related to the Middle East by so many close ties that it formed an integral part of the Levant. At Ugarit a large quarter of the city was occupied by Greek merchants, whose presence is also attested, among other places, at the gate of Mesopotamia, at Alalakh, in what is now Turkey. Thus, it is no surprise that, for example, the Greek myth about the succession of the divine kingship told in the *Theogony* of Hesiod and elsewhere is paralleled in a Hittite version of a Hurrian myth. In it, Anu, Kumarbi, and the storm god respectively,

parallel Uranus, Cronos, and Zeus in the *Theogony*. The Hittites had continuous diplomatic relations with the Achaeans of Greece, whose princes went to the royal court at Hattusa to perfect their skill with the chariot. The Greeks, therefore, had ample opportunity to become familiar with Hittite myths.

The *Epic of Gilgamesh* was then well-known in the Levant, as is indicated by discoveries of copies of it throughout this wide area. The *Odyssey* has many parallels with the *Epic of Gilgamesh*. The encounters of Odysseus with Circe and Calypso on their mythical isles, for instance, closely resemble the visit by Gilgamesh to a divine woman named Siduri, who keeps an inn in a marvellous garden of the sun god near the shores of ocean. Like the two Greek goddesses, Siduri tries to dissuade Gilgamesh from the pursuit of his journey by representing the pleasures of life, but the firm resolution of the hero finally obliges her to help him cross the waters of death. In the *Iliad*, Patroclus, who dies as a substitute for his king and dearest friend, Achilles, and then gives Achilles a description of the miserable condition of mortals after his death, bears striking similarities to the friend of Gilgamesh, Enkidu.

If these are indeed borrowings, it is all the more remarkable that they are used in Homer to express a view of life and a heroic temper radically different from those of the Sumerian epic of Mesopotamia. Gilgamesh persists in his quest of immortality even when Siduri shows him the vanity of such an ambition, but Odysseus shuns a goddess's offer of everlasting life, preferring to bear his human condition to the end. The loss of a beloved friend does not make Achilles seek desperately to escape from death. Instead he rushes into combat to revenge Patroclus, although he knows that he is condemning himself to an early death, and that the existence of a king in Hades will be incomparably less enviable than that of a slave on earth.

The Mesopotamian mind never tires of expressing deep human regret at mortality through stories about ancient heroes who, despite their superhuman strength and wisdom, and their intimacy with gods, failed to escape from death. A decisively different idea, however, is fundamental to the Greek heroic view of life. It has been demonstrated that the Greek view is derived from an Indo-European notion of justice—that each being has a fate (moira) assigned to him and marked clearly by boundaries that should never be crossed. Human energy and courage should, accordingly, be spent not in exceeding the proper limits of the human condition but in bearing it with style, pride, and dignity, gaining as much fame possible within the boundaries of individual moira. If induced by Folly (Ate, personified as a goddess of mischief) to commit an excess (hybris) with regard to his moira, a man will be punished without fail by the divine vengeance personified as Nemesis.

At the beginning of the Iliad, a plague decimates the Achaean army because its commander in chief, Agamemnon, refuses to return a captive, Chryseis, to her father, a priest of Apollo who offers a generous ransom. By unjustly insulting Achilles, Agamemnon commits another excess that causes the defeat of his army. Achilles, in the meantime, lets Ate take possession of his mind and refuses, to the point of excess, to resume his fight. He thus brings about a great misfortune, the loss of Patroclus, his dearest companion. Patroclus, however, also contributes to his own death by his hybris in pushing his triumph too far, ignoring Achilles' order to come back as soon as he has repulsed the enemy far from the Greek ships. The death of Hector also results from his hybris in rejecting the counsel of Polydamas and maintaining his army on the plain after the return of Achilles to combat. After so many disasters caused by the mischievous action of Ate among men, the last book of the Iliad presents a noble picture of Priam and Achilles, who submit piously to the orders of Zeus, enduring with admirable courage and moderation their respective fates.

Conversely, at the beginning of the Odyssey, Zeus evokes the ruin that Aegisthus will have to suffer for having acted "beyond his due share" by marrying Clytemnestra and murdering Agamemnon. This sets an antithesis to the story of the wise Odysseus, who, to accomplish his destiny as a mortal hero, never changes his purpose trying always to make the best of his countless misfortunes. He earns by this the favour of Athena and succeeds eventually in regaining Ithaca and punishing the wooers of Penelope for their *hybris* during his long absence. Present scholarship inclines to the view that such admirably well-structured poems as the *Iliad* and the *Odyssey* were probably shaped by Homer. This position contrasts with the extreme skepticism that marked all phases of Homeric criticism during the previous century. Yet the personality of Homer remains unknown and nothing certain is known about his life.

In comparison, information derived from his own works is fairly plentiful about the other great epic poet of Greece, Hesiod. He produced them presumably about 700 BCE, while tilling a farm in Askra, a small village of Boeotia. The social and geographical background of his poems, called didactic because of their occasionally moral and instructive tone, differs from the aristocratic society of Ionian Asia Minor that Homer addressed. Despite their different style, subjects, and view of life, however, Hesiod's *Theogony* and the *Works and Days* illustrate the same basic conception of justice as the Homeric epic. The *Theogony* describes a long sequence of primordial events that resulted in the present world order, in which man's inescapable lot is assigned by Zeus. The *Works and Days* explains, through a series of three myths, why the human lot is to work hard to produce riches. One must shut one's ears to the goddess who causes wars and lawsuits, listening only to the goddess who urges hard work in pursuit of riches. Pain and suffering have become unavoidable since Pandora—at

Prometheus's house and in conformity with the will of Zeus—opened the fatal jar containing all the ills of humankind. Moreover, the age of the race of iron has arrived when the fate of human beings is not to pass their lives in perpetual banquets or warfare, as did the preceding races, but to suffer constantly the fatigue and misery of labour. As long as the goddesses Aidos (a personification of the sense of shame) and Nemesis (a personification of divine retribution) stay with humankind, however, helping people observe their *moira* without committing excesses, one can still gain riches, merits, and glory by the sweat of one's brow. Only if one knows how to avoid all faults in daily work will one avoid offending Justice (Dikē), the sensitive virgin daughter of Zeus. This is why it is so vitally important for a farmer to know all the rules listed in the rest of the poem about seemingly trivial details of his work.

THE LATIN EPIC

Latin epic poetry was initiated in the 3rd century BCE by Livius Andronicus, who translated the *Odyssey* into the traditional metre of Saturnian verse. It was not until the 1st century BCE, however, that Rome possessed a truly national epic in the unfinished *Aeneid* of Virgil, who used Homer as his model. The story of Aeneas's journey, recounted in the first six books, is patterned after the *Odyssey*, with many imitative passages and even direct translations, while the description of the war in the last six books abounds with incidents modeled after those from the *Iliad*. More basically, however, Virgil made use of another model, Rome's own national legend about the war fought under Romulus against the Sabines. This legend preserves, in a historical disguise, an original Indo-European myth about a primitive conflict between the gods of sovereignty and war and the gods of fecundity, ending with the unification of the two divine races. In the development of this theme by Virgil, Aeneas and the Etruscans can be seen as representing the gods of sovereignty and war, and the Latins representing the gods of fecundity. Aeneas, who has brought the Trojan gods to Rome, is forced to fight with the help of the Etruscans against the Latins. It is the destiny of Aeneas to rule, and it is the fate of the Latins to share their land and women with the invaders and to accept Aeneas as their king. This resembles the unification of the warring races that climaxes the Indo-European myth.

The power exercised by the Indo-European ideological pattern on the Roman mind even under the empire is seen in the *Pharsalia* of Lucan (39–65 CE). In this historical epic, Cato, Caesar, and Pompey are depicted respectively as moral, warlike, and popular in a way that gives the story a clear trifunctional structure.

GERMANIC EPICS

A typical heroic age occurred during the wanderings of the Germanic tribes from the 3rd to the 6th century CE. Out of this too came a rich oral tradition, from which developed in the Middle Ages many epic poems. One of the greatest of these is the Old English *Beowulf*, written down in the 8th century. Archetypal Indo-European themes also reappear in these epics. For example, the theme of the fatal fight between father and son is recounted in the German *Hildebrandslied*, of which a 67-line fragment is extant. Again, a heroic version of the Indo-European myth about the rescue of the Sun Maiden from her captivity by the Divine Twins, which also provided the basic plot of the Greek Trojan cycle and the Indian *Ramayana*, is found in the German *Gudrun* (c. 1230).

CHANSONS DE GESTE

The French chansons de geste are epic poems whose action takes place during the reign of Charlemagne and his immediate successors. The *Chanson de Roland*, probably written down about the end of the 11th century, is by far the most refined of the group. The story of the poem had developed from a historical event, the annihilation of the rear guard of Charlemagne's army at Roncesvalles in the Pyrenees in 778 by Basque mountaineers. The Basques, however, are transformed in the epic to the Saracens, who to a later generation typified France's enemies in Spain. The other chansons de geste, none of which is comparable to *Roland* as a literary work, have been classified into three main cycles. The cycle of Guillaume d'Orange forms a biography

La Belle Dame Sans Merci, John William Waterhouse. *Arthurian romances, often told for amusement, tend to include a quest and a fervent love interest.* The Bridgeman Art Library/ Getty Images

of William (probably a historical count, William of Toulouse, who had, like the hero of the epic, a wife called Guibourg and a nephew, Vivien, and who became a monk in 806). Guibourg, the most faithful of wives, and the noble Vivien take prominent roles in the epic. The so-called Cycle of the Revolted Knights groups those poems that tell of revolts of feudal subjects against the emperor (Charlemagne or, more usually, his son, Louis). The Cycle of the King consists of the songs in which Charlemagne himself is a principal figure.

ARTHURIAN ROMANCE

The Arthurian romance seems to have developed first in the British Isles, before being taken to the Continent by Bretons, who migrated to Brittany in the 6th and 7th centuries. The core of the legend about Arthur and his knights derives from lost Celtic mythology. Many of the incidents in the former parallel the deeds of such legendary Irish characters as Cú Chulainn, an Ulster warrior said to have been fathered by the god Lug, and Finn, hero of the Fenian cycle about a band of warriors defending Ireland, both of whom are gods transformed into human heroes. The earliest extant works on Arthurian themes are four poems of Chrétien de Troyes, written in French between 1155 and 1185: *Erec, Yvain, Le Chevalier de la Charette* (left unfinished by Chrétien and completed by Godefroy de Lagny), and an unfinished *Perceval*. In German, after 1188, Hartmann von Aue (who also wrote

two legendary poems not belonging to the Arthurian cycle, *Gregorius* and *Poor Henry*) modeled his *Erec* and *Iwein* on those of Chrétien. The story of Perceval was given a full account by Wolfram von Eschenbach (c. 1170–1220) in his *Parzival* and in the unfinished *Titurel*. Another incomplete work of Wolfram, *Willehalm*, deals with the legend of William of Orange. *Tristan* of Gottfried von Strassburg is based directly on the older French version of Thomas of Britain (c. 1170–80). The romance proper, however, although it has similarities to the epic, differs in its lack of high purpose: fictions are told for their entertainment value rather than as models for national heroism. Developed in France in the Middle Ages, the romance is usually an adventure story with a strong love interest, intimately associated with the courtly love tradition of that time.

THE EPIC IN JAPAN

In Japan there were in ancient times families of reciters (*katari-be*) whose duty was to hand down myths and legends by word of mouth and to narrate them during official ceremonies and banquets. After the introduction of Chinese letters, however, from the 4th century CE onward, these traditional tales were put in writing and the profession of *katari-be* gradually died out. By the end of the 7th century, each clan of the ruling aristocracy seems to have possessed a written document that recounted the mythology and legendary history of Japan in a form biassed in favour of the clan concerned. These family documents were collected at the command of the emperor Temmu (672–686) and were used as basic materials for the compilation of the first national chronicles of Japan, the *Kojiki* (712; "Records of Ancient Matters") and the *Nihon shoki* (720; "Chronicles of Japan"). The myths and legends that are contained in the earlier parts of these two books derive, therefore, from the oral tradition of *katari-be*. Although no document preserves those narrations in their earliest form, it is generally assumed that they were originally in the form of poems. Many scholars believe that they were genuine epic poems, which were produced during a period of incessant warfare around the 4th century. At that time mounted aristocratic warriors of the future imperial family struggled to extend its power over the larger part of Japan. Exploits of warriors, such as the emperor Jimmu or Prince Yamato Takeru, in the earliest extant texts— the *Kojiki* and *Nihon shoki* of the 8th century—probably derive from a heroic epic about the wars of conquest of the first emperors, whose legendary feats were transformed into those of a few idealized heroic figures.

The middle of the Heian period (794–1185) saw the emergence of a new class of warrior known as samurai. They attached a greater importance to fame than to life. The battles they fought became the subject of epic narratives that were recited by itinerant blind priests to the accompaniment of a lutelike instrument called a *biwa*.

In the early part of the 13th century, tales about the wars of the preceding century, fought between the two strongest families of samurai, the Genji, or Minamoto, and the Heike, or Taira, were compiled in three significant war chronicles. The *Hōgen monogatari* and the *Heiji monogatari* deal with two small wars, the Hōgen (1156) and Heiji (1159), in which the Genji and Heike warriors fought for opposing court factions. The structure of the two works is roughly the same. Each celebrates the extraordinary prowess of a young Genji warrior, Minamoto Tametomo in the *Hōgen monogatari* and Minamoto Yoshihira in the *Heiji monogatari*. Each hero fights to the finish in exemplary manner not so much to win, for from the beginning each foresees the defeat of his own side, as for the sake of fame. And the consummate courage of the two heroes forms a striking contrast to the cowardice of court aristocrats. The bitterly fought Gempei War (1180–85), in which survivors of the Genji family challenged and defeated the Heike, is recounted in detail in the *Heike monogatari*, the greatest epic of Japanese literature. The sudden decline and ultimate extinction of the proud Heike, whose members had held the highest offices of the imperial court, illustrates the Buddhist philosophy of the transitory nature of all things. It invites the readers to seek deliverance from the world of sufferings through a faith that will take them to a land of eternal felicity at the moment of their death. The work is filled with tales of heroic actions of brave warriors. The most conspicuous is Minamoto Yoshitsune, one of the chief commanders of the Genji army: the legend of this man of military genius continued to develop in later literature, so that he has become the most popular hero of Japanese legend.

THE LATER WRITTEN EPIC

The vitality of the written epic is manifested by such masterworks as the 14th-century Italian *Divine Comedy* of Dante and the great Portuguese patriotic poem *The Lusíads* (1572) of Luís de Camões, which celebrates the voyage of Vasco da Gama to India. Novels and long narrative poems written by such major authors as Sir Walter Scott, Lord Byron, Alfred, Lord Tennyson, William Morris, and Herman Melville were patterned, to some extent, on the epic. Their fidelity to the genre, however, is found primarily in their large scope and their roots in a national soil. Their distance from the traditional oral epic tends to be considerable.

Among more modern epics, the Finnish *Kalevala* (1st ed. 1835; enlarged ed. 1849) occupies a special position. This is because its author, the 19th-century Finnish poet-scholar Elias Lönnrot, who composed it by combining short popular songs (*runot*) he himself had collected in Finland, had absorbed his material so well and identified himself so completely with the *runo* singers. He thus came close to showing what the oral epic, which he could study only at its

degenerative stage, might have been at its creative stage, on the lips of an exceptionally gifted singer.

EPIC: TERMS AND CONCEPTS

Across the world and through time, epic storytelling traditions have varied in many ways. Notwithstanding their tremendous diversity, they share certain characteristics across time and space. They are rule-governed. They use special languages and performance arenas while employing flexible patterns and structures that aid composition, retention, and reperformance. In addition, they assume an active role for the audience and fulfill a clear and important function for the societies that maintain them. The following short pieces reveal both the diversity and the shared features of world epics.

BYLINY

The traditional forms of Old Russian and Russian heroic narrative poetry transmitted orally are known as *byliny* (singular *bylina*) and are still a creative tradition in the 21st century. The oldest *byliny* belong to a cycle dealing with the golden age of Kievan Rus in the 10th–12th century. They centre on the deeds of Prince Vladimir I and his court. One of the favourite heroes is the independent Cossack Ilya of Murom, who defended Kievan Rus from the Mongols. Although these ancient songs are no longer known to the peasants around Kiev, they were discovered in the 19th century in the repertoire of peasants living around Lake Onega in the remote northwestern regions of European Russia. They are also known in the far northeastern outposts of Siberia.

Other *byliny*, dealing with all periods of Ukrainian and Russian history, have been collected throughout the country. They may relate events from the reigns of Ivan the Terrible or Peter the Great, or deal with the Cossack rebels Stenka Razin and Pugachov. A 20th-century *bylina*, the *Tale of Lenin*, converts the chief events of the Russian Revolution of 1917 into a formulaic hero tale. Taken together, the *byliny* constitute a folk history in which facts and sympathies are often at variance with official history.

Byliny may have originated with professional court minstrels, but they are now circulated and created by common folk. With the spread of literacy, the art of composing and chanting *byliny* is dying out.

CYCLE

A cycle in literature is a group of prose or poetic narratives, usually of different authorship, centring on a legendary hero and his associates. The term *cyclic poems* was first used in late Classical times to refer to the independent poems that appeared after Homer to supplement his account of the Trojan War and the heroes' homecomings. Another Classical Greek cycle is the "Theban" group, dealing with Oedipus and his descendants. This cycle is best known through Sophocles' tragedies *Oedipus Rex, Antigone,* and *Oedipus at Colonus,* and Aeschylus's *Seven Against Thebes*.

Medieval romance is classified into three major cycles: the "matter of Rome the great," the "matter of France," and the "matter of Britain" ("matter" here is a literal translation of the French *matière,* referring to subject matter, theme, topic, etc.). The matter of Rome, a misnomer, refers to all tales derived from Latin classics. The matter of France includes the stories of Charlemagne and his Twelve Noble Peers. The matter of Britain refers to stories of King Arthur and his knights, the Tristan stories, and independent tales having an English background, such as *Guy of Warwick.*

Groups of mystery plays that were regularly performed in various towns in England were also known as cycles. The word *cycle* is also used for a series of poems or novels that are linked in theme, such as Émile Zola's Rougon-Macquart cycle of 20 novels (1871–93), tracing the history of a single family.

SKALDIC POETRY

An oral court poetry called skaldic poetry originated in Norway but was developed chiefly by Icelandic poets (skalds) from the 9th to the 13th century. Skaldic poetry was contemporary with Eddaic poetry (that is, the poetry found in the *Poetic,* or *Elder, Edda*), but differed from it in metre, diction, and style. Eddaic poetry is anonymous, simple, and terse, often taking the form of an objective dramatic dialogue.

Skalds were identified by name. Their poems were descriptive and subjective and their metres strictly syllabic instead of free and variable. The language was ornamented with *heiti* and *kennings*. *Heiti* ("names") are uncompounded poetic nouns, fanciful art words rather than everyday terms (e.g., *brand* for "sword," or *steed* for "horse"). *Kennings* are metaphorical circumlocutions such as *sword liquid* for "blood" or *wave-horse* for "ship." Sometimes *kennings* are extremely indirect. For example, "the blue land of Haki" (a sea king) refers not to land but to the sea and requires a knowledge of Norse mythology to be understood.

Of the one hundred skaldic verse forms, the *dróttkvætt* (court metre), which uses a syllable count and a regular pattern of alliteration, internal rhyme, and assonance, was most popular. The formal subjects of the skalds were shield poems (descriptions of the mythological engravings on shields), praise of kings, epitaphs, and genealogies. There were also less formal occasional poems, dream songs, magic curses, lampoons, flytings (or poems of abuse), and (although forbidden by law) many love songs. Because they so often praised current feats of the kings, the poems have high historical value, limited only by their abstruse language. The greatest of the skalds was Egill Skallagrímsson, whose life and works are preserved in the *Egils Saga*.

CHAPTER 4

BALLAD

A short narrative folk song, the ballad crystallized in Europe in the late Middle Ages and persists to the present day in communities where literacy, urban contacts, and mass media have little affected the habit of folk singing.

France, Denmark, Germany, Russia, Greece, and Spain, as well as England and Scotland, possess impressive ballad collections. At least one-third of the three hundred extant English and Scottish ballads have counterparts in one or several of these continental balladries, particularly those of Scandinavia. In no two language areas, however, are the formal characteristics of the ballad identical. For example, British and American ballads are invariably rhymed and strophic (i.e., divided into stanzas). The Russian ballads known as *byliny* and almost all Balkan ballads are unrhymed and unstrophic. And, though the *romances* of Spain, as their ballads are called, and the Danish *viser* both use assonance instead of rhyme, the Spanish ballads are generally unstrophic while the Danish are strophic, parcelled into either quatrains or couplets.

In reception, however, the ballad's technique and form are often subordinated to its presentation of events—especially ones presented as historical, whether factually accurate or not—and their significance to the audience. The ballad also plays a critical role in the creation and maintenance of distinct national cultures. In contemporary literature and music, the ballad is primarily defined by its commitment to nostalgia, community histories, and romantic love.

ELEMENTS

The ballad, like the epic, possesses several features that are characteristic of the form. These include such devices as repetition, minimal characterization, and economy of narrative and a historical reliance on oral transmission.

NARRATIVE BASIS

Typically, the folk ballad tells a compact little story that begins eruptively at the moment when the narrative has turned decisively toward its catastrophe or resolution. Focusing on a single, climactic situation, the ballad leaves the inception of the conflict and the setting to be inferred or hurriedly sketches them in. Characterization is minimal, the characters revealing themselves in their actions or speeches. Overt moral comment on the characters' behaviour is suppressed and their motivation seldom explicitly detailed. Any description is brief and conventional. Transitions between scenes are abrupt, time shifts are only vaguely indicated, and crucial events and emotions are conveyed in crisp, poignant dialogue. In short, the ballad method of narration is directed toward achieving a bold, sensational, dramatic effect with purposeful starkness and abruptness. But despite the rigid economy of ballad narratives, a repertory of rhetorical devices is employed for prolonging highly charged moments in the story and thus thickening the emotional atmosphere. In the most famous of such devices, incremental repetition, a phrase or stanza is repeated several times with a slight but significant substitution at the same critical point. Suspense accumulates with each substitution, until at last the final and revelatory substitution bursts the pattern, achieving a climax and with it a release of powerful tensions. The following stanza is a typical example:

> *Then out and came the thick, thick blood,*
> *Then out and came the thin,*
> *Then out and came the bonny*
>   *heart's blood,*
> *Where all the life lay in.*

ORAL TRANSMISSION

Because ballads thrive among unlettered people and are freshly created from memory at each separate performance, they are subject to constant variation in both text and tune. Where tradition is healthy and not highly influenced by literary or other outside cultural influences, these variations keep the ballad alive by gradually bringing it into line with the style of life, beliefs, and emotional needs of the immediate folk audience. Ballad tradition, however, like all folk arts, is basically conservative, a trait that explains the references in several ballads to obsolete implements and customs, as well as the appearance of words and phrases that are so badly garbled as to indicate that the singer does not understand their meaning though he takes pleasure in their sound and respects their traditional right to a place in his version of the song. The new versions of ballads that arise as the result of cumulative variations are no less authentic than their antecedents. A poem is fixed in its final form when published, but the printed or taped record of a ballad is representative only of its appearance in one place, in one line of tradition, and at one moment in its protean history. The first record of a ballad is not its original form but merely its earliest recorded form, and the recording of a ballad does not inhibit tradition from varying it subsequently into other shapes, because tradition preserves by re-creating rather than by exact reproduction.

THEORIES OF COMPOSITION

How ballads are composed and set afloat in tradition has been the subject of bitter quarrels among scholars. The so-called communal school, which was led by two American scholars F.B. Gummere (1855–1919) and G.L. Kittredge (1860–1941), argued at first that ballads were composed collectively during the excitement of dance and song festivals. Under attack the communalists retreated to the position that although none of the extant ballads had been communally composed, the prototypical ballads that determined the style of the ballads had originated in this communal fashion. Their opponents were the individualists, who included the British men of letters W.J. Courthope (1842–1917) and Andrew Lang (1844–1912) and the American linguist Louise Pound (1872–1958). They held that each ballad was the work of an individual composer, who was not necessarily a folk singer, tradition serving simply as the vehicle

for the oral perpetuation of the creation. According to the widely accepted communal re-creation theory, put forward by the American collector Phillips Barry (1880–1937) and the scholar G.H. Gerould (1877–1953), the ballad is conceded to be an individual composition originally. This fact is considered of little importance because the singer is not expressing himself individually, but serving as the deputy of the public voice, and because a ballad does not become a ballad until it has been accepted by the folk community and been remolded by the inevitable variations of tradition into a communal product. Ballads have also been thought to derive from art songs, intended for sophisticated audiences, which happened to filter down to a folk level and become folk song. This view, though plausible in the case of certain folk lyrics, is inapplicable to the ballads, for if the ballads were simply miscellaneous castoffs, it would not be possible to discern so clearly in them a style that is unlike anything in sophisticated verse.

TECHNIQUE AND FORM

Ballads are normally composed in two kinds of stanzas. The first consists of a couplet of lines each with four stressed syllables, and with an interwoven refrain:

But it would have made your heart
   right sair,
With a hey ho and a lillie gay
To see the bridegroom rive his haire.
As the primrose spreads so sweetly

The second a stanza of alternating lines of four stresses and three stresses, the second and fourth lines rhyming:

There lived a wife at Usher's Well,
And a wealthy wife was she;
She had three stout and stalwart sons,
And sent them o'er the sea.

Reference to the tunes show that the three-stress lines actually end in an implied fourth stress to match the pause in the musical phrase at these points. The interwoven refrain is a concession to the musical dimension of the ballad. It may be a set of nonsense syllables (Dillum down dillum, Fa la la la) or irrelevant rigmaroles of flowers or herbs. A few ballads have stanza-length burdens interspersed between the narrative stanzas, a technique borrowed from the medieval carols. The lyrical and incantatory effect of refrains during the ballad performance is extremely appealing, but in cold print they often look ridiculous, which is perhaps why early collectors failed to note them. In the first example given previously, it will be noted that the gaiety of the refrain is at odds with the mood of the meaningful lines. Frequently, the ballad stanza satisfies the music's insistence on lyrical flourishes by repeating textual phrases and lines:

So he ordered the grave to be opened wide,
And the shroud to be turned down;
And there he kissed her clay cold lips
Till the tears came trickling down,
    down, down,
Till the tears came trickling down

The refrain is just one of the many kinds of repetition employed in ballads. Incremental repetition, already discussed, is the structural principle on which whole ballads ("The Maid Freed from the Gallows," "Lord Randal") are organized, and many other ballads contain long exchanges of similarly patterned phrases building cumulatively toward the denouement:

"Oh what will you leave to your
    father dear?"
"The silver-shod steed that brought
    me here."
"What will you leave to your mother dear?"
"My velvet pall and my silken gear."
"What will you leave to your brother John?"
"The gallows-tree to hang him on."

Any compressed narrative of sensational happenings told at a high pitch of feeling is bound to repeat words and phrases to accommodate the emotion that cannot be exhausted in one saying, a tendency that accounts for such stanzas as:

Then He says to His mother, "Oh: the
    withy [willow], oh: the withy,
The bitter withy that causes me to smart,
    to smart,
Oh: the withy, it shall be the very first tree
That perishes at the heart."

Much repetition in ballads is mnemonic as well as dramatic. Because ballads are performed orally, the hearer cannot turn back a page to recover a vital detail that slipped by in a moment of inattention. Crucial facts in narrative, therefore, are incised in the memory by skillful repetition. Instructions given in a speech are exactly repeated when the singer reports the complying action, and answers follow the form of the questions that elicited them.

The exigencies of oral performance also account for the conventional stereotyped imagery of the ballads. For unlike the poet, who reaches for the individualistic, arresting figure of speech, the ballad singer seldom ventures beyond a limited stock of images and descriptive adjectives. Knights are always gallant, swords royal, water wan, and ladies gay. Whatever is red is as red as blood, roses, coral, rubies, or cherries; white is stereotyped as snow white, lily white, or milk white. Such conventions fall into place almost by reflex action, easing the strain on the singer's memory and allowing him to give his full attention to the manipulation of the story. The resulting bareness of verbal texture, however, is more than compensated for by the dramatic rhetoric through which the narrative is projected. In any case, complex syntax and richness of language are forbidden to texts meant to be sung, for music engages too much of the hearer's attention for him to untangle an ambitious construction or relish an original image. Originality indeed, like anything else that exalts the singer, violates ballad decorum, which insists that the singer remain impersonal.

TYPES OF BALLADRY

The traditional folk ballad, sometimes called the Child ballad in deference to Francis Child, the scholar who compiled the definitive English collection, is the standard kind of folk ballad in English and is the type of balladry that this section is mainly concerned with. But there are peripheral kinds of ballads that must also be noticed in order to give a survey of balladry.

MINSTREL BALLAD

Minstrels, the professional entertainers of nobles, squires, rich burghers, and clerics until the 17th century, should properly have had nothing to do with folk ballads, the self-created entertainment of the peasantry. Minstrels sometimes, however, affected the manner of folk song or remodelled established folk ballads. Child included many minstrel ballads in his collection on the ground that fragments of traditional balladry were embedded in them. The blatant style of minstrelsy marks these ballads off sharply from folk creations. In violation of the strict impersonality of the folk ballads, minstrels constantly intrude into their narratives with moralizing comments and fervent assurances that they are not lying at the precise moment when they are most fabulous. The minstrels manipulate the story with coarse explicitness, begging for attention in a servile way, predicting future events in the story

FRANCIS J. CHILD

(b. Feb. 1, 1825, Boston, Mass., U.S.—d. Sept. 11, 1896, Boston)

The American scholar and educator Francis Child is noted for his systematic study, collecting, and cataloging of folk ballads.

Child graduated from Harvard University in 1846, and later, after studying in Europe, he succeeded Edward T. Channing in 1851 as Boylston professor of rhetoric, oratory, and elocution and in 1876 became professor of English at Harvard. Child studied English drama and Germanic philology, the latter at Berlin and Göttingen during a leave of absence (1849–51). He edited the poetic works of Edmund Spenser, 5 vol. (1855), and published an important treatise on Geoffrey Chaucer in the Memoirs of the American Academy of Arts and Sciences *for 1863.*

His largest undertaking grew out of an original collection of English and Scottish Ballads, *8 vol. (1857–58). Child accumulated in the Harvard library one of the largest folklore*

Francis J. Child. Library of Congress, Washington, D.C. (Digital File Number: cph 3e02266)

collections in existence, studied manuscript rather than printed versions of old ballads, and investigated songs and stories in other languages that were related to the English and Scottish ballads. His final collection was published as The English and Scottish Popular Ballads, *first in 10 parts (1882–98) and then in 5 quarto volumes, containing 305 ballads. Few significant additions have been made since, and in the 21st century Child's collection, though emended and corrected by later scholars, remains the authoritative treasury.*

and promising that it will be interesting and instructive, shifting scenes obtrusively, reflecting on the characters' motives with partisan prejudice. Often their elaborate performances are parcelled out in clear-cut divisions, usually called fits or cantos, to forestall tedium and build up suspense by delays and piecemeal revelations. Several surviving minstrel pieces are poems in praise of such noble houses as the Armstrongs ("Johnie Armstrong"), the Stanleys ("The Rose of England"), and the Percys ("The Battle of Otterburn," "The Hunting of the Cheviot," "The Earl

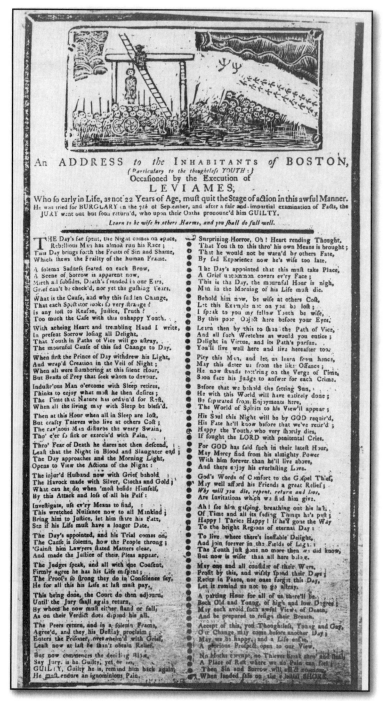

Detail of an undated broadside ballad distributed in Boston following the execution of Levi Ames for burglary and intended to warn "thoughtless Youth." Library of Congress, Washington, D.C.

of Westmoreland"), doubtless the work of propagandists in the employ of these families. The older Robin Hood ballads are also minstrel propaganda, glorifying the virtues of the yeomanry, the small independent landowners of preindustrial England. The longer, more elaborate minstrel ballads were patently meant to be recited rather than sung.

BROADSIDE BALLAD

Among the earliest products of the printing press were broadsheets about the size of handbills on which were printed the text of ballads. A crude woodcut often headed the sheet, and under the title it was specified that the ballad was to be sung to the tune of some popular air. Musical notation seldom appeared on the broadsides. Those who sold the ballads in the streets and at country fairs sang their wares so that anyone unfamiliar with the tune could learn it by listening a few times to the balladmonger's rendition. From the 16th century until the end of the 19th century, broadsides, known also as street ballads, stall ballads, or slip songs, were a lively commodity, providing employment for a troop of hack poets. Before the advent of newspapers, the rhymed accounts of current events provided by the broadside ballads were the chief source of spectacular news. Every sensational public happening was immediately clapped into rhyme and sold on broadsheets. Few of the topical pieces long survived the events that gave them birth, but

a good number of pathetic tragedies, such as "The Children in the Wood" and broadsides about Robin Hood, Guy of Warwick, and other national heroes, remained perennial favourites. Although the broadside ballad represents the adaptation of the folk ballad to the urban scene and middle class sensibilities, the general style more closely resembles minstrelsy, only with a generous admixture of vulgarized traits borrowed from book poetry. A few folk ballads appeared on broadsheets; many ballads, however, were originally broadside ballads the folk adapted.

LITERARY BALLADS

The earliest literary imitations of ballads were modelled on broadsides, rather than on folk ballads. In the early part of the 18th century, Jonathan Swift, who had written political broadsides in earnest, adapted the style for several jocular bagatelles. Poets such as Swift, Matthew Prior, and William Cowper in the 18th century and Thomas Hood, W.M. Thackeray, and Lewis Carroll in the 19th century made effective use of the jingling metres, forced rhymes, and unbuttoned style for humorous purposes. Lady Wardlaw's "Hardyknute" (1719), perhaps the earliest literary attempt at a folk ballad, was dishonestly passed off as a genuine product of tradition. After the publication of Thomas Percy's ballad compilation *Reliques of Ancient English Poetry* in 1765, ballad imitation enjoyed a considerable vogue, which properly

LEWIS CARROLL

(b. Jan. 27, 1832, Daresbury, Cheshire, Eng.—d. Jan. 14, 1898, Guildford, Surrey)

The British logician, mathematician, and novelist Charles Lutwidge Dodgson, better known by the pseudonym Lewis Carroll, is especially remembered for two enduring classics of children's literature: Alice's Adventures in Wonderland *(1865; illustrated by John Tenniel) and its sequel* Through the Looking-Glass *(1871). An unmarried deacon and a lecturer in mathematics at the University of Oxford, he enjoyed the company of young girls. His novel* Alice's Adventures in Wonderland *is based on stories he told to amuse young friends, especially Alice Liddell, the daughter of Henry George Liddell, dean of Christ Church. Its sequel describes Alice's further adventures. The two books, full of whimsy but also of sophisticated wit and mathematical and logical puzzles, became among the most famous and admired children's books in the world. Carroll's other works include the narrative nonsense poem* The Hunting of the Snark *(1876) and the children's novels* Sylvie and Bruno *(1889) and* Sylvie and Bruno Concluded *(1893). He was also an important early portrait photographer.*

belongs in the history of poetry rather than balladry.

SUBJECT MATTER

The stuff of ballads is the stuff of life, but with a starker light and contrast. Mystery, romance (in both the chivalric and the modern sense), crime and punishment, historical events, and many other topics are fair game for the balladeer.

THE SUPERNATURAL

The finest of the ballads are deeply saturated in a mystical atmosphere imparted by the presence of magical appearances and apparatus. The protagonist of "The Wife of Usher's Well" laments the death of her children so unconsolably that they return to her from the dead. The principal character in "Willie's Lady" cannot be delivered of her child because of her wicked mother-in-law's spells, an enchantment broken by a beneficent household spirit. In "The Great Silkie of Sule Skerry" a silkie (who is a man on land, but a seal in the sea) begets upon an "earthly" woman a son, who, on attaining maturity, joins his seal father in the sea, there shortly to be killed by his mother's human husband. The hero of "Kemp Owyne" removes a spell from a maiden by kissing her despite her bad breath and savage looks. An encounter between a demon and a maiden is the subject of "Lady Isabel and the Elf-Knight," the English counterpart of the ballads known to the Dutch-Flemish as "Herr Halewijn," to Germans as "Ulinger," to Scandinavians as "Kvindemorderen" and to the French as "Renaud le Tueur de Femme." In "The House Carpenter," a former lover (a demon in disguise) persuades a carpenter's wife to forsake her husband and children and come away with him, which proves to be a fatal decision. In American and in late British tradition the supernatural tends to get worked out of the ballads by being rationalized: instead of the ghost of his jilted sweetheart appearing to Sweet William of "Fair Margaret and Sweet William" as he lies in bed with his bride, it is rather a dream of the dead girl's image that kindles his fatal remorse. In addition to those ballads that turn on a supernatural occurrence, casual supernatural elements are found all through balladry.

ROMANTIC TRAGEDIES

The separation of lovers through a misunderstanding or the opposition of relatives is perhaps the commonest ballad story. "Barbara Allen" is typical: Barbara cruelly spurns her lover because of an unintentional slight; he dies of lovesickness, she of remorse. The Freudian paradigm operates rigidly in ballads: fathers oppose the suitors of their daughters, mothers the sweethearts of their sons. Thus "The Douglas Tragedy"—the Danish "Ribold and Guldborg"—occurs when an eloping couple is overtaken by the girl's father and brothers or "Lady Maisry," pregnant by an English lord, is burned by her fanatically Scottish brother. Incest, frequent in ballads recorded before 1800 ("Lizie Wan," "The Bonny Hind"), is shunned by modern tradition.

ROMANTIC COMEDIES

The outcome of a ballad love affair is usually, though not always, tragic. But even when true love is eventually rewarded, such ballad heroines as "The Maid Freed from the Gallows" and "Fair Annie," among others, win through to happiness after such bitter trials that the price they pay seems too great. The course of romance runs hardly more smoothly in the many ballads, influenced by the cheap optimism of broadsides, where separated lovers meet without recognizing each other. The girl is told by the "stranger" of her lover's defection or death. When her ensuing grief convinces him of her sincere love, he proves his identity and takes the joyful girl to wife. "The Bailiff's Daughter of Islington" is a classic of the type. Later tradition occasionally foists happy endings upon romantic tragedies: in the American "Douglas Tragedy" the lover is not slain but instead gets the irate father at his mercy and extorts a dowry from him. With marriage a consummation so eagerly sought in ballads, it is ironic that the bulk of humorous ballads deal with shrewish wives ("The Wife Wrapped in Wether's Skin") or gullible cuckolds ("Our Goodman").

CRIME

Crime, and its punishment, is the theme of innumerable ballads: his sweetheart poisons "Lord Randal"; "Little Musgrave" is killed by Lord Barnard when he is discovered in bed with Lady Barnard, and the lady, too, is gorily dispatched. The murders of "Jim Fisk," Johnny of "Frankie and Johnny," and many other ballad victims are prompted by sexual jealousy. One particular variety of crime ballad, the "last goodnight", represents itself falsely to be the contrite speech of a criminal as he mounts the scaffold to be executed. A version of "Mary Hamilton" takes this form, which was a broadside device widely adopted by the folk. "Tom Dooley" and "Charles Guiteau," the scaffold confession of the assassin of Pres. James A. Garfield, are the best known American examples.

MEDIEVAL ROMANCE

Perhaps a dozen or so ballads derive from medieval romances. As in "Hind Horn" and "Thomas Rymer," only the climactic scene is excerpted for the ballad. In general, ballads from romances have not worn well in tradition because of their unpalatable fabulous elements, which a more modern audience apparently regarded as childish. Thus "Sir Lionel" becomes in America "Bangum and the Boar," a humorous piece to amuse children. Heterodox apocryphal legends that circulated widely in the Middle Ages are the source of almost all religious ballads, notable "Judas," "The Cherry-Tree Carol," and "The Bitter Withy." The distortion of biblical narrative is not peculiarly British: among others, the Russian ballads of Samson and Solomon, the Spanish "Pilgrim to Compostela" and the French and Catalonian ballads on the penance of Mary Magdalence reshape canonical stories radically.

HISTORICAL BALLADS

Historical ballads date mainly from the period 1550–1750, though a few, like "The Battle of Otterburn," celebrate events of an earlier date, in this case 1388. "The Hunting of the Cheviot," recorded about the same time and dealing with the same campaign, is better known in a late broadside version called "Chevy Chase." The details in historical ballads are usually factually incorrect because of faulty memory or partisan alterations, but they are valuable in reflecting common attitudes toward the events they imperfectly report. For example, neither "The Death of Queen Jane," about one of the wives of Henry VIII, nor "The Bonny Earl of Murray" is correct in key details, but they accurately express the popular mourning for these figures. By far the largest number of ballads that can be traced to historical occurrences have to do with local skirmishes and matters of regional rather than national importance. The troubled border between England and Scotland in the 16th and early 17th century furnished opportunities for intrepid displays of loyalty, courage, and cruelty that are chronicled in such dramatic ballads as "Edom o Gordon," "The Fire of Frendraught," "Johnny Cock," "Johnie Armstrong," and "Hobie Noble." Closely analogous to these are Spanish *romances* such as "The Seven Princes of Lara," on wars between Moors and Christians.

JANE SEYMOUR.

Third queen of Henry the 8th king of England
(after Holbein.)

Married 1536.   Died 1537.

The anonymous ballad "The Death of Queen Jane," perhaps written about King Henry VIII's third wife, Jane Seymour, might not be factually accurate, but it does convey the sentiment of the time. Hulton Archive/Getty Images

DISASTER

Sensational shipwrecks, plagues, train wrecks, mine explosions– all kinds of shocking acts of God and man—were regularly chronicled in ballads, a few of which remained in tradition, probably because of some special charm in the language or the music. The shipwreck that lies in the background of one of the most poetic of all ballads "Sir Patrick Spens" cannot be fixed, but "The Titanic," "Casey Jones," "The Wreck on the C & O," and "The Johnstown Flood" are all circumstantially based on actual events, as was the 20th-century ballad "The Wreck of the *Edmund Fitzgerald*" by Canadian singer-songwriter Gordon Lightfoot.

OUTLAWS AND BADMEN

Epic and saga heroes figure prominently in Continental balladries, notable examples being the Russian Vladimir, the Spanish Cid Campeador, the Greek Digenes Akritas, and the Danish Tord of Havsgaard and Diderik. This kind of hero never appears in English and Scottish ballads. But the outlaw hero of the type of the Serbian Makro Kraljević or the Danish Marsk Stig is exactly matched by the English Robin Hood, who is the hero of some 40 ballads, most of them of minstrel or broadside provenance. His chivalrous style and generosity to the poor was imitated by later ballad highwaymen in "Dick Turpin," "Brennan on the Moor," and "Jesse James." "Henry Martyn" and "Captain Kidd" were popular

Robin Hood's gallantry and kindness made him the hero of more than 40 ballads. Rischgitz/Hulton Archive/Getty Images

pirate ballads, but the most widely sung was "The Flying Cloud," a contrite "goodnight" (written as if spoken shortly before execution) warning young men to avoid the curse of piracy. That so many folk heroes are sadistic bullies ("Stagolee"), robbers ("Dupree"), or pathological killers ("Sam Bass," "Billy the Kid") comments on commonplace hostility toward the church, constabulary, banks, and railroads. The kindly, law-abiding, devout, enduring steel driver "John Henry" is a rarity among ballad heroes.

OCCUPATIONAL BALLADS

A large section of balladry, especially American, deals with the hazards of such occupations as seafaring ("The Greenland Whale Fishery"), lumbering ("The Jam on Gerry's Rock"), mining ("The Avondale Mine Disaster"), herding cattle ("Little Joe the Wrangler"), and the hardships of frontier life ("The Arkansaw Traveler"). But men in these occupations sang ballads also that had nothing to do with their proper work: "The Streets of Laredo," for example, is known in lumberjack and soldier versions as well as the usual cowboy lament version, and the pirate ballad "The Flying Cloud" was much more popular in lumbermen's shanties than in forecastles.

BALLAD: TERMS AND CONCEPTS

Ballads of the minstrel, broadside, and literary type are treated in some detail in the preceding sections. These are perhaps the broadest categories described by scholars of the form. Some specific types and subtypes are discussed in the following text.

BORDER BALLAD

The border ballad is a type of spirited heroic ballad celebrating the raids, feuds, seductions, and elopements on the border between England and Scotland in the 15th and 16th centuries, where neither English nor Scottish law prevailed. Among the better known border ballads are "Johnny Cock," "Jock o' the Side," "Hobie Noble," and "The Bonny Earl of Murray." Though a few deal with events

of historical importance, most are concerned with the personal retributions of the outlaws and robber clans who maintained their own grim code on the border.

GOOD-NIGHT

A sensational subtype of broadside ballad, the good-night was popular in England from the 16th through the 19th century, purporting to be the farewell statement of a criminal made shortly before his execution. Good-nights are usually repentant in tone, containing a sketchy account of how the criminal first went astray, a detailed account of his grisly crime, his sentence by the judge, the grief of his aged parents, and a warning to others not to follow his example. An exception is "Sam Hall," in which the remorseless criminal boasts, "I hate you one and all," to the bitter end. Enterprising hack writers and broadside publishers often had the good-night printed in advance of the execution, ready for sale on the street (or at the scaffold if the execution were public) at the moment that it was accomplished. Many good-nights, originating in broadsides, have been incorporated into the folk tradition.

GWERSIOU

The *gwersiou* is a narrative ballad in the Breton language that dramatically describes local events, history, legends, and folklore. One of two major types of Breton folk poetry, the *gwersiou* was first published in an authenticated collection by François-Marie Luzel in *Gwersiou Breiz-Izel*, 2 vol. (1868–74; "Ballads of Lower Brittany").

KLEPHETIC BALLAD

Particular to the Mediterranean, Klephetic ballads are songs and poems extolling the adventures of the Klephts, Greek nationalists living as outlaws in the mountains during the period of Turkish domination over Greece (1453–1828). Containing some of the most beautiful and vivid verse in Modern Greek, the songs, mainly from the 18th century, are an entirely spontaneous poetry, composed in popular language and in 15-syllable verse, rhymed and unrhymed. They are pervaded with the spirit of the forests and the mountains and, like so much of Greek popular poetry, personify trees, rocks, and rivers. Even the mountains praise the prowess of the Klephts, bewail their deaths, and comfort the disconsolate wives and mothers. Klephtic ballads have been a constant source of inspiration and rejuvenation to Modern Greek poetry and to Greek nationalism.

CHAPTER 5

DRAMATIC LITERATURE

The term *dramatic literature* implies a contradiction in that *literature* originally meant something written and *drama* meant something performed. Most of the problems, and much of the interest, in the study of dramatic literature stem from this contradiction. Even though a play may be appreciated solely for its qualities as writing, greater rewards probably accrue to those who remain alert to the volatility of the play as a whole.

To appreciate this complexity in drama, however, each of its elements—acting, directing, staging, and so forth—should be studied, so that its relationship to all the others can be fully understood. It is the purpose of this chapter to study drama with particular attention to what the playwright sets down.

GENERAL CHARACTERISTICS

From the inception of a play in the mind of its author to the image of it that an audience takes away from the theatre, many hands and many physical elements help to bring it to life. Questions therefore arise as to what is and what is not essential to it. Is a play what its author thought he was writing, or the words he wrote? Is a play the way in which those words are intended to be embodied, or their actual interpretation by a director and the actors on a particular stage? Is a play in part the expectation an audience brings to the theatre, or is it the real response to what is seen and heard? Because drama is such a complex process of communication, its study and evaluation is as uncertain as it is mercurial.

All plays depend upon a general agreement by all participants—author, actors, and audience—to accept the operation of theatre and the conventions associated with it, just as players and spectators accept the rules of a game. Drama is a decidedly unreal activity, which can be indulged only if everyone involved admits it. Here lies some of the fascination of its study. For one test of great drama is how far it can take the spectator beyond his own immediate reality and to what use this imaginative release can be put. But the student of drama must know the rules with which the players began the game before he can make this kind of judgment. These rules may be conventions of writing, acting, or audience expectation. Only when all conventions are working together smoothly in synthesis, and the make-believe of the experience is enjoyed passionately with mind and emotion, can great drama be seen for what it is: the combined work of a good playwright, good players, and a good audience who have come together in the best possible physical circumstances.

Drama in some form is found in almost every society, primitive and civilized, and has served a wide variety of functions in the community. There are, for example, records of a sacred drama in Egypt two thousand years before the Common Era, and Thespis in the 6th century BCE in ancient Greece is accorded the distinction of being the first known playwright.

Elements of drama such as mime and dance, costume and decor long preceded the introduction of words and the literary sophistication now associated with a play. Moreover, such basic elements were not superseded by words, merely enhanced by them. Nevertheless, it is only when a play's script assumes a disciplinary control over the dramatic experience that the student of drama gains measurable evidence of what was intended to constitute the play. Only then can dramatic literature be discussed as such.

The texts of plays indicate the different functions they served at different times. Some plays embraced nearly the whole community in a specifically religious celebration, as when all the male citizens of a Greek city-state came together to honour their gods or when the annual Feast of Corpus Christi was celebrated with the great medieval Christian mystery cycles. Conversely, the ceremonious temple ritual of the early Noh drama of Japan was performed at religious festivals only for the feudal aristocracy. But the drama may also serve a more directly didactic purpose, as did the morality plays of the later Middle Ages, some 19th-century melodramas, and the 20th-century discussion plays of George Bernard Shaw and Bertolt Brecht. Plays can satirize society, or they can gently illuminate human weakness. They can divine the greatness and the limitations of humans in tragedy, or, in modern naturalistic playwriting, probe the human mind. Drama is the most wide-ranging of all the arts: it not only represents life but

Japanese Noh drama harkens back to Greek religious tragedy with, among other details, masked heroes and two actors with a chorus. Manan Vatsyayana/AFP/Getty Images

also is a way of seeing it. And it repeatedly proves Samuel Johnson's contention that there can be no certain limit to the modes of composition open to the dramatist.

Common Elements of Drama

Despite the immense diversity of drama as a cultural activity, all plays have certain elements in common. For one thing, drama can never become a "private" statement—in the way a novel or a poem may be—without ceasing to be meaningful theatre. The characters may be superhuman and godlike in appearance, speech, and deed or grotesque and ridiculous, perhaps even puppets, but as long as they behave in even vaguely recognizable human ways the spectator can understand them. Only if they are too abstract do they cease to communicate as theatre. Thus, the figure of Death in medieval drama reasons like a human being, and a god in Greek tragedy or in Shakespeare talks like any mortal. A play, therefore, tells its tale by the imitation of human behaviour. The remoteness or nearness of that behaviour to the real life of the audience can importantly affect the response of that audience: it may be in awe of what it sees, or it may laugh with detached superiority at clownish antics, or it may feel sympathy. These differences of alienation or empathy are important, because it is by opening or closing this aesthetic gap between the stage and the audience that a dramatist is able to control the spectator's experience of the play and give it purpose.

The second essential is implicit in the first. Although static figures may be as meaningfully symbolic on a stage as in a painting, the deeper revelation of character, as well as the all-important control of the audience's responses, depends upon a dynamic presentation of the figures in action. A situation must be represented on the stage, one recognizable and believable to a degree, which will animate the figures as it would in life. Some argue that action is the primary factor in drama, and that character cannot emerge without it. Because no play exists without a situation, it appears impossible to detach the idea of a character from the situation in which he is placed, though it may seem possible after the experience of the whole play. Whether the playwright conceives character before situation, or vice versa, is arbitrary. More relevant are the scope and scale of the character-in-situation—whether, for example, it is man confronting God or a man confronting his wife—for that comes closer to the kind of experience the play is offering its audience. Even here one must beware of passing hasty judgment, for it may be that the grandest design for heroic tragedy may be less affecting than the teasing vision of human madness portrayed in a good farce.

A third factor is style. Every play prescribes its own style, though it will be influenced by the traditions of its theatre and the physical conditions of performance. Style is not something imposed by actors upon the text after it is written, nor is it superficial to the business of the play. Rather, it is self-evident that a play will not communicate without it. Indeed, many a successful play has style and little else. By *style*, therefore, is implied the whole mood and spirit of the play, its degree of fantasy or realism, its quality of ritualism or illusion, and the way in which these qualities are signaled by the directions, explicit or implicit, in the text of the play. In its finer detail, a play's style controls the kind of gesture and movement of the actor, as well as his tone of speech, its pace and inflection. In this way the attitude of the audience is prepared also: nothing is more disconcerting than to be misled into expecting either a comedy or a tragedy and to find the opposite, although some great plays deliberately introduce elements of both. By means of signals of style, the audience may be led to expect that the play will follow known paths, and the pattern of the play will regularly echo the rhythm of response in the auditorium. Drama is a conventional game, and spectators cannot participate if the rules are constantly broken.

By presenting animate characters in a situation with a certain style and according to a given pattern, a playwright will endeavour to communicate thoughts and feelings and to have the audience consider those ideas or reproduce the emotion that inspired the writing of the play. In theatrical communication, however, audiences remain living and independent participants. In the process of performance, an actor has the duty of interpreting the author for the people watching the play and will expect to receive "feedback" in turn. The author must reckon with this circumstance. Ideas may not be accepted if they are offered forthrightly. And great dramatists who are intent on furthering social or political ideas, such as Henrik Ibsen, George Bernard Shaw, and Bertolt Brecht, quickly learned methods of having the spectators themselves reason the ideas as part of their response to the play. Nor will passions necessarily be aroused if overstatement of feeling ("sentimentality") is used without a due balance of thinking and even the detachment of laughter: Shakespeare and Anton Chekhov are two outstanding examples in Western drama of writers who achieved an exquisite balance of pathos with comedy in order to ensure the affective function of their plays.

DRAMATIC EXPRESSION

The language of drama can range between great extremes: on the one hand, an intensely theatrical and ritualistic manner and, on the other, an almost exact reproduction of real life of the kind commonly associated with motion picture and television drama. In the ritualistic drama of ancient Greece, the playwrights wrote in verse, and it may be assumed that

their actors rendered this in an incantatory speech halfway between speech and song. Both the popular and the coterie drama of the Chinese and Japanese theatre were also essentially operatic, with a lyrical dialogue accompanied by music and chanted rhythmically. The effect of such rhythmical delivery of the words was to lift the mood of the whole theatre onto the level of religious worship. Verse is employed in other drama that is conventionally elevated, like the Christian drama of the Middle Ages, the tragedy of the English Renaissance, the heroic Neoclassical tragedies of 17th-century France by Pierre Corneille and Jean Racine, the Romantic lyricism of Goethe and Friedrich Schiller, and modern attempts at a revival of a religious theatre like those of T.S. Eliot. Indeed, plays written in prose dialogue were at one time comparatively rare, and then associated essentially with the comic stage. Only at the end of the 19th century, when naturalistic realism became the mode, were characters in dramas expected to speak as well as behave as in real life.

Elevation is not the whole rationale behind the use of verse in drama. Some critics maintain that a playwright can exercise better control both over the speech and movement of the actors and over the responses of the audience by using the more subtle tones and rhythms of good poetry. The loose, idiomatic rhythms of ordinary conversation, it has been argued, give both actor and spectator too much freedom of interpretation and response. Certainly, the aural, kinetic, and emotive directives in verse are more direct than prose, though, in the hands of a master of prose dialogue like Shaw or Chekhov, prose can also share these qualities. Even more certain, the "aesthetic distance" of the stage, or the degree of unreality and make-believe required to release the imagination, is considerably assisted if the play uses elements of verse, such as rhythm and rhyme, not usually found in ordinary speech. Thus, verse drama may embrace a wide variety of nonrealistic aural and visual devices: Greek tragic choric speech provided a philosophical commentary upon the action, which at the same time drew the audience lyrically into the mood of the play. In the drama of India, a verse accompaniment made the actors' highly stylized system of symbolic gestures of head and eyes, arms and fingers a harmonious whole. The tragic soliloquy in

ANTON CHEKHOV

(b. Jan. 29 [Jan. 17, Old Style], 1860, Taganrog, Russia—d. July 14/15 [July 1/2], 1904, Badenweiler, Ger.)

Anton Chekhov, 1902. David Magarshack

Anton Chekhov is a major Russian playwright and a master of the modern short story. The son of a former serf, he supported his family by writing popular comic sketches while studying medicine in Moscow. During the time that he practiced as a doctor, he had his first full-length play, Ivanov *(1887–89), produced, but it was not well-received. He took up serious themes with stories such as "The Steppe" (1888) and "A Dreary Story" (1889). His later stories include "The Black Monk" (1894) and "Peasants" (1897). He converted his second long play,* The Wood Demon *(1888–89), into the masterpiece* Uncle Vanya *(1897). His play* The Seagull *(1896) was badly received until its successful revival in 1899 by Konstantin Stanislavsky and the Moscow Art Theatre. Chekhov moved to the Crimea to nurse his eventually fatal tuberculosis, and there he wrote his great last plays,* Three Sisters *(1901) and* The Cherry Orchard *(1904), for the Moscow Art Theatre. Chekhov's plays, which take a tragicomic view of the staleness of provincial life and the passing of the Russian gentry, received international acclaim after their translation into English and other languages, and as a short-story writer he is still regarded as virtually unmatched.*

Shakespeare permitted the hero, alone on the stage with the audience, to review his thoughts aloud in the persuasive terms of poetry. Thus, the soliloquy was not a stopping place in the action but rather an engrossing moment of drama when the spectator's mind could leap forward.

DRAMATIC STRUCTURE

The elements of a play do not combine naturally to create a dramatic experience but, rather, are made to work together through the structure of a play, a major factor in the total effect of the experience. A playwright will determine the shape of a play in part according to the conditions in which it will be performed: how long should it take to engage an audience's interest and sustain it? How long can an audience remain in their seats? Is the audience sitting in one place for the duration of performance, or is it moving from one pageant stage to the next, as in some medieval festivals? Structure is also dictated by the particular demands of the material to be dramatized: a revue sketch that turns on a single joke will differ in shape from a religious cycle, which may portray the whole history of humankind from the Creation to the Last Judgment. A realistic drama may require a good deal of exposition of the backgrounds and memories of the characters, while in a chronicle play the playwright may tell the whole story episodically from its beginning to the end. There is one general rule, as Aristotle originally suggested in his *Poetics*: a play must be long enough

to supply the information an audience needs to be interested and to generate the experience of tragedy, or comedy, on the senses and imagination.

In most plays it is necessary to establish a conventional code of place and time. In a play in which the stage must closely approximate reality, the location of the action will be precisely identified, and the scenic representation on stage must confirm the illusion. In such a play, stage time will follow chronological time almost exactly. And if the drama is broken into three, four, or five acts, the spectator will expect each change of scene to adjust the clock or the calendar. But the theatre has rarely expected realism, and by its nature it allows an extraordinary freedom to the playwright in symbolizing location and duration: as Samuel Johnson observed in his discussion of this freedom in Shakespeare, the spectators always allow the play to manipulate the imagination. It is sufficient for the witches in *Macbeth* to remark their "heath" with its "fog and filthy air" for their location to be accepted on a stage without scenery. And when Lady Macbeth later is seen alone reading a letter, she is without hesitation understood to be in surroundings appropriate to the wife of a Scottish nobleman. Simple stage symbolism may assist the imagination, whether the altar of the gods situated in the centre of the Greek *orchēstra*, a strip of red cloth to represent the Red Sea in a medieval miracle play, or a chair on which the Tibetan performer stands to represent a mountain. With this degree of fantasy, it is no wonder that the theatre can manipulate time as freely, passing from the past to the future, from this world to the next, and from reality to dream.

It is questionable, therefore, whether the notion of "action" in a play describes what happens on the stage or what is recreated in the mind of the audience. Certainly it has little to do with merely physical activity by the players. Rather, anything that urges forward the audience's image of the play and encourages the growth of its imagination is a valid part of the play's action. Thus, it was sufficient for the ancient Greek dramatist Aeschylus to have only two speaking male actors who wore various masks, typed for sex, age, class, and facial expression. In the Italian 16th- and 17th-century commedia dell'arte, the standard characters Pantalone and Arlecchino, each wearing his traditional costume and mask, appeared in play after play and were immediately recognized, so that an audience could anticipate the behaviour of the grasping old merchant and his rascally servant. On a less obvious level, a speech that in reading seems to contribute nothing to the action of the play can provide in performance a striking stimulus to the audience's sense of the action, its direction and meaning. Thus, both the Greek chorus and the Elizabethan actor in soliloquy might be seen to "do" nothing, but their intimate speeches of evaluation and reassessment teach the spectator how to think and feel about the action of the main stage and lend great weight

to the events of the play. For drama is a reactive art, moving constantly in time, and any convention that promotes a deep response while conserving precious time is of immeasurable value.

DRAMA AS AN EXPRESSION OF A CULTURE

In spite of the wide divergencies in purpose and convention of plays as diverse as the popular Kabuki of Japan and the coterie comedies of the Restoration in England, a Javanese puppet play and a modern social drama by the American dramatist Arthur Miller, all forms of dramatic literature have some points in common. Differences between plays arise from differences in conditions of performance, local conventions, the purpose of theatre within the community, and cultural history. Of these, the cultural background is the most important, if the most elusive. It is cultural difference that makes the drama of the East immediately distinguishable from that of the West.

EAST-WEST DIFFERENCES

Asian drama consists chiefly of the classical theatre of Hindu India and its derivatives in Peninsular Malaysia and of Myanmar (Burma), Thailand, China, Japan, Java, and Bali. It was at its peak during the period known in the West as the Middle Ages and the Renaissance. Stable and conservative, perpetuating its customs with reverence, Asian culture showed little of the interest in chronology and advancement shown by the West and placed little emphasis on authors and their individual achievements. Thus the origins of Asian drama are lost in time, although its themes and characteristic styles probably remain much the same as before records were kept. The civilizations of the East have only relatively recently been affected by Western theatre, just as the West has only relatively recently become conscious of the theatrical wealth of the East and what it could do to fertilize the modern theatre (as in the 20th-century experimental drama of William Butler Yeats and Thornton Wilder in English, of Paul Claudel and Antonin Artaud in French, and of Brecht in German).

In their representations of life, classical Japanese and Chinese drama are the most conventional and nonrealistic in world theatre. Performed over the centuries by actors selflessly devoted to the profession of a traditional art, conventions of performance became highly stylized, and traditions of characterization and play structure became formalized to a point of exceptional finesse, subtlety, and sophistication. In these and other types of Asian drama, all the elements of the performing arts are made by usage to combine to perfection: dance and mime, speech and song, narrative and poetry. The display and studied gestures of the actors, their refined dance patterns, and the all-pervasive instrumental accompaniment to the voices of the players and the action of the play suggest to Western eyes an exquisite combination of ballet with opera, in which the written text assumes a subordinate role. In this drama, place could be shifted with a license that would have astonished the most romantic of Elizabethan dramatists, the action could leap back in time in a way reminiscent of the flashback of the modern cinema, and events could be telescoped with the abandon of Expressionism. This extreme theatricality lent to artists and audiences an imaginative freedom upon which great theatre could thrive.

Significantly, most Asian cultures also nourished a puppet theatre, in which stylization of character, action, and staging were particularly suitable to equally stylized puppets. In Bunraku, the classical puppet theatre of Japan, the elocutionary art of a chanted narration and the manipulative skill with the dolls diminished the emphasis on the script except in the work of the 17th-century master Chikamatsu Monzaemon, who enjoyed a creative freedom in writing for puppets rather than for the actors of Kabuki. By contrast, Western drama during and after the Renaissance has offered increasing realism, not only in decor and costume but also in the treatment of character and situation.

It is generally thought that Asian drama, like that of the West, had its beginnings in religious festivals. Dramatists retained the moral tone of religious drama while using popular legendary stories to imbue their plays with a romantic and sometimes sensational quality. This was never the sensationalism of novelty that Western dramatists sometimes used: Eastern invention is merely a variation on what is already familiar, so that the slightest changes of emphasis could give pleasure to the cognoscenti. This kind of subtlety is not unlike that found in the repeatedly depicted myths of Greek tragedy. What is always missing in Asian drama is that restlessness for change characteristic of modern Western drama. In the West, religious questioning, spiritual disunity, and a belief in the individual vision combined finally with commercial pressures to produce comparatively rapid changes. None of the moral probing of Greek tragedy, the character psychology of Shakespeare and Racine, the social and spiritual criticism of Ibsen and August Strindberg, nor the contemporary drama of shock and argument, is imaginable in the classical drama of the East.

Greek Origins

Ancient Greek tragedy flowered in the 5th century BCE in Athens. Its form and style—influenced by religious ritual, traditionally thought to have contributed to the emergence of Greek theatre—were dictated by its performance in the great dramatic competitions of the spring and winter festivals of Dionysus. Participation in ritual requires that the audience largely knows what to expect. Ritual dramas were written on the same legendary stories of Greek heroes in festival after festival. Each new drama provided the spectators with a reassessment of the meaning of the legend along with a corporate religious exercise. Thus, the chorus of Greek tragedy played an important part in conveying the dramatist's intention. The chorus not only provided a commentary on the action but also guided the moral and religious thought and emotion of the audience throughout the play: for Aeschylus (c. 525–456 BCE) and Sophocles (c. 496–406 BCE) it might be said that the chorus was the play, and even for Euripides (c. 480–406 BCE) it remained lyrically powerful. Other elements of performance also controlled the dramatist in the form and style he could use in these plays: in particular, the great size of the Greek arena demanded that the players make grand but simple gestures and intone a poetry that could never approach modern conversational dialogue. Today the superhuman characters of these plays, Agamemnon and Clytemnestra, Orestes and Electra, Oedipus and Antigone, seem unreal, for they display little "characterization" in the modern sense and their fates are sealed. Nevertheless, these great operatic tableaux—built, as one critic has said, for weight and not speed—were evidently able to carry their huge audiences to a catharsis of feeling. It is a mark of the piety of those audiences that the same reverent festivals supported a leavening of satyr plays and comedies, bawdy and irreverent comments on the themes of the tragedies, culminating in the wildly inventive satires of Aristophanes (c. 445–c. 385 BCE).

The main characters in Greek tragedy, such as Orestes and Electra in Aeschylus' Oresteia, *usually made sweeping but unadorned gestures to covey their emotions to the vast Greek arena.* The Washington Post/Getty Images

The study of Greek drama demonstrates how the ritual function of theatre shapes both play and performance. This ritual aspect was lost when the Romans assimilated Greek tragedy and comedy. The Roman comedies of Plautus (c. 254–184 BCE) and Terence (c. 186/185–159 BCE) were brilliant but inoffensive entertainments, while the oratorical tragedies of Seneca (c. 4 BCE–65 CE) on themes from the Greek were written probably only to be read by the ruling caste. Nevertheless, some of the dramatic techniques of these playwrights influenced the shape and content of plays of later times. The bold prototype characters of Plautus (the boasting soldier, the old miser, the rascally parasite), with the intricacies of his farcical plotting, and the sensational content and stoical attitudes of Seneca's drama reappeared centuries later when classical literature was rediscovered.

BIBLICAL PLAYS

Western drama had a new beginning in the medieval church, and, again, the texts reflect the ritual function of the theatre in society. The Easter liturgy, the climax of the Christian calendar, explains much of the form of medieval drama as it developed into the giant mystery cycles. From at least the 10th century the clerics of the Roman Catholic Church enacted the simple Latin liturgy of the *Quem quaeritis?* (literally "Whom do you seek?"), the

account of the visit to Jesus Christ's tomb by the three Marys, who are asked this question by an angel. The liturgical form of Lent and the Passion, indeed, embodies the drama of the Resurrection to be shared mutually by actor-priest and audience-congregation. When the Feast of Corpus Christi was instituted in 1246, the great lay cycles of biblical plays (the mystery plays and miracle cycles) developed rapidly, eventually treating the whole story of humankind from the Creation to the Last Judgment, with the Crucifixion still the climax of the experience. The other influence controlling their form and style was their manner of performance. The vast quantity of material that made up the story was broken into many short plays, and each was played on its own stage in the vernacular by members of the craft guilds. Thus, the authors of these dramas gave their audience not a mass communal experience, as the Greek dramatists had done, but rather many small and intimate dramatizations of the Bible story. In stylized and alliterative poetry, they mixed awesome events with moments of extraordinary simplicity, embodying local details, familiar touches of behaviour, and the comedy and the cruelty of medieval life. Their drama consists of strong and broad contrasts, huge in perspective but meaningful in human terms, religious and appropriately didactic in content and yet popular in its manner of reaching its simple audiences.

INTO THE 16TH AND 17TH CENTURIES

In an account of dramatic literature, the ebullient but unscripted farces and romances of the commedia dell'arte properly have no place, but much in it became the basis of succeeding comedy. Two elements are worth noting. First, the improvisational spirit of the commedia troupes, in which the actor would invent words and comic business (*lazzi*) to meet the occasion of the play and the audience he faced, encouraged a spontaneity in the action that has affected the writing and playing of Western comedy ever since. Second, basic types of comic character derived from the central characters, who reappeared in the same masks in play after play. As these characters became well known everywhere, dramatists could rely on their audience to respond to them in predictable fashion. Their masks stylized the whole play and allowed the spectator freedom to laugh at the unreality of the action. An understanding of the commedia illuminates a great deal in the written comedies of Shakespeare in England, Molière and Pierre Marivaux in France, and Carlo Goldoni and Carlo Gozzi in Italy.

In the 16th century, England and Spain provided all the conditions necessary for a drama that could rival ancient Greek drama in scope and subtlety. In both nations, there were public as well as private playhouses, audiences of avid imagination, a developing language that invited its poetic expansion, a rapid growth of professional acting companies, and a simple but flexible stage. All these factors combined to provide the dramatist with an opportunity to create a varied and exploratory new drama of outstanding interest. In Elizabethan London, dramatists wrote in an extraordinary range of dramatic genres, from native comedy and farce to Senecan tragedy, from didactic morality plays to popular chronicle plays and tragicomedies, all before the advent of Shakespeare. Although Shakespeare developed certain genres, such as the chronicle play and the tragedy, to a high degree, Elizabethan dramatists characteristically used a medley of styles. With the exception of Ben Jonson and a few others, playwrights mixed their ingredients without regard for classical rule. The result was a rich body of drama, exciting and experimental in character. A host of new devices were tested, mixing laughter and passion; shifting focus and perspective by slipping from verse to prose and back again; extending the use of the popular clown; exploiting the double values implicit in boy actors playing the parts of girls; exploring the role of the actor in and out of character; but, above all, developing an extraordinarily flexible dramatic poetry. These dramatists produced a visually and aurally exciting hybrid drama that could stress every subtlety of thought and feeling. It is not surprising that they selected their themes from every Renaissance problem of order and authority, of passion and reason, of good and evil and explored every comic attitude to people and society with unsurpassed vigour and vision.

Quite independently in Spain, dramatists embarked upon a parallel development of genres ranging from popular farce to chivalric tragedy. The hundreds of plays of Spain's greatest playwright, Lope de Vega, cover every subject from social satire to religion with equal exuberance. The drama of Paris of the 17th century, however, was determined by two extremes of dramatic influence. On the one hand, some playwrights developed a tragedy rigidly based in form upon Neoclassical notions of Aristotelian unity, controlled by verse that is more regular than that of the Spanish or English dramatists. On the other hand, the French theatre developed a comedy strongly reflecting the work of the itinerant troupes of the commedia dell'arte. The Aristotelian influence resulted in the plays of Pierre Corneille and Jean Racine, tragedies of honour using classical themes, highly sophisticated theatrical instruments capable of searching deeply into character and motive, and capable of creating the powerful tension of a tightly controlled plot. The other influence produced the brilliant plays of Molière, whose training as an actor in the masked and balletic commedia tradition supplied him with a perfect mode for a more sophisticated comedy. Molière's work established the norm of French comedy, bold in plotting, exquisite in style, irresistible in comic suggestion. Soon after, upon the return

of Charles II to the throne of England in 1660, a revival of theatre started the English drama on a new course. Wits such as William Wycherley and William Congreve wrote for the intimate playhouses of the Restoration and an unusually homogeneous coterie audience of the court circle. They developed a comedy of manners, replete with social jokes that the actor, author, and spectator could share—a unique phase in the history of drama. These plays started a characteristic style of English domestic comedy still recognizable in London comedy today.

German dramatists of the later part of the 18th century achieved stature through a quite different type of play: Goethe, Friedrich Schiller, and others of the passionate, poetic Sturm und Drang ("Storm and Stress") movement tried to echo the more romantic tendencies in Shakespeare's plays. Dramatists of the 19th century, however, lacking the discipline of classical form, wrote derivative melodramas that varied widely in quality, often degenerating into mere sensationalism. Melodrama rapidly became the staple of the theatre across Europe and America. Bold in plotting and characterization, simple in its evangelical belief that virtue will triumph and providence always intervene, it pleased vast popular audiences and was arguably the most prolific and successful drama in the history of the theatre. Certainly, melodrama's elements of essential theatre should not be ignored by those interested in drama as a social phenomenon. At least melodramas encouraged an expansion of theatre audiences ready for the most recent phase in dramatic history.

The time grew ripe for a new and more adult drama at the end of the 19th century. As novelists developed greater naturalism in both content and style, dramatists too looked to new and more realistic departures: the dialectical comedies of ideas of George Bernard Shaw; the problem plays associated with Henrik Ibsen; the more lyrical social portraits of Anton Chekhov; the fiercely personal, social, and spiritual visions of August Strindberg. These dramatists began by staging the speech and behaviour of real life, in devoted detail, but became more interested in the symbolic and poetic revelation of the human condition. Where Ibsen began by modeling his tightly structured dramas of humans in society upon the formula for the well-made play, which carefully controlled the audience's interest to the final curtain, Strindberg, a generation later, developed a free psychological and religious dream play that bordered on Expressionism. As sophisticated audiences grew interested more in causes rather than in effects, the great European playwrights of the turn of the century mixed their realism increasingly with symbolism. Thus the Naturalistic movement in drama, though still not dead, had a short but vigorous life. Its leaders freed the drama of the 20th century and beyond to pursue every kind of style, and subsequent dramatists have been wildly experimental. The contemporary playwright can adopt any dramatic mode, mixing effects to shock the spectator into an awareness of self, beliefs, and environment.

DRAMA IN EASTERN CULTURES

Because of its inborn conservatism, the dramatic literature of the East does not show such diversity, despite its variety of cultures and subcultures. The major features of Asian drama may be seen in the three great classical sources of India, China, and Japan. The simplicity of the Indian stage, a platform erected for the occasion in a palace or a courtyard, like the simplicity of the Elizabethan stage, lent great freedom to the imagination of the playwright. In the plays of India's greatest playwright, Kalidasa (*fl.* 5th century CE), there is an exquisite refinement of detail in presentation. His delicate romantic tales leap time and place by simple suggestion and mingle courtly humour and lighthearted wit with charming sentiment and religious piety. Quite untrammeled by realism, lyrical in tone and refined in feeling, his fanciful love and adventure stories completely justify their function as pure entertainment. His plots are without the pain of reality, and his characters never descend from the ideal: such poetic drama is entirely appropriate to the Hindu aesthetic of blissful idealism in art.

Some contrast may be felt between the idealistic style of the Sanskrit drama and the broader, less courtly manner of the Chinese and its derivatives in Southeast Asia. These plays cover a large

Kabuki is based on household stories and popular history and can include slapstick as well as fervour. Jemal Countess/WireImage/Getty Images

variety of subjects and styles, but all combine music, speech, song, and dance, as does all Asian drama. Heroic legends, pathetic moral stories, and brilliant farces all blended spectacle and lyricism and were as acceptable to a sophisticated court audience as to a popular street audience. The most important Chinese plays stem from the Yuan dynasty (1206–1368), in which an episodic narrative is carefully structured and unified. Each scene introduces a song whose lines have a single rhyme, usually performed by one singer, with a code of symbolic gestures and intonations that has been refined to an extreme. The plays have strongly typed heroes and villains, simple plots, scenes of bold emotion, and moments of pure mime.

The drama of Japan, with its exquisite artistry of gesture and mime and its symbolism of setting and costume, took two major directions. Noh drama, emerging from religious ritual, maintained a special refinement appropriate to its origins and its aristocratic audiences. Kabuki (its name suggesting its composition: *ka*, "singing"; *bu*, "dancing";

ki, "acting") in the 17th century became Japan's popular drama. Noh theatre is reminiscent of the religious tragedy of the Greeks in the remoteness of its legendary content, in its masked heroic characters, in its limit of two actors and a chorus, and in the static, oratorical majesty of its style. Kabuki, however, finds its material in domestic stories and in popular history, and the actors, without masks, move and speak more freely, without seeming to be realistic. Kabuki plays are less rarefied and are often fiercely energetic and wildly emotional, as befitting their presentation before a broader audience. The written text of the Noh play is highly poetic and pious in tone, compressed in its imaginative

KALIDASA

(b. c. 5th century CE, India)

The Sanskrit-language poet and dramatist Kalidasa is one of the greatest Indian writers of any epoch. The six works identified as genuine are the dramas Abhijnanashakuntala *("The Recognition of Shakuntala"),* Vikramorvashi *("Urvashi Won by Valour"), and* Malavikagnimitra *("Malavika and Agnimitra"); the epic poems* Raghuvamsha *("Dynasty of Raghu") and* Kumarasambhava *("Birth of the War God"); and the lyric "Meghaduta" ("Cloud Messenger").*

Little is known about him. His poems suggest that he was a Brahman (priest), liberal yet committed to the orthodox Hindu worldview. His name, literally "servant of Kali," presumes that he was a Shaivite (follower of the god Shiva, whose consort was Kali), though occasionally he eulogizes other gods, notably Vishnu. The society reflected in Kalidasa's work is that of a courtly aristocracy sure of its dignity and power. Kalidasa has perhaps done more than any other writer to wed the older, Brahmanic religious tradition, particularly its ritual concern with Sanskrit, to the needs of a new and brilliant secular Hinduism. The fusion, which epitomizes the renaissance of the Gupta period, did not, however, survive its fragile social base. With the disorders following the collapse of the Gupta Empire, Kalidasa became a memory of perfection that neither Sanskrit nor the Indian aristocracy would know again.

ideas, fastidious and restrained in verbal expression, and formal in its sparse plotting, whereas the text of a Kabuki play lends plentiful opportunities for spectacle, sensation, and melodrama. In Kabuki there can be moments of realism but also whole episodes of mime and acrobatics. There can be moments of slapstick but also moments of violent passion. In all, the words are subordinate to performance in Kabuki.

DRAMA AND COMMUNAL BELIEF

The drama that is most meaningful and pertinent to its society is that which arises from it. The religious drama of ancient Greece, the temple drama of early India and Japan, the mystery cycles of medieval Europe, all have in common more than their religious content: when the theatre is a place of worship, its drama goes to the roots of belief in a particular community. The dramatic experience becomes a natural extension of human life—both of the individual and of the social being. The content of the mystery cycles speaks formally for the orthodox dogma of the church, thus seeming to place the plays at the centre of medieval life, like the church itself. Within such a comprehensive scheme, particular needs could be satisfied by comic or pathetic demonstration. For example, such a crucial belief as that of the Virgin Birth of Jesus was presented in the York (England) cycle of mystery plays, of the 14th–16th centuries, with a nicely balanced didacticism when

Joseph wonders how a man of his age could have got Mary with child and an angel explains what has happened. The humour reflects the simplicity of the audience and at the same time indicates the perfect faith that permitted the near-blasphemy of the joke. In the tragedies Shakespeare wrote for the Elizabethan theatre, he had the same gift of satisfying deep communal needs while meeting a whole range of individual interests present in his audience.

When the whole community shares a common heritage, patriotic drama and drama commemorating national heroes, as are seen almost universally in Asian theatre, is of this kind. Modern Western attempts at a religious didactic drama, or indeed at any drama of "ideas," have had to reckon with the disparate nature of the audience. Thus the impact of Ibsen's social drama both encouraged and divided the development of the theatre in the last years of the 19th century. Plays such as *A Doll's House* (1879) and *Ghosts* (published 1881), which challenged the sanctity of marriage and questioned the loyalty a wife owed to her husband, took their audiences by storm: some violently rejected the criticism of their cherished social beliefs, and thus such plays may be said to have failed to persuade general audiences to examine their moral position. Conversely, there were sufficient numbers of enthusiasts (so-called Ibsenites) to stimulate a new drama of ideas. Problem plays appeared all over Europe and undoubtedly rejuvenated the theatre for the 20th century.

Shaw's early Ibsenite plays in London, which presented drawing-room comedy with such sober themes as slum landlordism (*Widowers' Houses*, 1892) and prostitution (*Mrs. Warren's Profession*, 1902), resulted only in failure, but Shaw quickly found a comic style that was more disarming. In his attack on false patriotism (*Arms and the Man*, 1894) and the motives for middle-class marriage (*Candida*, 1897), he does not affront his audiences. He leads them by gentle laughter and surprise to review their own positions.

DRAMA: TERMS AND CONCEPTS

The reader of plays may be confronted with a variety of unfamiliar references in critical literature. The following definitions provide a sampling of play cycles, subgenres of dramas, and particular examples and elements of dramatic literature.

Auto Sacramental

The Spanish dramatic genre known as *auto sacramental* (Spanish: "sacramental act") reached its height in the 17th century with *autos* written by the playwright Pedro Calderón de la Barca. Performed outdoors as part of the Corpus Christi feast day celebrations, *autos* were short allegorical plays in verse dealing with some aspect of the mystery of the Holy Eucharist, which the feast of Corpus Christi solemnly celebrated. They derived from tableaus, which had been part of the procession that accompanied the Eucharist as it was carried through the streets at Corpus Christi. The tableaus became animated, then developed a dramatic form, and finally were detached from the Eucharistic procession to form one of their own. Mounted on carts, they were pulled to selected places in the municipality, and the actors presented their *autos,* one after another, much as the scriptural plays of the Netherlands and northern England had been presented on pageant wagons during the Middle Ages. Expenses for these superbly set and dressed *autos* were paid by the municipality.

These little plays had begun to appear in the late 16th century, but they were at first rough and primitive, a rustic form of pious entertainment. Important names in the development of the *autos* into works of polished art were a bookseller from Valencia, Juan de Timoneda, and the playwrights Jose de Valdivielso and his contemporary Lope de Vega. It was Calderón, however, who seized the opportunity that they offered for allegory to cover a wide range of nonsacramental subjects. He took the *auto* form to new heights of artistic achievement.

Accused of displaying irreverence toward the sacrament during the 18th century, their performance was in 1765 prohibited by royal decree. Some 20th-century poets imitated their form and wrote secularized versions of the old *autos*.

CHRONICLE PLAY

A chronicle play (also called chronicle history, or history play) is drama with a theme from history consisting usually of loosely connected episodes chronologically arranged. Plays of this type typically lay emphasis on the public welfare by pointing to the past as a lesson for the present, and the genre is often characterized by its assumption of a national consciousness in its audience. It has flourished in times of intensely nationalistic feeling, notably in England from the 1580s until the 1630s, by which time it was "out of fashion," according to the prologue of John Ford's play *Perkin Warbeck*. Early examples of the chronicle play include *The Famous Victories of Henry the Fifth*, *The Life and Death of Jacke Straw*, *The Troublesome Raigne of John King of England*, and *The True Tragedie of Richard III*. The genre came to maturity with the work of Christopher Marlowe (*Edward II*) and William Shakespeare (*Henry VI*, parts 2 and 3).

In *An Apology for Actors* (1612), the dramatist Thomas Heywood wrote that chronicle plays

are writ with this ayme, and carryed with this methode, to teach their subjects obedience to their king, to shew the people the untimely ends of such as have moved tumults, commotions, and insurrections, to present them with the flourishing estate of such

as live in obedience, exhorting them to allegeance, dehorting them from all trayterous and fellonious stratagems.

At the same time, it was argued that the overthrow of a tyrant (such as Richard III, according to the Tudor reading of events) was right and proper.

Elizabethan dramatists drew their material from the wealth of chronicle writing for which the age is renowned, notably Edward Hall's *The Union of the Two Noble and Illustre Famelies of Lancastre & Yorke* and the *Chronicles of England, Scotlande, and Irelande* of Raphael Holinshed. The genre was a natural development from the morality plays of the Middle Ages. In a forerunner of the chronicle play, John Bale's *Kynge Johan,* all the characters except the king himself are allegorical and have names such as Widow England, Sedition, and Private Wealth.

No age has matched the Elizabethan, either in England or elsewhere, in this kind of play. But chronicle plays are still sometimes written—for example, by the 20th-century English playwright John Arden (*Left-Handed Liberty, Armstrong's Last Goodnight*)—and the genre corresponds in many respects, especially in its didactic purpose and episodic structure, with the influential 20th-century epic theatre of Bertolt Brecht in Germany and Tony Kushner in the United States, specifically Kushner's AIDS drama *Angels in America*, which debuted on Broadway in 1993.

CLOAK AND SWORD DRAMA

The Spanish cloak and sword drama (*comedia de capa y espada*; also called cloak and dagger theatre) is a 17th-century genre of upper–middle-class manners and intrigue. The name derives from the cloak and sword that were part of the typical street dress of students, soldiers, and cavaliers, the favourite heroes of these plays. The type was anticipated by the plays of Bartolomé de Torres Naharro, but its popularity was established by the inventive dramas of Lope de Vega and Tirso de Molina. The extremely complicated plots deal with the frustration of an idealized love by the conventional Spanish *pundonor* ("point of honour"). The affairs of the lady and her gallant are mirrored or parodied in the actions of the servants. The hero's valet (the *gracioso*) also supplies a common-sense commentary on the manners of his masters. After many misunderstandings, duels, renunciations, and false alarms about honour, the plays usually end happily with several marriages. In the 19th and 20th centuries, the term *cloak-and-dagger* referred to espionage, both real and fictional.

COMÉDIE LARMOYANTE

The comédie larmoyante ("tearful comedy") is an 18th-century genre of French sentimental drama, which formed a bridge between the decaying tradition of aristocratic Neoclassical tragedy and the rise of serious bourgeois drama. Such comedies made no pretense of being amusing; virtuous characters were subjected to distressing domestic crises, but, even if the play ended unhappily, virtue never went unrewarded. If the heroine died, for example, her "moral" triumph was made clear to the audience.

The form is best exemplified in the 40 or so verse plays of Nivelle de La Chaussée, such as *Le Préjugé à la mode* (performed and published 1735; "Fashionable Prejudice"). The effect of the comédie larmoyante was to blur the distinctions between comedy and tragedy, drive both from the French stage, and form the basis for the *drame bourgeois*, realistic contemporary comedy heralded by Denis Diderot's *Le Fils naturel* (published 1757, performed 1771). The comédie larmoyante also set the stage for the appearance of melodrama in the late 18th century.

DIALOGUE

Defined in its widest sense, dialogue is the recorded conversation of two or more persons, especially as an element of drama or fiction. As a literary form, it is a carefully organized exposition, by means of invented conversation, of contrasting philosophical or intellectual attitudes. The oldest known dialogues are the Sicilian mimes, written in rhythmic prose by Sophron of Syracuse in the early 5th century BCE. Although none of these has survived, Plato knew and admired them. But the form of philosophic dialogue that he perfected by 400 BCE was sufficiently original to be an independent literary creation. With due attention to characterization and the dramatic situation from which the discussion arises, it develops dialectically the main tenets of Platonic philosophy. To Lucian in the 2nd century CE the dialogue owes a new tone and function. His influential *Dialogues of the Dead,* with their coolly satirical tone, inspired innumerable imitations in England and France during the 17th and 18th centuries, for example, dialogues by the French writers Bernard de Fontenelle (1683) and François Fénelon (1700–12).

The revival of interest in Plato during the Renaissance encouraged numerous imitations and adaptations of the Platonic dialogue. In Spain, Juan de Valdés used it to discuss problems of patriotism and humanism (written 1533), and Vincenzo Carducci, theories of painting (1633). In Italy, dialogues on the Platonic model were written by Torquato Tasso (1580), Giordano Bruno (1584), and Galileo (1632). The Renaissance also adapted the dialogue form to uses unsuspected by either Plato or Lucian, such as the teaching of languages.

In the 16th and 17th centuries, dialogue lent itself easily and frequently to the presentation of controversial religious, political, and economic ideas. George Berkeley's *Three Dialogues Between Hylas and Philonous* (1713) are perhaps the best of the English imitations of Plato. The best-known 19th-century examples of the form are Walter Savage Landor's *Imaginary Conversations* (vols. 1 and 2, 1824; vol. 3, 1828; thereafter sporadically to 1853), sensitive re-creations of such historical personages as Dante and Beatrice. André Gide's *Interviews imaginaires* (1943), which explore the psychology of the supposed participants, and George Santayana's *Dialogues in Limbo* (1925) illustrate the survival of this ancient form in the 20th century.

DOMESTIC TRAGEDY

A drama in which the tragic protagonists are ordinary middle- or lower-class individuals is called a domestic tragedy. It is in contrast to classical and Neoclassical tragedy, in which the protagonists are of kingly or aristocratic rank and their downfall is an affair of state as well as a personal matter.

The earliest known examples of domestic tragedy are three anonymous late Elizabethan dramas: *Arden of Feversham* (c. 1591), the story of the murder of Mr. Arden by his wife and her lover and their subsequent execution; *A Warning for Faire Women* (1599), which deals with the murder of a merchant by his wife; and *A Yorkshire Tragedy* (c. 1606), in which a father destroys his family. To these may be added Thomas Heywood's less sensational but no less tragic *A Woman Kilde with Kindnesse* (1607). Domestic tragedy did not take hold, however, until reintroduced in the 18th century by George Lillo with *The London Merchant, or the History of George Barnwell* (1731). The popularity of this sordid drama of an apprentice who murders his uncle-guardian influenced domestic tragedy in France and

Germany, where the dramatist and critic G.E. Lessing, in his *Hamburgische Dramaturgie* (1767–69), paved the way for its critical acceptance.

Domestic tragedy found its mature expression in the plays of Henrik Ibsen toward the end of the 19th century. In earlier domestic dramas by other playwrights the protagonists were sometimes villains and at other times merely pathetic, but the bourgeois heroes of Ibsen's *Brand* (1866), *Rosmersholm* (1886), *The Master Builder* (1892), and *When We Dead Awaken* (1899) are endowed with some of the isolated grandeur of the heroes of classical tragedy.

A tragedy on a humbler social level than that of the middle class, *Woyzeck,* was written as early as 1836 by the German dramatist Georg Büchner. Its hero, a poor soldier and former serf, is so reduced in status he finds employment as a doctor's guinea pig. Yet the work has a shattering tragic impact and bears out the precept stated by another German tragic dramatist of the 19th century, Friedrich Hebbel: "One need only be a man, after all, to have a destiny." *Woyzeck* was well in advance of its time. Lower-class tragedy did not come to the fore until the turn of the 20th century with such works as Gerhart Hauptmann's *Die Weber* (1892; *The Weavers*) and *Rose Bernd* (1903). Other outstanding examples are Eugene O'Neill's *Long Day's Journey into Night* (1956), Arthur Miller's *Death of a Salesman* (1949), and Lillian Hellman's *The Children's Hour* (1934).

DROLL

A droll (the short form of droll-humour, or drollery) is a short comic scene or farce adapted from an existing play or created by actors, performed in England during the period of the Civil Wars and the Commonwealth (1642–60) while the London theatres were closed down by the Puritans. Because stage plays were prohibited at this time, actors developed other, shorter means of entertainment to circumvent the restrictions, performing drolls in inns and at fairs on improvised stages.

Robert Cox was the leading performer of drolls, and his repertoire included "The Merry Conceits of Bottom the Weaver" from *A Midsummer Night's Dream* and "The Bouncing Knight, or The Robbers Rob'd" from *Henry IV, Part 1.* Other subjects of drolls were Falstaff, the gravediggers' scene in *Hamlet,* and, occasionally, biblical adaptations. Francis Kirkman published a collection of 26 drolls in 1662 titled *The Wits; or, Sport upon Sport.*

EVERYMAN

An English morality play of the 15th century, *Everyman* was probably a version of a Dutch play, *Elckerlyc*. It achieves a beautiful, simple solemnity in treating allegorically the theme of death and the fate of the human soul—of the character Everyman's soul as he tries to justify his time on earth. Though morality plays on the whole failed to achieve the vigorous realism of the Middle Ages' scriptural drama, this short play (about nine hundred lines) is more than an allegorical sermon because vivid characterization gives it dramatic energy. It is generally regarded as the finest of the morality plays.

HOCKTIDE PLAY

A folk play once given at Coventry, Eng., on Hock Tuesday (the second Tuesday after Easter), the Hocktide play was suppressed at the Protestant Reformation because of disorders attendant on it but was revived for the entertainment of Queen Elizabeth I at the Kenilworth Revels in 1575. As described by one of her courtiers, the action of the play consisted mainly of a mock battle between parties of men representing English and Danish knights, in which the Danes were defeated and led away as captives by English women. This was meant to represent the massacre of the Danes by King Ethelred in 1002, although some scholars believe that the play had its beginnings in hocking, a still older custom of the folk festivals. On Hock Monday women went out with ropes, hocking, or capturing, any man they met and exacting a forfeit. Men were allowed to retaliate in kind on Hock Tuesday. The forfeit money seems to have been used to defray parish expenses. The bishop of Worcester forbade this practice in 1450, but traces of it are found in records well into the 17th century.

JESUIT DRAMA

Jesuit drama was a program of theatre developed for educational and propagandist purposes in the colleges of the Society of Jesus during the 16th, 17th, and 18th centuries. Cultivated as a medium for disseminating Roman Catholic doctrine, drama flourished in the Jesuit schools for more than two hundred years, evolving from modest student exercises to elaborate productions that often rivaled the contemporary public stage in polish and technical skill.

The earliest recorded performance of a Jesuit play was in 1551, at the newly founded Collegio Mamertino at Messina, in Sicily. In less than 20 years, plays were being performed at more than a dozen of the new Jesuit colleges springing up in cities across the Continent, including Rome, Sevilla (Seville), Córdoba, Innsbruck, Munich, and Vienna. By the mid-17th century there were nearly three hundred Jesuit colleges in Europe, and in almost every one at least one play was given each year.

Originally, these plays were to be pious in nature, expressing true religious and moral doctrines. They were to be acted in Latin, decorously, and with little elaboration. And no female characters or costumes were to appear. All these rules were relaxed or revised as Jesuit drama evolved. Favourite subjects came from biblical histories, the lives of saints and martyrs, and incidents in the life of Christ, but Jesuit playwrights also drew upon material from pagan mythology, ancient history, and contemporary events, all reinterpreted in terms of Catholic doctrine. Dramas were frequently performed in the national languages or with vernacular prologues that explained the Latin text. Jesuit plays became increasingly elaborate, and their stagecraft kept pace with all the newest technical developments of European theatre.

Music was an important element in most of the plays, ranging from simple songs to works that called for a large orchestra and chorus. The elaborate musical productions of Austria and southern Germany reflected the influence of Italian opera as well as the long tradition of music in the church. The colleges of France even included ballet in their performances.

The extravagance and luxury of many of the Jesuit productions came under heavy attack. Many productions were enormously expensive, and it was charged that students in some colleges did little more than prepare and perform plays. Opponents of the Jesuit order seized upon such charges and made them part of the wave of anti-Jesuit feeling that grew in the mid-18th century. Dramatic performances were prohibited or limited in many areas, and they ceased altogether in 1773, when the Society of Jesus was temporarily suppressed.

LITURGICAL DRAMA

Liturgical drama is the name of a type of play acted in the Middle Ages within or near the church and relating stories from the Bible and of the saints. Although they had their roots in the Christian liturgy, such plays were not performed as essential parts of a standard church service. The language of the liturgical drama was Latin, and the dialogue was frequently chanted to simple monophonic melodies. Music was also used in the form of incidental dance and processional tunes.

The earliest traces of the liturgical drama are found in manuscripts dating from the 10th century. Its genesis may perhaps be found in the chant "Quem quaeritis" ("Whom do you seek"), a trope to the Introit of the Easter mass. In *Regularis concordia* (mid-10th century), Aethelwold, bishop of Winchester described in some detail the manner in which the "Quem quaeritis" trope was performed as a small scene during the Matins service on Easter morning. The dialogue represents the well-known story of the three Marys approaching the tomb of Christ: "Whom do you seek?" "Jesus of Nazareth." "He is not here. He has arisen as was prophesied. Go. Announce that he has arisen from the dead."

The liturgical drama gradually increased in both length and sophistication and flourished particularly during the 12th and 13th centuries. The most popular themes were derived from colourful biblical tales (Daniel in the lion's den, the foolish virgins, the story of the Passion and death of Jesus, etc.) as well as from the stories of the saints (as the Virgin Mary and St. Nicholas). Eventually, the connection between the liturgical drama and the church was severed completely, as the plays came under secular sponsorship and adopted the vernacular.

MELODRAMA

A sentimental drama having an improbable plot that concerns the vicissitudes suffered by the virtuous at the hands of the villainous but ends happily with virtue triumphant is called a melodrama. Featuring stock characters such as the noble hero, the long-suffering heroine, and the cold-blooded villain, the melodrama focusses not on character development but on sensational incidents and spectacular staging. In music, melodrama signifies lines spoken to a musical accompaniment.

The melodramatic stage play is generally regarded as having developed in France as a result of the impact of Jean-Jacques Rousseau's *Pygmalion* (1762; first performed 1770) on a society torn by violent political and social upheaval and exposed to the influences of the English Gothic novel and of Sturm und Drang (Storm and Stress) and Romanticism from Germany. The pioneer and prime exponent of the 18th-century French melodrama with its music, singing, and spectacular effects was Guilbert de Pixérécourt. His *Coelina, ou l'enfant de mystère* (1800) was translated as *A Tale of Mystery* (1802) by Thomas Holcroft and established the new genre in England. It was not utterly new to England, however. The restrictions of the Licensing Act of 1737 had been habitually evaded by combining drama with music, singing, and dancing.

Another prominent dramatist whose melodrama influenced other countries was the German August von Kotzebue. His *Menschenhass und Reue* (1789) became tremendously popular in England as *The Stranger* (1798). He also provided the original of Richard Brinsley Sheridan's *Pizarro* (1799). In the early 19th century, melodrama spread throughout the European theatre. In Russia the authorities welcomed it as diverting attention from more serious issues.

During the 19th century, music and singing were gradually eliminated. As technical developments in the theatre made greater realism possible, more emphasis was given to the spectacular (e.g., snowstorms, shipwrecks, battles, train wrecks, conflagrations, earthquakes, and horse races). Among the best known and most representative of the melodramas popular in England and the United States are *The Octoroon* (1859) and *The Colleen Bawn* (1860), both by Dion Boucicault. More sensational were *The Poor of New York* (1857), *London by Night* (1844), and *Under the Gaslight* (1867). The realistic staging and the social evils touched upon, however perfunctorily and sentimentally, anticipated the later theatre of the Naturalists.

With the growing sophistication of the theatre in the early 20th century, the theatrical melodrama declined in popularity. It was a vigorous form, though, in motion picture adventure serials until the advent of sound. The exaggerated gestures, dramatic chases, emotional scenes, simple flat characters, and impossible situations were later revived and parodied. Melodrama makes up a good part of contemporary television drama.

PASSION PLAY

Any religious drama of medieval origin that treats the suffering, death, and Resurrection of Christ is termed a Passion play. Early Passion plays (in Latin) consisted of readings from the Gospel with interpolated poetical sections on the events of Christ's Passion and related subjects, such as Mary Magdalene's life and repentance, the raising of Lazarus, the Last Supper, and the lament of the Virgin Mary. Use of the vernacular in these interpolations led to the development of independent vernacular plays, the earliest surviving examples being in German. Such plays were at first only preludes to dramatic presentations of the Resurrection. The introduction of Satan (which became typical of German and Czech plays), and thus of introductory representations of the fall of Lucifer and the Fall of man (as in the early 14th-century Vienna Passion), and of scenes from the Hebrew Bible and of the Last Judgment, led to development of cyclic plays similar to the Corpus Christi cycles. The great Celtic Passion cycles of Cornwall and Brittany, and the St. Gall Passion play (which begins with the entry of St. Augustine, who introduces the prophets and patriarchs of the Hebrew Bible, and also includes the marriage at Cana), exemplify this type of Passion play.

The Tirol plays early formed a separate group, representing only scenes from the Passion and Resurrection. The Bohemian plays, such as the St. Eger Passion, developed from a simpler version of the Vienna Passion, were also distinct in style and incident.

The earliest Passion plays of France and Flanders are thought to have their source in a nondramatic narrative poem of the 13th century, the *Passion des jongleurs*. These plays became highly elaborated in the course of their development, culminating in performances (Mons, 1501; Valenciennes, 1547) lasting more than a week. Confraternities were founded for performance of Passion plays, the most famous being the Confrérie de la Passion (1402). Passion plays were also performed in Spain, Italy, and elsewhere, with local variations.

By the 16th century, many of the Passion plays, debased by secular influences, had degenerated into mere popular entertainments, full of crude slapstick and buffoonery. Many were forbidden by ecclesiastical authorities, and many more were suppressed after the Reformation.

The most famous of the Passion plays to survive into the 20th century is that performed at Oberammergau, in the Bavarian Alps. According to tradition, the play has been presented every 10 years since 1634, in fulfillment of a vow made after the village was spared an epidemic of plague (shifting to decennial years in 1700), except in 1870 during the Franco-Prussian War and World War II, when religious plays were banned. It remains an entirely local production, with villagers taking all the parts and singing in the chorus. Since 1930 roofed seats have protected the audience from

The most famous Passion play is presented at Oberammergau, in the Bavarian Alps, where it has been performed every decade since 1634. Johannes Simon/Getty Images

the weather. The production runs from May through September. Some villagers and some Jewish organizations have protested anti-Semitic overtones in the 1860 text. Traditional Passion plays have also been revived in villages in the Austrian Tirol. In northern Spain, during Lent and Holy Week, a Catalan Passion play is performed by villagers. And in Tegelen, in the Netherlands, a modern play by the Dutch poet Jacques Scheurs is given every five years.

PROLOGUE AND EPILOGUE

The prefatory and supplementary pieces to a literary work, especially a verse drama, are called, respectively, the prologue and the epilogue. The ancient Greek *prologos* was of wider significance than the modern prologue, effectively taking the place of an explanatory first act. A character, often a deity, appeared on the empty stage to explain events prior to the action of the drama, which consisted mainly of a catastrophe. On the Latin stage, the prologue was generally more elaborately written, as in the case of Plautus's *Rudens*, which contains some of his finest poetry.

In England the mystery and miracle plays began with a homily. Thomas Sackville used a dumb show as a prologue to the first English tragedy, *Gorboduc* (performed 1561). Shakespeare began *Henry IV, Part 2* with the character of Rumour to set the scene and *Henry V* with a chorus. The Plautine prologue was revived by Molière in France during the 17th century.

The epilogue, at its best, was a witty piece intended to send the audience home in good humour. Its form in the English theatre was established by Ben Jonson in *Cynthia's Revels* (c. 1600). Jonson's epilogues typically asserted the merits of his play and defended it from anticipated criticism.

The heyday of the prologue and epilogue in the English theatre was the Restoration period. From 1660 to the decline of the drama in the reign of Queen Anne, scarcely a play was produced in London without a prologue and epilogue. Playwrights asked their friends to write these poems for them. Poems supplied by writers of established reputation conferred prestige on the works of novices.

Though epilogues were rarely written after the 18th century, prologues have been used effectively in such 20th-century plays as Hugo von Hofmannsthal's *Jedermann* (1911; *Everyman*, 1912), Thornton Wilder's *Our Town* (1938), Tennessee Williams' *Glass Menagerie*, and Jean Anouilh's *Antigone* (both 1944).

SACRA RAPPRESENTAZIONE

The *sacra rappresentazione* (meaning "holy performance") is a type of 15th-century Italian ecclesiastical drama similar to the mystery plays of France and England and the *auto sacramental* of Spain. Originating and flourishing in Florence, these religious dramas represented scenes from the Old and New Testaments, from pious legends, and from the lives of the saints. The plays were didactic, using dialogues drawn from the sacred Scriptures to instruct the audience in lessons of good conduct by dramatizing the punishment of vice and the reward of virtue.

The origin of the *sacra rappresentazione* can be traced to the Middle Ages, when the Italian theatre was inextricably linked to the Roman Catholic Church. The liturgical dramas were performed by priests as part of the worship service, and, unlike later *rappresentazioni*, were in Latin, not vernacular. The *sacra rappresentazione* also drew inspiration from sacred chants of the 13th century and from the Florentine festivals, which were more spectacle than drama. Although *rappresentazioni* were performed throughout Italy, the *sacra rappresentazione* of Florence was the only truly theatrical genre. The others were pantomimed, with only a few spoken words of explanation.

SOTIE

Popular in France in the 15th and early 16th centuries, the *sotie* (*sottie*) is a short satirical play in which a company of *sots* ("fools") exchanged badinage on contemporary persons and events. The *sots*, wearing the traditional short jacket, tights, bells, and dunce cap of the fool, also introduced acrobatics and farcical humour into the sketches. At first the *sotie* was used as an introductory piece to mystery and morality plays. Developing into an independent form, *soties* were created and staged by the Clercs de la Basoche, an association of law clerks; the Enfants sans Souci, a group of nobles; and other, more permanent companies. Pierre Gringore became the preeminent *sotie* dramatist. The *sotie* was openly satirical and was used as a weapon in political battles. It was forbidden in the 16th century and replaced by more general forms of satire.

THEATRE OF THE ABSURD

The Theatre of the Absurd consists of the dramatic works of certain European and American dramatists of the 1950s and early '60s who agreed with the existentialist philosopher Albert Camus's assessment, in his essay "The Myth of Sisyphus" (1942), that the human situation is essentially absurd, devoid of purpose. The term is also loosely applied to those dramatists and the production of those works. Though no formal Absurdist movement existed as such, dramatists as diverse as Samuel Beckett, Eugène Ionesco, Jean Genet, Arthur Adamov, Harold Pinter, and a few others shared a pessimistic vision of humanity struggling vainly to find a purpose and to control its fate. Humankind in this view is left feeling hopeless, bewildered, and anxious.

The ideas that inform the plays also dictate their structure. Absurdist playwrights, therefore, did away with most of the logical structures of traditional theatre. There is little dramatic action as conventionally understood. However frantically the characters perform, their busyness serves to underscore the fact that nothing happens to change their existence. In Beckett's *Waiting for Godot* (1952), plot is eliminated, and a timeless, circular quality emerges as two lost creatures, usually played as tramps, spend their days waiting—but without any certainty of whom they are waiting for or of whether he, or it, will ever come.

Language in an Absurdist play is often dislocated, full of cliches, puns, repetitions, and non sequiturs. The characters in Ionesco's *The Bald Soprano* (1950) sit and talk, repeating the obvious until it sounds like nonsense, thus revealing the inadequacies of verbal communication. The ridiculous, purposeless behaviour and talk give the plays a sometimes dazzling comic surface, but there is an underlying serious message of metaphysical distress. This reflects the influence of comic tradition drawn from such sources as commedia dell'arte, vaudeville, and music hall combined with such theatre arts as mime and acrobatics. At the same time, the impact of ideas as expressed by the Surrealist, existentialist, and Expressionist schools and the writings of Franz Kafka is evident.

Originally shocking in its flouting of theatrical convention while popular for its apt expression of the preoccupations of the mid-20th century, the Theatre of

SAMUEL BECKETT

(b. April 13?, 1906, Foxrock, County Dublin, Ire.—d. Dec. 22, 1989, Paris, France)

Samuel Beckett was an author, a critic, and a playwright and the winner of the Nobel Prize for Literature in 1969. He wrote in both French and English and is perhaps best known for his plays, especially En attendant Godot *(1952;* Waiting for Godot*). After studying in Ireland and traveling, he settled in Paris in 1937. During World War II he supported himself as a farmworker and joined the underground resistance. In the postwar years he wrote, in French, the narrative trilogy* Molloy *(1951),* Malone Dies *(1951), and* The Unnamable *(1953). His play* Waiting for Godot *was an immediate success in Paris and gained wider acclaim when he translated it into English. Marked by minimal plot and action, existentialist ideas, and humour, it typifies the Theatre of the Absurd. His later plays, also sparsely staged, abstract works that deal with the mystery and despair of human existence, include* Endgame *(1957),* Krapp's Last Tape *(1958), and* Happy Days *(1961). Beckett's later works tended toward extreme concentration and brevity.* Come and Go *(1967), a playlet, or "dramaticule," as he called it, contains only 121 words that are spoken by the three characters. The prose fragment "Lessness" consists of but 60 sentences, each of which occurs twice. His series* Acts Without Words *are exactly what the title denotes, and one of his last plays,* Rockaby, *lasts for 15 minutes. Such brevity is merely an expression of Beckett's determination to pare his writing to essentials, to waste no words on trivia.*

the Absurd declined somewhat by the mid-1960s. Some of its innovations had been absorbed into the mainstream of theatre even while serving to inspire further experiments. Various chief authors of the Absurd have sought new directions in their art, while others continue to work in the same vein.

TRAGICOMEDY

A dramatic work that incorporates both tragic and comic elements is called a tragicomedy. When coined by the Roman dramatist Plautus in the 2nd century BCE, the word denoted a play in which gods and men, masters and slaves reverse the roles traditionally assigned to them, gods and heroes acting in comic burlesque and slaves adopting tragic dignity. This startling innovation may be seen in Plautus' *Amphitryon.*

In the Renaissance, tragicomedy became a genre of play that mixed tragic elements into drama that was mainly comic. The Italian writer Battista Guarini defined tragicomedy as having most of tragedy's elements (e.g., a certain gravity of diction, the depiction of important public events, and the arousal of compassion) but never carrying the action to tragedy's conclusion, and judiciously including such comic elements as low-born characters, laughter, and jests. Central to this kind of tragicomedy were danger, reversal, and a happy ending. Despite its affront to the strict Neoclassicism of the day, which forbade the mixing of genres, tragicomedy flourished, especially in England, whose writers largely ignored the edicts of Neoclassicism. John Fletcher provides a good example of the genre in *The Faithful Shepherdess* (c. 1608), itself a reworking of Guarini's *Il pastor fido,* first published in 1590. Notable examples of tragicomedy by William Shakespeare are *The Merchant of Venice* (1596–97), *The Winter's Tale* (1610–11), and *The Tempest* (1611–12).

Nineteenth-century Romantic writers espoused Shakespeare's use of tragicomedy in the belief that his plays closely mirrored nature, and they used him as a model for their works. The dramas of Georg Büchner, Victor Hugo, and Christian Dietrich Grabbe reflect his influence. With the advent of realism later in the 19th century, tragicomedy underwent yet another revision. Still intermingling the two elements, comic interludes now highlighted the ironic counterpoints inherent in a play, making the tragedy seem even more devastating. Such works as Henrik Ibsen's *Ghosts* (1881) and *The Wild Duck* (1884) reflect this technique. George Bernard Shaw said of Ibsen's work that it established tragicomedy as a more meaningful and serious entertainment than tragedy. Anton Chekhov's tragicomedies include *Uncle Vanya* (1897) and *The Cherry Orchard* (1904).

Modern tragicomedy is sometimes used synonymously with Absurdist drama, which suggest that laughter is the only response left to us when faced with the tragic emptiness and meaninglessness of existence. Examples of this modern type of tragicomedy are Samuel Beckett's *Endgame* (1958) and Harold Pinter's *The Dumb-Waiter* (1960).

UNITIES

The three principles derived by French classicists from Aristotle's *Poetics* are called the unities. They require a play to have a single action represented as occurring in a single place and within the course of a day. These principles were called, respectively, unity of action, unity of place, and unity of time.

These three unities were redefined in 1570 by the Italian humanist Lodovico Castelvetro in his interpretation of Aristotle, and they are usually referred to as "Aristotelian rules" for dramatic structure. Actually, Aristotle's observations on tragedy are descriptive rather than prescriptive, and he emphasizes only one unity, that of plot, or action.

In the French classical tragedy, the unities were adhered to literally and became the source of endless critical polemics. Disputes arose over such problems as whether a single day meant 12 or 24 hours and whether a single place meant one room or one city. Some believed that the action represented in the play should occupy no more time than that required for the play's performance—about two hours. In spite of such severe restrictions, the great 17th-century French dramatists Pierre Corneille and Jean

Racine, confining the crises of their characters' lives to a single setting and a brief span of hours, produced a unique form of tragedy that derives its austere power from its singleness of concentration. The prestige of the unities continued to dominate French drama until the Romantic era, when it was destroyed, in an evening of catcalls and violence, with the opening of Victor Hugo's Romantic tragedy *Hernani* (1830).

In England, where playwrights often had two or more plots in a play, comedy and tragedy were mixed and the setting switched to "another part of the forest" freely. The unities were esteemed in theory but ignored in practice.

WELL-MADE PLAY

The well-made play is a type of play that is constructed according to certain strict technical principles. It dominated the stages of Europe and the United States for most of the 19th century and continued to exert influence into the 20th.

The technical formula of the well-made play, developed around 1825 by the French playwright Eugène Scribe, called for complex and highly artificial plotting, a build-up of suspense, a climactic scene in which all problems are resolved, and a happy ending. Conventional romantic conflicts were a staple subject of such plays (for example, the problem of a pretty girl who must choose between a wealthy, unscrupulous suitor and a poor but honest young man). Suspense was created by misunderstandings between

characters, mistaken identities, secret information (the poor young man is really of noble birth), lost or stolen documents, and similar contrivances. Later critics, such as Émile Zola and George Bernard Shaw, denounced Scribe's work and that of his successor, Victorien Sardou, for exalting the mechanics of playmaking at the expense of honest characterizations and serious content, but both playwrights were enormously popular in their day. Scribe, with the aid of assistants, wrote literally hundreds of plays and librettos that were translated,

LILLIAN HELLMAN

(b. June 20, 1905, New Orleans, La., U.S.— d. June 30, 1984, Vineyard Haven, Martha's Vineyard, Mass.)

Lillian Hellman was an American playwright and motion-picture screenwriter whose dramas forcefully attacked injustice, exploitation, and selfishness. After working as a book reviewer, press agent, and play reader, she began writing plays in the 1930s. Her first major success, The Children's Hour *(1934), concerned two schoolteachers falsely accused of lesbianism. She examined family infighting in her hit* The Little Foxes *(1939) and political injustice in* Watch on the Rhine *(1941). All were made into successful films. Called before the House Un-American Activities Committee in 1952, she refused to testify. She wrote several memoirs—*An Unfinished Woman *(1969),* Pentimento *(1973), and* Maybe *(1980)—and edited the works of her longtime companion, the novelist Dashiell Hammett.*

adapted, and imitated all over Europe. In England the well-made play was taken up by such practitioners as Wilkie Collins, who summed up the formula succinctly: "Make 'em laugh; make 'em weep; make 'em wait." Henry Arthur Jones and Arthur Pinero used the technique successfully, with somewhat improved characterizations and emotional tension, and Pinero brought it to the level of art with *The Second Mrs. Tanqueray* in 1893. The polished techniques of the well-made play were also turned to serious purposes in the plays of Émile Augier and Alexandre Dumas *fils*, which dealt with social conditions, such as prostitution and the emancipation of women, and are regarded as the precursors of the problem play. Lillian Hellman and Terence Rattigan are among 20th-century playwrights whose works draw on the principles of the well-made play.

CHAPTER 6

COMEDY

The chief object of comedy, in drama or other art forms, according to modern notions, is to amuse. It is contrasted on the one hand with tragedy and on the other with farce, burlesque, and other forms of humorous amusement.

The classic conception of comedy, which began with Aristotle in ancient Greece of the 4th century BCE and persists through the present, holds that it is primarily concerned with humans as social beings, rather than as private persons, and that its function is frankly corrective. The comic artist's purpose is to hold a mirror up to society to reflect its follies and vices, in the hope that they will, as a result, be mended. The 20th-century French philosopher Henri Bergson shared this view of the corrective purpose of laughter. Specifically, he felt, laughter is intended to bring the comic character back into conformity with his society, whose logic and conventions he abandons when "he slackens in the attention that is due to life." Here comedy is considered primarily as a literary genre.

ORIGINS AND DEFINITIONS

The word *comedy* seems to be connected by derivation with the Greek verb meaning "to revel," and comedy arose out of the revels associated with the rites of Dionysus, a god of vegetation. The origins of comedy are thus bound up with vegetation ritual. Aristotle, in his *Poetics*, states that comedy

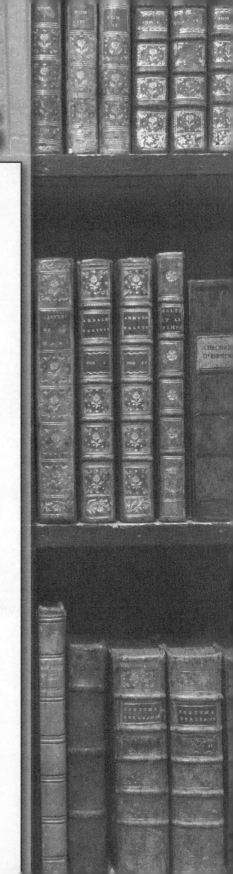

Comedy has its roots in vegetation ritual, as it evolved from revels associated with Dionysus (Bacchus), god of vegetation. Vuillermoz/AgenceImages/Getty Image

originated in phallic songs and that, like tragedy, it began in improvisation. Though tragedy evolved by stages that can be traced, the progress of comedy passed unnoticed because it was not taken seriously. When tragedy and comedy arose, poets wrote one or the other, according to their natural bent. Those of the graver sort, who might previously have been inclined to celebrate the actions of the great in epic poetry, turned to tragedy. Poets of a lower type, who had set forth the doings of the ignoble in invectives, turned to comedy. The distinction is basic to the Aristotelian differentiation between tragedy and comedy: tragedy imitates men who are better than the average and comedy men who are worse.

For centuries, efforts at defining comedy were to be along the lines set down by Aristotle: the view that tragedy deals with personages of high estate, and comedy deals with lowly types; tragedy treats of matters of great public import, while comedy is concerned with the private affairs of mundane life; and the characters and events of tragedy are historic and so, in some sense, true, while the humbler materials of comedy are but feigned. Implicit, too, in Aristotle is the distinction in styles deemed appropriate to the treatment of tragic and comic story. As long as there was at least a theoretical separation of comic and tragic styles, either genre could, on occasion, appropriate the stylistic manner of the other to a striking effect, which was never possible after the crossing of stylistic lines became commonplace.

The ancient Roman poet Horace, who wrote on such stylistic differences, noted the special effects that can be achieved when comedy lifts its voice in pseudo-tragic rant and when tragedy adopts the prosaic but affecting language of comedy. Consciously combined, the mixture of styles produces the burlesque, in which the grand manner (epic or tragic) is applied to a trivial subject, or the serious subject is subjected to a vulgar treatment, to ludicrous effect.

The English novelist Henry Fielding, in the preface to *Joseph Andrews* (1742), was careful to distinguish between the comic and the burlesque. The latter centres on the monstrous and unnatural and gives pleasure through the surprising absurdity it exhibits in appropriating the manners of the highest to the lowest, or vice versa. Comedy, however, confines itself to the imitation of nature, and, according to Fielding, the comic artist is not to be excused for deviating from it. His subject is the ridiculous, not the monstrous, as with the writer of burlesque; and the nature he is to imitate is human nature, as viewed in the ordinary scenes of civilized society.

THE HUMAN CONTRADICTION

In dealing with humans as social beings, all great comic artists have known that they are in the presence of a contradiction: that behind the social being lurks an animal being, whose behaviour often accords very ill with the canons dictated by society. Comedy, from its ritual beginnings, has celebrated creative energy. The primitive revels out of which comedy arose frankly acknowledged the animal nature of humankind. The animal masquerades and the phallic processions are the obvious witnesses to it. Comedy testifies to physical vitality, delight in life, and the will to go on living. Comedy is at its merriest, its most festive, when this rhythm of life can be affirmed within the civilized context of human society. In the absence of this sort of harmony between creatural instincts and the dictates of civilization, sundry strains and discontents arise, all bearing witness to the contradictory nature of humanity, which in the comic view is a radical dualism. Efforts to follow the way of rational sobriety are forever being interrupted by the infirmities of the flesh. The duality that tragedy views as a fatal contradiction in the nature of things, comedy views as one more instance of the incongruous reality that everyone must live with as best they can.

"Wherever there is life, there is contradiction," says Søren Kierkegaard, the 19th-century Danish existentialist, in the *Concluding Unscientific Postscript* (1846), "and wherever there is contradiction, the comical is present." He went on to say that the tragic and the comic are both based on contradiction but "the tragic is the suffering contradiction, comical, painless contradiction." Comedy makes the contradiction manifest along with a way out, which is why the contradiction is painless. Tragedy, however, despairs of a way out of the contradiction.

The incongruous is "the essence of the laughable," said the English essayist William Hazlitt, who also declared, in his essay "On Wit and Humour" in *English Comic Writers* (1819), "Man is the only animal that laughs and weeps; for he is the only animal that is struck with the difference between what things are, and what they ought to be."

COMEDY, SATIRE, AND ROMANCE

Comedy's dualistic view of the individual as an incongruous mixture of bodily instinct and rational intellect is an essentially ironic view—implying the capacity to see things in a double aspect. The comic drama takes on the features of satire as it fixes on professions of virtue and the practices that contradict them. Satire assumes standards against which professions and practices are judged. To the extent that the professions prove hollow and the practices vicious, the ironic perception darkens and deepens. The element of the incongruous points in the direction of the grotesque, which implies an admixture of elements that do not match. The ironic gaze

eventually penetrates to a vision of the grotesque quality of experience, marked by the discontinuity of word and deed and the total lack of coherence between appearance and reality. This suggests one of the extreme limits of comedy, the satiric extreme, in which the sense of the discrepancy between things as they are and things as they might be or ought to be has reached to the borders of tragedy. For the tragic apprehension, as Kierkegaard states, despairs of a way out of the contradictions that life presents.

As satire may be said to govern the movement of comedy in one direction, romance governs its movement in the other. Satiric comedy dramatizes the discrepancy between the ideal and the reality and condemns the pretensions that would mask reality's hollowness and viciousness. Romantic comedy also regularly presents the conflict between the ideal shape of things as hero or heroine could wish them to be and the hard realities with which they are confronted, but typically it ends by invoking the ideal, despite whatever difficulties reality has put in its way. This is never managed without a good deal of contrivance, and the plot of the typical romantic comedy is a medley of clever scheming, calculated coincidence, and wondrous discovery, all of which contribute ultimately to making the events answer precisely to the hero's or heroine's wishes. Plotting of this sort has had a long stage tradition and not exclusively in comedy. It is first encountered in the tragicomedies of the ancient

JEAN ANOUILH

(b. June 23, 1910, Bordeaux, France—d. Oct. 3, 1987, Lausanne, Switz.)

A French playwright who became one of the strongest personalities of the French theatre, Jean Anouilh achieved an international reputation. His plays are intensely personal messages. Often they express his love of the theatre as well as his grudges against actors, wives, mistresses, critics, academicians, bureaucrats, and others. After studying law, he wrote his first play, The Ermine *(1932), followed by the successful* Traveler Without Luggage *(1937). He is best remembered for* Antigone *(1944),* The Lark *(1953), and* Becket *(1959), in which he used techniques such as the play within the play, flashbacks and flash-forwards, and the exchange of roles. A skillful exponent of the well-made play, he rejected naturalism and realism in favour of a return to theatricalism. Technically he showed a great versatility, from the stylized use of Greek myth, to the rewriting of history, to the* comédie-ballet, *to the modern comedy of character. Although not a systematic ideologist, Anouilh developed his own view of life highlighting the contradictions within human reality, for example, or the ambiguous relationships between good and evil. He called two major collections of his plays* Pièces roses *("Rose-coloured Plays") and* Pièces noires *("Black Plays"), in which similar subjects are treated more or less lightly.*

Greek dramatist Euripides (e.g., *Alcestis, Iphigeneia in Tauris, Ion, Helen*). Shakespeare explored the full range of dramatic possibilities of the romantic mode of comedy. The means by which the happy ending is accomplished in romantic comedy—the document or the bodily mark that establishes identities to the satisfaction of all the characters of goodwill—are part of the stock-in-trade of all comic dramatists, even such 20th-century playwrights as Jean Anouilh (in *Traveler Without Luggage*, 1937) and T.S. Eliot (in *The Confidential Clerk*, 1953).

There is nothing necessarily inconsistent in the use of a calculatedly artificial dramatic design to convey a serious dramatic statement. The contrived artifice of Shakespeare's mature comic plots is the perfect foil against which the reality of the characters' feelings and attitudes assumes the greater naturalness. The strange coincidences, remarkable discoveries, and wonderful reunions are unimportant compared with the emotions of relief and awe that they inspire. Their function, as Shakespeare uses them, is precisely to give rise to such emotions, and the emotions, thanks to the plangent poetry in which they are expressed, end by transcending the circumstances that occasioned them. But when such artifices are employed simply for the purpose of eliminating the obstacles to a happy ending—as is the case in the sentimental comedy of the 18th and early 19th centuries—they stand forth as imaginatively impoverished dramatic clichés. The dramatists of sentimental comedy were committed to writing exemplary plays, wherein virtue would be rewarded and vice frustrated. If hero and heroine were to be rescued from the distresses that had encompassed them, any measures were apparently acceptable. The important thing was that the play's action should reach an edifying end. It is but a short step from comedy of this sort to the melodrama that flourished in the 19th-century theatre. The distresses that the hero and heroine suffer are, in melodrama, raised to a more than comic urgency, but the means of deliverance have the familiar comic stamp: the secret at last made known, the long-lost child identified, the hard heart made suddenly capable of pity. Melodrama is a form of fantasy that proceeds according to its own childish and somewhat egoistic logic. Hero and heroine are pure, anyone who opposes them is a villain, and the purity that has exposed them to risks must ensure their eventual safety and happiness. What melodrama is to tragedy, farce is to comedy, and the element of fantasy is equally prominent in farce and in melodrama. If melodrama provides a fantasy in which the protagonist suffers for his virtues but is eventually rewarded for them, farce provides a fantasy in which the protagonist sets about satisfying his most roguish or wanton, mischievous or destructive, impulses and manages to do so with impunity.

THEORIES

The treatise that Aristotle is presumed to have written on comedy is lost. There is, however, a fragmentary treatise on comedy that bears an obvious relation to Aristotle's treatise on tragedy, *Poetics*, and is generally taken to be either a version of a lost Aristotelian original or an expression of the philosophical tradition to which he belonged. This is the *Tractatus Coislinianus*, preserved in a 10th-century manuscript in the De Coislin Collection in Paris. The *Tractatus* divides the substance of comedy into the same six elements that are discussed in regard to tragedy in the *Poetics*: plot, character, thought, diction, melody, and spectacle. The characters of comedy, according to the *Tractatus*, are of three kinds: the impostors, the self-deprecators, and the buffoons. The Aristotelian tradition from which the *Tractatus* derives probably provided a fourth, the churl, or boor. The list of comic characters in the *Tractatus* is closely related to a passage in Aristotle's *Nicomachean Ethics*, in which the boaster (the person who says more than the truth) is compared with the mock-modest person (the person who says less), and the buffoon (who has too much wit) is contrasted with the boor (who has too little).

COMEDY AS A RITE

The *Tractatus* was not printed until 1839, and its influence on comic theory is thus of relatively modern date. It is frequently cited in the studies that attempt to combine literary criticism and anthropology, in the manner in which James George Frazer combined studies of primitive religion and culture in *The Golden Bough* (1890–1915). In such works, comedy and tragedy alike are traced to a prehistoric death-and-resurrection ceremonial, a seasonal pantomime in which the old year, in the guise of an aged king (or hero or god), is killed, and the new spirit of fertility, the resurrection or initiation of the young king, is brought in. This rite typically featured a ritual combat, or agon, between the representatives of the old and the new seasons, a feast in which the sacrificial body of the slain king was devoured, a marriage between the victorious new king and his chosen bride, and a final triumphal procession in celebration of the reincarnation or resurrection of the slain god. Implicit in the whole ceremony is the ancient rite of purging the tribe through the expulsion of a scapegoat, who carries away the accumulated sins of the past year. Frazer, speaking of scapegoats in *The Golden Bough*, noted that this expulsion of devils was commonly preceded or followed by a period of general license, an abandonment of the ordinary restraints of society during which all offenses except the gravest go unpunished. This quality of Saturnalia is characteristic of comedy from ancient Greece through medieval Europe.

The seasonal rites that celebrate the yearly cycle of birth, death, and rebirth were seen by the Canadian critic Northrop Frye as the basis for the generic plots of comedy, romance, tragedy, and irony and satire. The four prefigure the fate of a hero and the society he brings into being. In comedy (representing the season of spring), the hero appears in a society controlled by obstructing characters and succeeds in wresting it from their grasp. The movement of comedy of this sort typically replaces falsehood with truth, illusion with reality. The hero, having come into possession of his new society, sets forth upon adventures, and these are the province of romance (summer). Tragedy (autumn) commemorates the hero's passion and death. Irony and satire (winter) depict a world from which the hero has disappeared, a vision of "unidealized existence." With spring, the hero is born anew.

The Moral Force of Comedy

The characters of comedy specified in the *Tractatus* arrange themselves in a familiar pattern: a clever hero is surrounded by fools of sundry varieties (impostors, buffoons, boors). The hero is something of a trickster, dissimulating his own powers, while exploiting the weaknesses of those around him. The comic pattern is a persistent one. It appears not only in ancient Greek comedy but also in the farces of ancient Italy, in the commedia dell'arte that came into being in 16th-century Italy, and even in the routines of late-night television comedians and their straight men. Implicit here is the tendency to make folly ridiculous, to laugh it out of countenance, which has always been a prominent feature of comedy.

Renaissance critics, elaborating on the brief and cryptic account of comedy in Aristotle's *Poetics*, stressed the derisive force of comedy as an adjunct to morality. The Italian scholar Gian Giorgio Trissino's account of comedy in his *Poetica*, apparently written in the 1530s, is typical: as tragedy teaches by means of pity and fear, comedy teaches by deriding things that are vile. Attention is directed here, as in other critical treatises of this kind, to the source of laughter. According to Trissino, laughter is aroused by objects that are in some way ugly and especially by that from which better qualities were hoped. His statement suggests the relation of the comic to the incongruous. Trissino was as aware as the French poet Charles Baudelaire was three centuries later that laughter betokens the fallen nature of man (Baudelaire would term it the Satanic nature). Man laughs, says Trissino (echoing Plato's dialogue *Philebus*), because he is envious and malicious and never delights in the good of others except when he hopes for some good from it for himself.

The most important English Renaissance statement concerning comedy is that of Sir Philip Sidney in *The Defence of Poesie* (1595):

Comedy is an imitation of the common errors of our life, which [the comic dramatist] representeth in the most ridiculous and scornful sort that may be, so as it is impossible that any beholder can be content to be such a one.

Like Trissino, Sidney notes that, while laughter comes from delight, not all objects of delight cause laughter, and he demonstrates the distinction as Trissino had done: "We are ravished with delight to see a fair woman, and yet are far from being moved to laughter. We laugh at deformed creatures, wherein certainly we cannot delight." The element of the incongruous is prominent in Sidney's account of scornful laughter. He cites the image of the hero of Greek legend Heracles, with his great beard and furious countenance, in woman's attire, spinning at the command of his beloved queen, Omphale, and declares that this arouses both delight and laughter.

COMEDY AND CHARACTER

Another English poet, John Dryden, in *Of Dramatick Poesie, an Essay* (1668), makes the same point in describing the kind of laughter produced by the ancient Greek comedy *The Clouds*, by Aristophanes. In it the character of Socrates is made ridiculous by acting extremely unlike the true Socrates—that is, by appearing childish and absurd rather than with the gravity of the true Socrates. Dryden was concerned with analyzing the laughable quality of comedy and with demonstrating the different forms it has taken in different periods of dramatic history. Aristophanic comedy sought its laughable quality not so much in the imitation of a person as in the representation of "some odd conceit which had commonly somewhat of unnatural or obscene in it." In the so-called New Comedy, introduced by Menander late in the 4th century BCE, writers sought to express the ethos, or character, as in their tragedies they expressed the pathos, or suffering, of humankind. This distinction goes back to Aristotle, who in the *Rhetoric* distinguished between ethos (natural bent, disposition, or moral character) and pathos (emotion) displayed in a given situation. And the Latin rhetorician Quintilian, in the 1st century CE, noted that ethos is akin to comedy and pathos to tragedy. The distinction is important to Renaissance and Neoclassical assumptions concerning the respective subject of comic and tragic representation. In terms of emotion, ethos is viewed as a permanent condition characteristic of the average person and relatively mild in its nature. Pathos, however, is a temporary emotional state, often violent. Comedy thus expresses human character in the ordinary circumstances of everyday life, and tragedy expresses the sufferings of a particular individual in extraordinary periods of intense emotion.

In dealing with persons engaged in normal affairs, the comic dramatists tended to depict the individual in terms of some single but overriding personal trait or habit. They adopted a method based on the physiological concept of the four humours, or bodily fluids (blood, phlegm, choler, melancholy), and the belief that an equal proportion of these constituted health, while an excess or deficiency of any one of them brought disease. Because the humours governed temperament, an irregular distribution of them was considered to result not only in bodily sickness but also in derangements of personality and behaviour, as well. The resultant comedy of humours is distinctly English, as Dryden notes, and particularly identified with the comedies of Ben Jonson.

THE ROLE OF WIT

Humour is native to humankind. Folly need only be observed and imitated by the comic dramatist to give rise to laughter. Observers as early as Quintilian, however, have pointed out that, though folly is laughable in itself, such jests may be improved if the writer adds something of his own—namely, wit. A form of repartee, wit implies both a mental agility and a linguistic grace that is very much a product of conscious art. Quintilian describes wit at some length in his *Institutio oratoria*. It partakes of urbanity, a certain tincture of learning, charm, saltiness, or sharpness, and polish and elegance. In the preface (1671) to *An Evening's Love*, Dryden distinguishes between the comic talents of Jonson, on the one hand, and of Shakespeare and his contemporary John Fletcher, on the other, by virtue of their excelling respectively in humour and in wit. Jonson's talent lay in his ability "to make men appear pleasantly ridiculous on the stage," while Shakespeare and Fletcher excelled in wit, or "the

Characters such as Shakespeare's Falstaff add to the humour of a comedy by saying the unexpected. Patrick Riviere/Getty Images

Humour is the describing the ludicrous as it is in itself; wit is the exposing it, by comparing or contrasting it with something else. Humour is, as it were, the growth of nature and accident; wit is the product of art and fancy.

The distinctions persist into the most sophisticated treatments of the subject. Sigmund Freud, for example, in *Wit and its Relation to the Unconscious* (1905), said that wit is made, but humour is found. Laughter, according to Freud, is aroused at actions that appear immoderate and inappropriate, at excessive expenditures of energy: it expresses a pleasurable sense of the superiority felt on such occasions.

sharpness of conceit," as seen in their repartee. The distinction is noted as well in *Of Dramatick Poesie, an Essay*, where a comparison is made between the character of Morose in Jonson's play *Epicoene*, who is characterized by his humour (namely, his inability to abide any noise but the sound of his own voice), and Shakespeare's Falstaff, who, according to Dryden, represents a miscellany of humours and is singular in saying things that are unexpected by the audience.

The distinctions that Hazlitt arrives at, then, in his essay "On Wit and Humour" are very much in the classic tradition of comic criticism:

BAUDELAIRE ON THE GROTESQUE

The view that laughter comes from superiority is referred to as a commonplace by Baudelaire, who states it in his essay "On the Essence of Laughter" (1855). Laughter, says Baudelaire, is a consequence of the human notion of one's own superiority. It is a token both of an infinite misery, in relation to the absolute being of whom humans have an inkling, and of infinite grandeur, in relation to the beasts, and results from the perpetual collision of these two infinities. The crucial part of Baudelaire's essay, however, turns on his distinction between the comic and the grotesque. The comic, he says, is an imitation mixed with a certain creative faculty, and the grotesque is a creation mixed with a certain imitative faculty— imitative of elements found in nature. Each gives rise to laughter expressive of an idea of superiority—in the comic, the superiority of man over man and, in the grotesque, the superiority of man over nature. The laughter caused by the grotesque has about it something more profound and primitive, something much closer to the innocent life, than has the

CHARLES BAUDELAIRE

(b. April 9, 1821, Paris, France—d. Aug. 31, 1867, Paris)

The reputation of the French poet, translator, and literary and art critic Charles Baudelaire rests primarily on Les Fleurs du mal *(1857;* The Flowers of Evil*), perhaps the most important and influential poetry collection published in Europe in the 19th century. While a law student he became addicted to opium and hashish and contracted syphilis. His early reckless spending on fine clothes and furnishings led to a life dogged by debt. In 1844 he formed an association with Jeanne Duval, a woman of mixed black and white ancestry who inspired some of his finest poetry. He published a single novel,* La fanfarlo, *in 1847. His discovery of the works of Edgar Allan Poe in 1852 led to years of work on Poe, which produced many masterly translations and critical articles. His masterpiece,* Les fleurs du mal, *dealt with erotic, aesthetic, and social themes in ways that appalled many of his middle-class readers, and he was accused of obscenity and blasphemy. Though the title of his book became a byword for depravity, the book itself became a classic. His* Petits poèmes en prose *(1868) was an important and innovative experiment in prose poetry. He also wrote provocative essays in art criticism. Baudelaire's later years were darkened by disillusionment, despair, and mounting debt. His death at 46 resulted from syphilis. He is regarded as the earliest and finest poet of modernism in French.*

Baudelaire, photograph by Étienne Carjat, 1863. Courtesy of the Bibliothèque Nationale, Paris

laughter caused by the comic in human behaviour. In France the great master of the grotesque was the 16th-century author François Rabelais, while some of the plays of Molière in the next century best expressed the comic.

BERGSON'S AND MEREDITH'S THEORIES

The French philosopher Henri Bergson (1859–1941) analyzed the dialectic of comedy in his essay "Laughter," which deals directly with the spirit of contradiction that is basic both to comedy and to life. Bergson's central concern is with the opposition of the mechanical and the living. Stated in its most general terms, his thesis holds that the comic consists of something mechanical encrusted on the living. Bergson traces the implications of this view in the sundry elements of comedy: situations, language, characters. Comedy expresses a lack of adaptability to society; any individual is comic who goes his own way without troubling to get into touch with his fellow beings. The purpose of laughter is to wake him from his dream. Three conditions are essential for the comic: the character must be unsociable, for that is enough to make him ludicrous; the spectator must be insensible to the character's condition, for laughter is incompatible with emotion; and the character must act automatically (Bergson cites the systematic absentmindedness of Don Quixote). The essential difference between comedy and tragedy, says Bergson, invoking a distinction that goes back to that maintained between ethos and pathos, is that tragedy is concerned with individuals and comedy with classes. And the reason that comedy deals with the general is bound up with the corrective aim of laughter: the correction must reach as great a number of persons as possible. To this end, comedy focusses on peculiarities that are not indissolubly bound up with the individuality of a single person.

It is the business of laughter to repress any tendency on the part of the individual to separate himself from society. The comic character would, if left to his own devices, break away from logic (and thus relieve himself from the strain of thinking); give over the effort to adapt and readapt himself to society (and thus slacken in the attention that is due to life); and abandon social convention (and thus relieve himself from the strain of living).

The essay "On the Idea of Comedy and the Uses of the Comic Spirit" (1877), by Bergson's English contemporary George Meredith, is a celebration of the civilizing power of the comic spirit. The mind, he affirms, directs the laughter of comedy, and civilization is founded in common sense, which equips one to hear the comic spirit when it laughs folly out of countenance and to participate in its fellowship.

Both Bergson's and Meredith's essays have been criticized for focussing so exclusively on comedy as a socially corrective force and for limiting the scope of laughter to its derisive power. The charge is more damaging to Meredith's essay than it is to Bergson's. Whatever the limitations of the latter, it nonetheless explores the implications of its own thesis with the utmost thoroughness, and the result is a rigorous analysis of comic causes and effects for which any student of the subject must be grateful. It is with farce that Bergson's remarks on comedy have the greatest connection and on which they seem chiefly to have been founded. It is no accident that most of his examples are drawn from Molière, in whose work the farcical element is strong, and from the farces of Bergson's own contemporary Eugène-Marin Labiche. The laughter of comedy is not always derisive, however, as some of Shakespeare's greatest comedies prove. And there are plays, such as Shakespeare's last ones, which are well within an established tradition of comedy but in which laughter hardly sounds at all. These suggest regions of comedy on which Bergson's analysis of the genre sheds hardly any light at all.

THE COMIC AS A FAILURE OF SELF-KNOWLEDGE

Aristotle said that comedy deals with the ridiculous, and Plato, in the *Philebus*, defined the ridiculous as a failure of self-knowledge. Such a failure is there shown to be laughable in private individuals (the personages of comedy) but terrible in persons who wield power (the personages of tragedy). In comedy, the failure is often mirrored in a character's efforts to live up to an ideal of self that may be perfectly worthy but

the wrong ideal for that particular character. Shakespearean comedy is rich in examples: the King of Navarre and his courtiers, who must be made to realize that nature meant them to be lovers, not academicians, in *Love's Labour's Lost*; Beatrice and Benedick, who must be made to know that nature meant them for each other, not for the single life, in *Much Ado About Nothing*; Duke Orsino in *Twelfth Night*, who is brought to see that it is not Lady Olivia whom he loves but the disguised Viola, and Lady Olivia herself, who, when the right man comes along, decides that she will not dedicate herself to seven years of mourning for a dead brother, after all; and Angelo in *Measure for Measure*, whose image of himself collapses when his lust for Isabella makes it clear that he is not the ascetic type. The movement of all these plays follows a familiar comic pattern, wherein characters are brought from a condition of affected folly amounting to self-delusion to a plain recognition of who they are and what they want. For the five years or so after he wrote *Measure for Measure*, in 1603–04, Shakespeare seems to have addressed himself exclusively to tragedy, and each play in the sequence of masterpieces he produced during this period—*Othello, King Lear, Macbeth, Antony and Cleopatra*, and *Coriolanus*—turns in some measure on a failure of self-knowledge. This is notably so in the case of *Lear*, which is the tragedy of a man who (in the words of one of his daughters) "hath ever but slenderly known himself" and whose fault (as the Fool suggests) is to have grown old before he grew wise.

The plots of Shakespeare's last plays (*Pericles, Cymbeline, The Winter's Tale, The Tempest*) all contain a potential tragedy but one that is resolved by nontragic means. They contain, as well, an element of romance of the kind purveyed from Greek New Comedy through the plays of the ancient Roman comic dramatists Plautus and Terence. Children lost at birth are miraculously restored, years later, to their parents, thereby providing occasion for a recognition scene that functions as the denouement of the plot. Characters find themselves—they come to know themselves—in all manner of ways by the ends of these plays. Tragic errors have been made, tragic losses have been suffered, tragic passions—envy, jealousy, wrath—have seemed to rage unchecked, but the miracle that these plays celebrate lies in the discovery that the errors can be forgiven, the losses restored, and the passions mastered by the godly spirit of reason. The near tragedies experienced by the characters result in the ultimate health and enlightenment of the soul. What is learned is of a profound simplicity: the need for patience under adversity, the need to repent of one's sins, the need to forgive the sins of others. In comedy of this high and sublime sort, patience, repentance, and forgiveness are opposed to the viciously circular pattern of crime, which begets vengeance, which begets more crime. Comedy of this sort deals in regeneration and rebirth. There is always about it something of the religious, as humankind is absolved of its guilt and reconciled one to another and to whatever powers that be.

DIVINE COMEDIES IN THE WEST AND EAST

The 4th-century Latin grammarian Donatus distinguished comedy from tragedy by the simplest terms: comedies begin in trouble and end in peace, while tragedies begin in calms and end in tempest. Such a differentiation of the two genres may be simplistic, but it provided sufficient grounds for Dante to call his great poem *La Commedia* (*The Comedy*; later called *The Divine Comedy*), because, as he says in his dedicatory letter, it begins amid the horrors of hell but ends amid the pleasures of heaven. This suggests the movement of Shakespeare's last plays, which begin amid the distresses of the world and end in a supernal peace. Comedy conceived in this sublime and serene mode is rare but recurrent in the history of the theatre. The Spanish dramatist Pedro Calderón de la Barca's *Life Is a Dream* (1635) is an example. On the operatic stage, so is Mozart's *Magic Flute* (1791), in spirit and form so like Shakespeare's *Tempest*, to which it has often been compared. In later drama, Henrik Ibsen's *Little Eyolf* (1894) and August Strindberg's *To Damascus* (1898-1904)—both of which are among the late works of these Scandinavian dramatists—have affinities with this type, and this is the comic mode in which T.S. Eliot's last play, *The Elder Statesman* (1958), is conceived. It may represent the most universal mode of comedy. The American philosopher Susanne K. Langer writes:

In Asia the designation "Divine Comedy" would fit numberless plays; especially in India triumphant gods, divine lovers united after various trials [as in the perennially popular romance of Rama and Sita], are the favourite themes of a theater that knows no "tragic rhythm." The classical Sanskrit drama was heroic comedy—high poetry, noble action, themes almost always taken from the myths—a serious, religiously conceived drama, yet in the "comic" pattern, which is not a complete organic development reaching a foregone, inevitable conclusion, but is episodic, restoring a lost balance, and implying a new future. The reason for this consistently "comic" image of life in India is obvious enough: both Hindu and Buddhist regard life as an episode in the much longer career of the soul which has to accomplish many incarnations before it reaches its goal, nirvana. Its struggles in the world do not exhaust it; in fact they are scarcely worth recording except in entertainment theater, "comedy" in our sense—satire, farce, and dialogue. The characters whose fortunes are seriously interesting are the eternal gods; and

for them there is no death, no limit of potentialities, hence no fate to be fulfilled. There is only the balanced rhythm of sentience and emotion, upholding itself amid the changes of material nature.

(From *Feeling and Form*; Charles Scribner's Sons, 1953)

COMEDY: TERMS AND CONCEPTS

Among the many terms associated with comedy are several that arose in ancient Greece. Also differentiated in the following selection are a sampling of later developments in the genre, such as comedies of humour, intrigue, and manners.

AGON

An agon is a debate or contest between two characters in Attic comedy, constituting one of several formal conventions in these highly structured plays. More generally, an agon is the contest of opposed wills in Classical tragedy or any subsequent drama.

The Old Comedy of Greece, introduced into Dionysian festivals in 487 BCE and surviving in the works of Aristophanes, adhered to a rigid structure within which some variation was allowed. The plays begin with a prologos, which outlines the dilemma of the plot, followed by the parodos, or chorus entrance, which in Aristophanic comedies often revealed the chorus dressed as animals. Next, a debate, or agon, develops between an actor and the chorus or between two actors, each supported by half the chorus. Representing opposing principles, the actors argue in a fashion similar to the dialectical dialogues of Plato. In Aristophanes's *The Clouds,* for example, the agon concerns right and wrong logic. Following the debate is the parabasis, or "coming forward," at which time the chorus steps forward to address the audience directly, speaking in the name of the poet and often haranguing the audience by attacking prominent people or social and political principles.

The probable source of the agon and the other elaborate conventions of Old Comedy is the mimetic ritual from which comedy evolved, namely ancient fertility rituals in which men attempted to imitate the life cycles of regeneration and rebirth.

COMEDY OF HUMOURS

A dramatic genre most closely associated with the English playwright Ben Jonson from the late 16th century, the comedy of humours derives its name from the Latin *humor* (more properly *umor*), meaning "liquid." In medieval and Renaissance medical theory, it was held that the human body contained a balance of four liquids, or humours: blood, phlegm, yellow bile (choler), and black bile (melancholy). When properly balanced, these humours were thought to give the individual a healthy mind in a healthy body.

In his play *Every Man Out of His Humour* (1599), Jonson explains that the system of humours governing the body may by metaphor be applied to the general disposition, so that a peculiar quality may so possess a person as to make him or her act in one way. Jonson's characters usually represent one humour and, thus unbalanced, are basically caricatures. Jonson distinguished two kinds of humour: true humour, in which one peculiar quality actually possessed a person, body and soul; and an adopted humour, or mannerism, in which a person went out of his way to appear singular by affecting certain fashions of clothing, speech, and social habits.

COMEDY OF INTRIGUE

The comedy of intrigue, or comedy of situation, is a comic form in which complicated conspiracies and stratagems dominate the plot. The complex plots and subplots of such comedies are often based on ridiculous and contrived situations with large doses of farcical humour. An example of comedy of intrigue is William Shakespeare's *Comedy of Errors* (first performed 1592–93), a humorous exploitation of the confusion resulting from twin masters and their twin servants. Shakespeare's play is itself a version of two plays by the Roman comedy writer Plautus (c. 254–184 BCE), *Menaechmi* and *Amphitruo.*

In the hands of a master such as Molière, the comedy of intrigue often shades into a comedy of manners. Thus, *Le Médecin malgré lui* (1666; *The Doctor in Spite of Himself*), which begins as a farce based on the simple joke of mistaking the ne'er-do-well woodcutter Sganarelle for a doctor, gradually becomes a satire on learned pretension and bourgeois credulity as Sganarelle fulfills his role as a doctor with great success.

COMEDY OF MANNERS

The comedy of manners is a witty, cerebral form of dramatic comedy that depicts and often satirizes the manners and affectations of a contemporary society. It is concerned with social usage and the question of whether or not characters meet certain social standards. Often the governing social standard is morally trivial but exacting. The plot of such a comedy, usually concerned with an illicit love affair or similarly scandalous matter, is subordinate to the play's brittle atmosphere, witty dialogue, and pungent commentary on human foibles.

The comedy of manners, which was usually written by sophisticated authors for members of their own coterie or social class, has historically thrived in periods and societies that combined material prosperity and moral latitude. Such was the case in ancient Greece when Menander (c. 342–c. 292 BCE) inaugurated New Comedy, the forerunner of comedy of manners. Menander's smooth style, elaborate plots, and stock characters were imitated by the Roman poets Plautus (c. 254–184 BCE) and Terence (186/185–159 BCE), whose comedies were widely known and copied during the Renaissance.

One of the greatest exponents of the comedy of manners was Molière, who satirized the hypocrisy and pretension of 17th-century French society in such plays as *L'École des femmes* (1662; *The School for Wives*) and *Le Misanthrope* (1666; *The Misanthrope*).

In England the comedy of manners had its great day during the Restoration period. Although influenced by Ben Jonson's comedy of humours, the Restoration comedy of manners was lighter, defter, and more vivacious in tone. Playwrights declared themselves against affected wit and acquired follies and satirized these qualities in caricature characters with label-like names such as Sir Fopling Flutter (in Sir George Etherege's *Man of Mode*, 1676) and Tattle (in William Congreve's *The Old Batchelour*, 1693). The masterpieces of the genre were the witty, cynical, and epigrammatic plays of William Wycherley (*The Country-Wife*, 1675) and William Congreve (*The Way of the World*, 1700). In the late 18th century Oliver Goldsmith (*She Stoops to Conquer*, 1773) and Richard Brinsley Sheridan (*The Rivals*, 1775; *The School for Scandal*, 1777) revived the form.

The tradition of elaborate, artificial plotting and epigrammatic dialogue was carried on by the Anglo-Irish playwright Oscar Wilde in *Lady Windermere's Fan* (1892) and *The Importance of Being Earnest* (1895). In the 20th century the comedy of manners reappeared in the witty, sophisticated drawing-room plays of the British dramatists Noël Coward and

In The Importance of Being Earnest *(1895), Oscar Wilde carried on a tradition of intricate, simulated plotting and succinct dialogue in his comedy of manners.* Eileen Darby/Time & Life Pictures/Getty Images

Somerset Maugham and the Americans Philip Barry and S.N. Behrman.

FABULA ATELLANA

The earliest native Italian farce was the *fabula Atellana*, presumably a rustic improvisational comedy featuring masked stock characters. The farces derived their name from the town of Atella in the Campania region of southern Italy and seem to have originated among Italians speaking the Oscan dialect. They became a popular entertainment in ancient republican and early imperial Rome, by which time they were performed in Latin but possibly spiced with Oscan words and place-names. Originally based on scenarios handed down by oral tradition, they became a literary genre in the 1st century BCE, but only a few fragments survive of works by Lucius Pomponius of Bononia, Novius, and other writers. The farces had stock characters: Maccus, the clown; Bucco ("Fat Cheeks"), the simpleton; Pappus, the old fool; Dossennus, whose name has been taken to mean "Hunchback"; and Manducus, perhaps meaning "the Glutton." There is no record of these farces after the 1st century CE, but certain of the stock characters of the 16th-century Italian commedia dell'arte reflect the influence of the Atellan plays.

FABULA PALLIATA

Fabula palliata (plural form *fabula palliatae*) is the name given to any of the Roman comedies that were translations or adaptations of Greek New Comedy. It derives from the *pallium*, the Latin name for the himation (a Greek cloak), and means roughly "play in Greek dress." All surviving Roman comedies written by Plautus and Terence belong to this genre.

The comedies retained the Greek stock characters and conventionalized plots of romantic intrigue as a framework to the satire of everyday contemporary life. The *fabula palliata* became something more than mere translation in the works of Plautus, who introduced Roman manners and customs, Italian place-names, and Latin puns into the Greek form, writing in a style that is characterized by boisterous humour, nimbleness and suppleness of diction, and high spirits. Plautus sometimes turned scenes of iambic dialogue in his Greek originals into musical scenes composed in various metres. Terence, though closer in spirit to his Greek originals, often combined materials from two different plays into one (*contaminatio*). His style is graceful and correct, more polished but less lively than that of Plautus, and his characters are well delineated. Statius Caecilius, famed for his emotional power and well-constructed plots, and Sextus Turpilius, who kept close to Greek models, are other prominent representatives. By the mid-2nd century BCE, the *fabula palliata* had been replaced by the *fabula togata* (from the Roman toga, "play in Roman dress"), but no complete work survives of this naturalized Roman comedy. It is through the *fabulae palliatae* of Plautus and Terence that Greek New Comedy was preserved and influenced succeeding generations of comedy in Europe from the Renaissance on.

FARCE

A comic dramatic piece, the farce uses highly improbable situations, stereotyped characters, extravagant exaggeration, and violent horseplay. The term also refers to the class or form of drama made up of such compositions. Farce is generally regarded as intellectually and aesthetically inferior to comedy in its crude characterizations and implausible plots, but it has been sustained by its popularity in performance and has persisted throughout the Western world to the present.

Antecedents of farce are found in ancient Greek and Roman theatre, both in the comedies of Aristophanes and Plautus and in the popular native Italian *fabula Atellana*, entertainments in which the actors played stock character types—such as glutton, graybeard, and clown—who were caught in exaggerated situations.

It was in 15th-century France that the term *farce* was first used to describe the elements of clowning, acrobatics, caricature, and indecency found together within a single form of entertainment. Such pieces were initially bits of impromptu buffoonery inserted by actors into the texts of religious plays—hence the use of the Old French word

farce, "stuffing." Such works were afterward written independently, the most amusing of the existing texts being *Maistre Pierre Pathelin* (c. 1470). French farce spread quickly throughout Europe, notable examples being the interludes of John Heywood in 16th-century England. Shakespeare and Molière eventually came to use elements of farce in their comedies.

Farce continued throughout the 18th and 19th centuries. In France, Eugène-Marin Labiche's *Le Chapeau de paille d'Italie* (1851; *An Italian Straw Hat*) and Georges Feydeau's *La Puce à l'oreille* (1907; *A Flea in Her Ear*) were notable successes. Farce also surfaced

JOHN HEYWOOD

(b. 1497?, London, Eng.?—d. after 1575, Mechelen, Belg.)

The British playwright John Heywood is known for his witty, satirical interludes (dialogues on a set subject), which helped put English drama on the road to the fully developed stage comedy of the Elizabethans. His interludes, which replace biblical allegory and the moral instruction of the morality play with representations of everyday life and manners, include The Play of the Wether, A Play of Love, *and* Wytty and Wytless *(all printed 1533), and* The Playe Called the Foure P.P.: A Palmer, a Pardoner, a Potycary, a Pedler *(printed c. 1544). He also wrote epigrams, ballads, and a verse allegory,* The Spider and the Flie *(1556).*

in music hall, vaudeville, and boulevard entertainments.

Farce survived in the late 19th and early 20th centuries in such plays as *Charley's Aunt* (1892) by Brandon Thomas and found new expression in film comedies with Charlie Chaplin, the Keystone Kops, and the Marx Brothers. The farces presented at the Aldwych Theatre, London, between the world wars were enormously popular, and numerous successful television comedy shows attest to the durability of the form. Examples from the second half of the century are the Italian Dario Fo's *Morte accidentale di un anarchico* (1974; *Accidental Death of an Anarchist*), Michael Frayn's *Noises Off* (1982), and Alan Ayckbourn's *Communicating Doors* (1995).

LOW COMEDY

A dramatic or literary entertainment with no underlying purpose except to provoke laughter by boasting, boisterous jokes, drunkenness, scolding, fighting, buffoonery, and other riotous activity is known as a low comedy. Used either alone or added as comic relief to more serious forms, low comedy has origins in the comic improvisations of actors in ancient Greek and Roman comedy. Low comedy can also be found in medieval religious drama, in the works of William Shakespeare (as in, for example, the porter scene in Act 2, scene 3, of *Macbeth*), in farce and vaudeville,

and in the various media available in the 21st century.

MIDDLE COMEDY

The style of drama that prevailed in Athens from about 400 BCE to about 320 BCE is known as Middle Comedy. Preoccupied with social themes, Middle Comedy represents a transition from Old Comedy, which presented literary, political, and philosophical commentary interspersed with scurrilous personal invective, to New Comedy, with its gently satiric observation of contemporary domestic life. Aristophanes' last play, the *Plutus,* is an extant work that reflects this transition. Antiphanes and Alexis were preeminent Middle Comedy dramatists, but none of their plays has survived except in later quotations of individual words or sentences.

MOCK-EPIC

The form of satire that adapts the elevated heroic style of the classical epic poem to a trivial subject is the mock-epic (also called mock-heroic). The tradition, which originated in classical times with an anonymous burlesque of Homer, the *Batrachomyomachia* (*Battle of the Frogs and the Mice*), was honed to a fine art in the late 17th- and early 18th-century Neoclassical period. A double-edged satirical weapon, the mock-epic was sometimes used by the "moderns" of this period to ridicule contemporary "ancients" (classicists). More often it was used by "ancients" to point up the unheroic character of the modern age by subjecting thinly disguised contemporary events to a heroic treatment. The classic example of this

ALEXANDER POPE

(b. May 21, 1688, London, Eng.—d. May 30, 1744, Twickenham, near London)

Alexander Pope, English poet and satirist of the Augustan period, is best known for his poems An Essay on Criticism *(1711),* The Rape of the Lock *(1712–14),* The Dunciad *(1728), and* An Essay on Man *(1733–34). He is one of the most epigrammatic of all English authors. A precocious boy precluded from formal education by his Roman Catholicism, Pope was mainly self-educated. A spinal deformity and other health problems limited his growth and physical activities, leading him to devote himself to reading and writing. His first major work was* An Essay on Criticism, *a poem on the art of writing that contains several brilliant epigrams (e.g., "To err is human, to forgive, divine"). His witty mock-epic* The Rape of the Lock *ridicules fashionable society. The great labour of his life was his verse translation of Homer's* Iliad *(1720) and* Odyssey *(1726), whose success made him financially secure. He became involved in many literary battles, prompting him to write poems such as the scathing mock-epic* The Dunciad *and* An Epistle to Dr. Arbuthnot *(1735). The philosophical* An Essay on Man *was intended as part of a larger work that Pope never completed.*

is Nicolas Boileau's *Le Lutrin* (1674–83; "The Lectern"), which begins with a quarrel between two ecclesiastical dignitaries about where to place a lectern in a chapel and ends with a battle in a bookstore in which champions of either side hurl their favourite "ancient" or "modern" authors at each other. Jonathan Swift's "Battle of the Books" (1704) is a variation of this theme in mock-heroic prose. The outstanding English mock-epic is Alexander Pope's brilliant tour de force *The Rape of the Lock* (1712–14), which concerns a society beau's theft of a lock of hair from a society belle. Pope treated the incident as if it were comparable to events that sparked the Trojan War.

Most mock-epics begin with an invocation to the muse and use the familiar epic devices of set speeches, supernatural interventions, and descents to the underworld, as well as infinitely detailed descriptions of the protagonist's activities. Thus, they provide much scope for display of the author's ingenuity and inventiveness. An American mock-epic, Joel Barlow's *The Hasty Pudding* (written 1793), celebrates in three four hundred-line cantos his favourite New England dish, cornmeal mush.

NEW COMEDY

The variety of Greek drama prevalent from roughly 320 BCE to the mid-3rd century BCE is known as New Comedy. It offers a mildly satiric view of contemporary Athenian society, especially in its familiar and domestic aspects. Unlike Old Comedy, which parodied public figures and events, New Comedy features fictional average citizens and has no supernatural or heroic overtones. Thus, the chorus, the representative of forces larger than life, recedes in importance and becomes a small band of musicians and dancers who periodically provide light entertainment.

The plays commonly deal with the conventionalized situation of thwarted lovers and contain such stock characters as the cunning slave, the wily merchant, the boastful soldier, and the cruel father. One lover is usually a foundling, the discovery of whose true birth and identity makes marriage possible in the end. Although it does not realistically depict contemporary life, New Comedy accurately reflects the disillusioned spirit and moral ambiguity of the bourgeois class of this period.

Menander introduced the New Comedy in his works about 320 BCE and became its most famous exponent, writing in a quiet, witty style. Although most of his plays are lost, *Dyscolus* ("The Grouch") survives, along with large parts of *Perikeiromenē* ("The Shorn Girl"), *Epitrepontes* ("The Arbitration"), and *Samia* ("The Girl from Samos"). Menander's plays are mainly known through the works of the Roman dramatists Plautus and Terence, who translated and adapted them, along with other stock plots and characters of Greek New Comedy, for the Roman stage. Revived during the Renaissance, New Comedy influenced

MENANDER

(b. c. 342—d. c. 292 BCE)

Athenian dramatist whom ancient critics considered the supreme poet of Greek New Comedy (i.e., the last flowering of Athenian stage comedy). He produced his first play in 321 BCE and in 316 he won a festival prize with Dyscolus *("The Misanthrope"), the only one of his plays for which a complete text still exists. By the end of his career he had written more than one hundred plays and had won eight victories at Athenian dramatic festivals. Menander was considered by ancient critics the supreme poet of Greek New Comedy. He excelled at presenting characters such as stern fathers, young lovers, and intriguing slaves. As adapted by the Romans Plautus and Terence, his plays influenced the later development of Renaissance comedy.*

European drama down to the 18th century. The commedia erudita, plays from printed texts popular in Italy in the 16th century, and the improvisational commedia dell'arte that flourished in Europe from the 16th to the 18th century used characters and plot conventions that originated in Greek New Comedy. They were also used by Shakespeare and other Elizabethan and Restoration dramatists. Rodgers and Hart's *The Boys from Syracuse* (1938) is a musical version of Shakespeare's *Comedy of Errors,* which in turn is based on Plautus's *Menaechmi* and *Amphitruo,* which are adaptations of Greek New Comedy.

OLD COMEDY

The initial phase of ancient Greek comedy (c. 5th century BCE), Old Comedy is known through the works of Aristophanes. Old Comedy plays are characterized by an exuberant and high-spirited satire of public persons and affairs. Composed of song, dance, personal invective, and buffoonery, the plays also include outspoken political criticism and comment on literary and philosophical topics. The plays, consisting of loosely related episodes, were first performed in Athens for the religious festival of Dionysus. They gradually took on a six-part structure: an introduction, in which the basic fantasy is explained and developed; the *parodos,* entry of the chorus; the contest, or *agon,* a ritualized debate between opposing principals, usually stock characters; the *parabasis,* in which the chorus addresses the audience on the topics of the day and hurls scurrilous criticism at prominent citizens; a series of farcical scenes; and a final banquet or wedding. The chorus often were dressed as animals, while the characters wore street dress and masks with grotesque features.

Old Comedy sometimes is called Aristophanic comedy, after its most famous exponent, whose 11 surviving plays include *The Clouds* (423 BCE), a satire on the misuse of philosophical argument directed chiefly against Socrates, and *The Frogs* (405 BCE), a satire on Greek drama directed chiefly against Euripides. Other Old Comedy writers include Cratinus, Crates, Pherecrates, and Eupolis.

Athens's defeat in the Peloponnesian War signaled the end of Old Comedy, because a sense of disillusionment with the heroes and gods who had played a prominent role in Old Comedy became marked.

SATYR PLAY

The satyr play is a genre of ancient Greek drama that preserves the structure and characters of tragedy while adopting a happy atmosphere and a rural background. The satyr play can be considered the reversal of Attic tragedy, a kind of "joking tragedy." The actors play mythical heroes engaged in action drawn from traditional mythical tales, but the chorus members are satyrs, guided by old Silenus. Satyrs are nature spirits who combine male human traits (beards, hairy bodies, flat noses, and an erect phallus) with the ears and tails of horses. The satyrs are contrasted with the main characters—who are more or less serious—by their dancing, their love of wine, and their diverting banter, often expressed in low language. This contrast, which is the special trait of satyric drama, served to alleviate the emotional tension of the tragic trilogy.

The usual interpretation is that the satyr plays were presented directly after the tragic trilogy, as the fourth play in competitions. They are regularly listed fourth in lists of plays put on at the Great (or City) Dionysia in Athens. Some satyr plays by Aeschylus seem to

In the ancient Greek satyr play, the merry, frolicking satyr contrasts with the more serious main characters. The Bridgeman Art Library/Getty Images

make more sense as the second play of the group, however, such as the *Sphinx* in his Theban trilogy and *Proteus* in his *Oresteia*. According to tradition, Pratinas of Phlius was the first to produce a satyr play, at Athens in the 70th Olympiad (499–496 BCE).

Under the influence of comedy, the growing sophistication of Athenian audiences reduced the need for satyr plays to produce comic relief, as is seen in *Alcestis* (438 BCE), the fourth drama produced by Euripides, which is almost completely lacking in the genre's

traditional characteristics. Only one traditional satyr play, Euripides' *Cyclops*, survives. However, papyrus discoveries have revealed significant fragments of others, especially the *Dictyulci* ("Net Fishers") of Aeschylus and the *Ichneutae* ("Trackers") of Sophocles.

SENTIMENTAL COMEDY

A dramatic genre of the 18th century, the sentimental comedy is a play in which middle-class protagonists triumphantly overcome a series of moral trials. Such comedy aimed at producing tears rather than laughter. Sentimental comedies reflected contemporary philosophical conceptions of humans as inherently good but capable of being led astray through bad example. By an appeal to his noble sentiments, a man could be reformed and set back on the path of virtue. Although the plays contained characters whose natures seemed overly virtuous, and whose trials were too easily resolved, they were nonetheless accepted by audiences as truthful representations of the human predicament. Sentimental comedy had its roots in early 18th century tragedy, which had a vein of morality similar to that of sentimental comedy but had loftier characters and subject matter than sentimental comedy.

Writers of sentimental comedy included Colley Cibber and George Farquhar, with their respective plays *Love's Last Shift* (1696) and *The Constant Couple* (1699). The best-known sentimental comedy is Sir Richard Steele's *The Conscious Lovers* (1722), which deals with the trials and tribulations of its penniless heroine Indiana. The discovery that she is an heiress affords the necessary happy resolution. Steele, in describing the affect he wished the play to have, said he would like to arouse "a pleasure too exquisite for laughter." Sentimental comedies continued to coexist with such conventional comedies as Oliver Goldsmith's *She Stoops to Conquer* (1773) and Richard Brinsley Sheridan's *The Rivals* (1775) until the sentimental genre waned in the early 19th century.

In France comédie larmoyante, similar to sentimental comedy, was written principally by Pierre-Claude Nivelle de La Chaussée, whose *Le Préjugé à la mode* (1735; "Fashionable Prejudice") is a good example of the genre.

CHAPTER 7

TRAGEDY

Tragedy is a major branch of drama, which treats in a serious and dignified style the sorrowful or terrible events encountered or caused by a heroic individual. By extension the term may be applied to other literary works, such as the novel.

Although the word *tragedy* is often used loosely to describe any sort of disaster or misfortune, it more precisely refers to a work of art that probes with high seriousness questions concerning the role of man in the universe. The Greeks of Attica, the ancient state whose chief city was Athens, first used the word in the 5th century BCE to describe a specific kind of play, which was presented at festivals in Greece. Sponsored by the local governments, these plays were attended by the entire community, a small admission fee being provided by the state for those who could not afford it themselves. The atmosphere surrounding the performances was more like that of a religious ceremony than entertainment. There were altars to the gods, with priests in attendance, and the subjects of the tragedies were the misfortunes of the heroes of legend, religious myth, and history. Most of the material was derived from the works of Homer and was common knowledge in the Greek communities. So powerful were the achievements of the three greatest Greek dramatists—Aeschylus (525–456 BCE), Sophocles (c. 496–406 BCE), and Euripides (c. 480–406 BCE)— that the word they first used for their plays survived and came to describe a literary genre that, in spite of many transformations and lapses, has proved its viability through 25 centuries.

Historically, tragedy of a high order has been created in only four periods and locales: Attica, in Greece, in the 5th century BCE; England in the reigns of Elizabeth I and James I, from 1558 to 1625; 17th-century France; and Europe and America during the second half of the 19th century and the first half of the 20th. Each period saw the development of a special orientation and emphasis, a characteristic style of theatre. In the modern period, roughly from the middle of the 19th century, the idea of tragedy found embodiment in the collateral form of the novel.

ORIGINS IN GREECE

The questions of how and why tragedy came into being and of the bearing of its origins on its development in subsequent ages and cultures have been investigated by historians, philologists, archaeologists, and anthropologists with results that are suggestive but conjectural. Even the etymology of the word *tragedy* is far from established. The most generally accepted source is the Greek *tragōidia*, or "goat-song," from *tragos* ("goat") and *aeidein* ("to sing"). The word could have referred either to the prize, a goat, that was awarded to the dramatists whose plays won the earliest competitions or to the dress (goat skins) of the performers, or to the goat that was sacrificed in the rituals from which tragedy developed.

In these communal celebrations, a choric dance may have been the first formal element and perhaps for centuries was the principal element. A speaker was later introduced into the ritual, in all likelihood as an extension of the role of the priest, and dialogue was established between him and the dancers, who became the chorus in the Athenian drama. Aeschylus is usually regarded as the one who, realizing the dramatic possibilities of the dialogue, first added a second speaker and thus invented the form of tragedy. That so sophisticated a form could have been fully developed by a single artist, however, is scarcely credible. Hundreds of early tragedies have been lost, including some by Aeschylus himself. Of some 90 plays attributed to him, only seven have survived.

Four Dionysia, or Bacchanalia, feasts of the Greek god Dionysus (Bacchus), were held annually in Athens. Because Dionysus once held place as the god of vegetation and the vine, and the goat was believed sacred to him, it has been conjectured that tragedy originated in fertility feasts to commemorate the harvest and the vintage and the associated ideas of the death and renewal of life. The purpose of such rituals is to exercise some influence over these vital forces. Whatever the original religious connections of tragedy may have been, two elements have never entirely been lost: (1) its high seriousness, befitting matters in which survival is at issue and (2) its involvement of the entire community in matters of ultimate and common concern. When either element diminishes, when the form is overmixed with satiric, comic, or sentimental elements, or when the theatre of concern succumbs to the theatre of entertainment, then tragedy falls from its high estate and is on its way to becoming something else.

As the Greeks developed it, the tragic form, more than any other, raised questions about human existence. Why must humans suffer? Why must humans be forever torn between the seeming irreconcilable forces of good and evil, freedom and necessity, truth and deceit? Are the causes of suffering outside of oneself, in blind chance, in the evil designs of others, in the malice of the gods? Are its causes internal, and does one bring suffering upon oneself through arrogance, infatuation, or the tendency to overreach? Why is justice so elusive?

AESCHYLUS: THE FIRST GREAT TRAGEDIAN

It is this last question that Aeschylus asks most insistently in his two most famous works, the *Oresteia* (a trilogy comprising *Agamemnon*, *Choephoroi*, and *Eumenides*) and *Prometheus Bound* (the first part of a trilogy of which the last two parts have been lost): Is it right that Orestes, a young man in no way responsible for his situation, should be commanded by a god, in the name of justice, to avenge his father by murdering his mother? Is there no other way out of his dilemma than through the ancient code of blood revenge, which will only compound the dilemma? Again: Was it right that Prometheus, in befriending humankind with the gifts of fire

Aeschylus, marble bust. Photos.com/ Jupiterimages

and the arts, should offend the presiding god Zeus and himself be horribly punished? Aeschylus opened questions whose answers in the Homeric stories had been taken for granted. In Homer, Orestes' patricide is regarded as an act of filial piety, and Prometheus's punishment is merely the inevitable consequence of defying the reigning deity. All the materials of tragedy, all its cruelty, loss, and suffering, are present in Homer and the ancient myths but are dealt with as absolutes—self-sufficient and without the questioning spirit that was necessary to raise them to the level of tragedy. It remained for Aeschylus and his fellow tragedians first to treat these "absolutes" critically and creatively in sustained dramatic form. They were true explorers of the human spirit.

In addition to their remarkable probing into the nature of existence, their achievements included a degree of psychological insight for which they are not generally given credit. Though such praise is usually reserved for Shakespeare and the moderns, the Athenian dramatists conveyed a vivid sense of the living reality of their characters' experience: of what it felt like to be caught, like Orestes, in desperately conflicting loyalties or to be subjected, like Prometheus, to prolonged and unjust punishment. The mood of the audience as it witnessed the acting out of these climactic experiences has been described as one of impassioned contemplation. From their myths and epics and from their history in the 6th century, the people of Athens learned that they could extend an empire and lay the foundations of a great culture. From their tragedies of the 5th century, they learned who they were, something of the possibilities and limitations of the spirit, and of what it meant, not merely what it felt like, to be alive in a world both beautiful and terrible.

Aeschylus has been called the most theological of the Greek tragedians. His *Prometheus* has been compared to the Book of Job of the Bible both in its structure (i.e., the immobilized heroic figure maintaining his cause in dialogues with visitors) and in its preoccupation with the problem of suffering at the hands of a seemingly unjust deity. Aeschylus tended to resolve the dramatic problem into some degree of harmony, as scattered evidence suggests he did in the last two parts of the *Promethiad* and as he certainly did in the conclusion of the *Oresteia*. This tendency would conceivably lead him out of the realm of tragedy and into religious assurance. But his harmonies are never complete. In his plays evil is inescapable, loss is irretrievable, suffering is inevitable. What the plays say positively is that one can learn through suffering. The chorus in *Agamemnon*, the first play of the *Oresteia*, says this twice. The capacity to learn through suffering is a distinguishing characteristic of the tragic hero, preeminently of the Greek tragic hero. He has not merely courage, tenacity, and endurance but also the ability to grow, by means of these qualities, into an understanding of himself, of his fellows, and of the conditions of existence. Suffering, says Aeschylus, need not be embittering but can be a source of knowledge. The moral force of his plays and those of his fellow tragedians can hardly be exaggerated. They were shaping agents in the Greek notion of education. It has been said that from Homer the Greeks learned how to be good Greeks and from the tragedies they learned an enlarged humanity. If it cannot be proved that Aeschylus "invented" tragedy, it is clear that he at least set its tone and established a model that is still operative. Such 20th-century dramatists as T.S. Eliot, in *The Family Reunion* (1939), and Jean-Paul Sartre, in *The Flies* (1943), found modern relevance in its archetypal characters, situations, and themes, and in the 21st century the *Oresteia* is still considered one of the greatest spiritual works written.

SOPHOCLES: THE PUREST ARTIST

Sophocles' life spanned almost the whole of the 5th century. He is said to have written his last play, *Oedipus at Colonus*, at age 90. Only seven of his plays, of some 125 attributed to him, survive. He won the prize in the tragic competitions 20 times and never placed lower than second.

Sophocles has been called the great mediating figure between Aeschylus and Euripides. Of the three, it might be said that Aeschylus tended to resolve tragic tensions into higher truth, to look beyond, or above, tragedy; that Euripides' irony and bitterness led him the other way to fix on the disintegration of the individual; and that Sophocles, who is often called the "purest" artist of the three, was truest to the actual state of human experience. Unlike the others, Sophocles seems never to insinuate himself into his characters or situations, never to manipulate them into preconceived patterns. He sets them free on a course seemingly of their own choosing. He neither preaches nor rails. If life is hard and often destructive, the question Sophocles asks is not how did this come to be or why did such a misfortune have to happen but rather, given the circumstances, how must one conduct oneself, how should one act, and what must one do.

His greatest play, *Oedipus the King*, may serve as a model of his total dramatic achievement. Embodied in it, and suggested with extraordinary dramatic tact, are all the basic questions of tragedy, which are presented in such a way as almost to define the form itself. It is not surprising that Aristotle, a century later, analyzed it for his definition of tragedy in the *Poetics*. It is the nuclear Greek tragedy, setting the norm in a way that cannot be claimed for any other work, not even the *Oresteia*.

In *Oedipus*, as in Sophocles' other plays, the chorus is much less prominent than in Aeschylus's works. The action is swifter and more highly articulated. The dialogue is sharper, more staccato, and bears more of the meaning of the play. Though much has been made of the influence of fate on the action of the play, later critics emphasize the freedom with which Oedipus acts throughout. Even before the action of the play begins, the oracle's prediction that Oedipus was doomed to kill his father and marry his mother had long since come true, though he did not realize it. Though he was fated, he was also free throughout the course of the play—free to make decision after decision, to carry out his freely purposed action to its completion. In him, Sophocles achieved one of the enduring definitions of the tragic hero—that of a man for whom the liberation of the self is a necessity. The action of the play, the purpose of which is to discover the murderer of Oedipus's father and thereby to free the city from its curse, inevitably leads to Oedipus's suffering—the loss of his wife, kingdom, and sight. The messenger who reports Oedipus's self-blinding might well have summarized the play with "All ills that there are names for, all are here." And the chorus's final summation deepens the note of despair: "Count no man happy," they say in essence, "until he is dead."

But these were not Sophocles' ultimate verdicts. The action is so presented that the final impression is not of human helplessness at the hands of maligning gods nor of man as the pawn of fate. Steering his own course, with great courage, Oedipus has ferreted out the truth of his identity and administered his own punishment, and, in his suffering, learned a new humanity. The final impression of the *Oedipus*, far from being one of unmixed evil and nihilism, is of massive integrity, powerful will, and magnanimous acceptance of a horribly altered existence.

Some 50 years later, Sophocles wrote a sequel to *Oedipus the King*. In *Oedipus at Colonus*, the old Oedipus, further schooled in suffering, is seen during his last day alive. He is still the same Oedipus in many ways: hot-tempered, hating his enemies, contentious. Though he admits his "pollution" in the murder of his father and the marriage to his mother, he denies that he had sinned, because he had done both deeds unwittingly. Throughout the play, the theme of which has been described as the "heroization" of Oedipus, he grows steadily in nobility and awesomeness. Finally, sensing the approach of the end, he leaves the scene, to be elevated in death to a demigod, as the messenger describes the miraculous

event. In such manner Sophocles leads his tragedy toward an ultimate assertion of values. His position has been described as "heroic humanism," as making a statement of belief in the human capacity to transcend evils, within and without, by means of the human condition itself.

Tragedy must maintain a balance between the higher optimisms of religion or philosophy, or any other beliefs that tend to explain away the enigmas and afflictions of existence, on the one hand, and the pessimism that would reject the whole human experiment as valueless and futile on the other. Thus the opposite of tragedy is not comedy but the literature of cynicism and despair, and the opposite of the tragic artist's stance, which is one of compassion and involvement, is that of the detached and cynical ironist.

EURIPIDES: THE DARK TRAGEDIAN

The tragedies of Euripides test the Sophoclean norm in this direction. His plays present in gruelling detail the wreck of human lives under the stresses that the gods often seem willfully to place upon them. Or, if the gods are not willfully involved through jealousy or spite, they sit idly by while an individual wrecks himself through passion or heedlessness. No Euripidean hero approaches Oedipus in stature. The margin of freedom is narrower, and the question of justice, so central and absolute an ideal for Aeschylus, becomes a subject for irony. In *Hippolytus*, for example, the goddess

Aphrodite never thinks of justice as she takes revenge on the young Hippolytus for neglecting her worship. She acts solely out of personal spite. In *Medea*, Medea's revenge on Jason through the slaughter of their children is so hideously unjust as to mock the very question. In the *Bacchae*, when the frenzied Agave tears her own son, Pentheus, to pieces and marches into town with his head on a pike, the god Dionysus, who had engineered the situation, says merely that Pentheus should not have scorned him. The Euripidean gods, in short, cannot be appealed to in the name of justice. Euripides' tendency toward moral neutrality, his cool tacking between sides (e.g., between Pentheus versus Dionysus and the bacchantes) leave the audience virtually unable to make a moral decision. In Aeschylus's *Eumenides* (the last play of the *Oresteia*), the morals of the gods improve. Athena is there, on the stage, helping to solve the problem of justice. In Sophocles, while the gods are distant, their moral governance is not questioned. *Oedipus* ends as if with a mighty "So be it." In Euripides, the gods are destructive, wreaking their capricious wills on the defenseless. Aristotle called Euripides the most tragic of the three dramatists. Surely his depiction of the arena of human life is the grimmest.

Many qualities, however, keep his tragedies from becoming literature of protest, of cynicism, or of despair. He reveals profound psychological insight, as in the delineation of such antipodal characters as Jason and Medea, or of the forces, often subconscious, at work in the

Euripides, marble herm copied from a Greek original, c. 340–330 BCE; in the Museo Archeologico Nazionale, Naples. Courtesy of the Soprintendenza alle Antichita della Campania, Naples

group frenzy of the *Bacchae*. His Bacchic odes reveal remarkable lyric power. And he has a deep sense of human values, however external and self-conscious. Medea, even in the fury of her hatred for Jason and her lust for revenge, must steel herself to the murder of her children, realizing the evil of what she is about to do. In this realization, Euripides suggests a saving hope: here is a great nature gone wrong—but still a great nature.

LATER GREEK DRAMA

After Euripides, Greek drama reveals little that is significant to the history of tragedy.

Performances continued to be given in theatres throughout the Mediterranean world, but, with the decline of Athens as a city-state, the tradition of tragedy eroded. As external affairs deteriorated, the high idealism, the exalted sense of human capacities depicted in tragedy at its height, yielded more and more to the complaints of the Skeptics. The Euripidean assault on the gods ended in the debasement of the original lofty conceptions. A 20th-century British Classical scholar, Gilbert Murray, used the phrase "the failure of nerve" to describe the late Greek world. It may, indeed, provide a clue to what happened. Conversely, according to the 19th-century German philosopher Friedrich Nietzsche, in *The Birth of Tragedy* (1872), a quite different influence may have spelled the end of Greek tragedy: the so-called Socratic optimism, the notion underlying the dialogues of Plato that an individual could "know himself" through the exercise of reason in patient, careful dialectic—a notion that diverted questions of human existence away from drama and into philosophy. In any case, the balance for tragedy was upset, and the theatre of Aeschylus, Sophocles, and Euripides gave way to what seems to have been a theatre of diatribe, spectacle, and entertainment.

THE LONG HIATUS

The Roman world failed to revive tragedy. Seneca (4 BCE–65 CE) wrote at least eight tragedies, mostly adaptations of Greek materials, such as the stories of Oedipus, Hippolytus, and Agamemnon, but with little of the Greek tragic feeling for character and theme. The emphasis is on sensation and rhetoric, tending toward melodrama and bombast. The plays are of interest in this context mainly as the not entirely healthy inspiration for the precursors of Elizabethan tragedy in England.

The long hiatus in the history of tragedy between the Greeks and the Elizabethans has been variously explained. In the Golden Age of Roman literature, roughly from the birth of Virgil in 70 BCE to the death of Ovid in 17 CE, the Roman poets followed the example of Greek literature. Although they produced great lyric and epic verse, their tragic drama lacked the probing freshness and directness fundamental to tragedy.

With the collapse of the Roman world and the invasions of the barbarians came the beginnings of the long, slow development of the Christian church. Churchmen and philosophers gradually forged a system, based on Christian revelation, of human nature and destiny. The mass, with its daily reenactment of the sacrifice of Jesus Christ, its music, and its dramatic structure, may have provided something comparable to tragic drama in the lives of the people.

With the coming of the Renaissance, the visual arts more and more came to represent the afflictive aspects of life, and the word *tragedy* again came into currency. Geoffrey Chaucer used the word in *Troilus and Criseyde*, and in *The Canterbury Tales* it is applied to a series of stories in the medieval style of *de casibus virorum illustrium,* meaning "the downfalls (more or less inevitable) of princes." Chaucer used the word to signify little more than the turn of the wheel of fortune, against whose force no meaningful human effort is possible. It remained for the Elizabethans to develop a theatre and a dramatic literature that reinstated the term on a level comparable to that of the Greeks.

ELIZABETHAN

The long beginning of the Elizabethan popular theatre, like that of the Greek theatre, lay in religious ceremonials, probably in the drama in the liturgy of the two greatest events in the Christian year, Christmas and Easter. In the early church, exchanges between two groups of choristers, or between the choir and a solo voice, led to the idea of dialogue, just as it had in the development of Greek tragedy. The parts became increasingly elaborate, and costumes were introduced to individualize the characters. Dramatic gestures and actions were a natural development. More and more biblical stories were dramatized, much as Homer's material was used by the Greek tragedians, although piously in this instance, with none of the tragic skepticism of the Greeks. In the course of generations, the popularity of the performances grew to such an extent that, to accommodate the crowds, they were moved, from inside the church to the porch, or square, in front of the church. The next step was

the secularization of the management of the productions, as the towns and cities took them over. Daylong festivals were instituted, involving, as in the Greek theatre, the whole community. Cycles of plays were performed at York, Chester, and other English religious centres, depicting in sequences of short dramatic episodes the whole human story, from the Fall of Lucifer and the Creation to the Day of Doom. Each play was assigned to an appropriate trade guild (the story of Noah and the Ark, for example, went to the shipwrights), which took over complete responsibility for the production. Hundreds of actors and long preparation went into the festivals. These "miracle" and "mystery" plays, however crude they may now seem, dealt with the loftiest of subjects in simple but often powerful eloquence. Although the audience must have been a motley throng, it may well have been as involved and concerned as those of the Greek theatre.

Once the drama became a part of the secular life of the communities, popular tastes affected its religious orientation. Comic scenes, like those involving Noah's nagging wife, a purely secular creation who does not appear in the Bible, became broader. The "tragic" scenes—anything involving the Devil or Doomsday—became more and more melodramatic. With the Renaissance came the rediscovery of the Greek and Roman cultures and the consequent development of a world view that led away from moral and spiritual absolutes and toward an increasingly skeptical individualism. The high poetic spirits of the mid-16th century began to turn the old medieval forms of the miracles and mysteries to new uses and to look to the ancient plays, particularly the lurid tragedies of Seneca, for their models. A bloody play, *Gorboduc*, by Thomas Sackville and Thomas Norton, first acted in 1561, is now known as the first formal tragedy in English, though it is far from fulfilling the high offices of the form in tone, characterization, and theme. Thomas Kyd's *Spanish Tragedie* (c. 1589) continued the Senecan tradition of the "tragedy of blood" with somewhat more sophistication than *Gorboduc* but even more bloodletting. Elizabethan tragedy never freed itself completely from certain melodramatic aspects of the influence of Seneca.

MARLOWE AND THE FIRST CHRISTIAN TRAGEDY

The first tragedian worthy of the tradition of the Greeks was Christopher Marlowe. Of Marlowe's tragedies, *Tamburlaine* (1587), *Doctor Faustus* (c. 1588), *The Jew of Malta* (1589), and *Edward II* (1594), the first two are the most famous and most significant. In *Tamburlaine*, the material was highly melodramatic. The historical figure's popular image was that of the most ruthless and bloody of conquerors. In a verse prologue, when Marlowe invites the audience to "View but his [Tamburlaine's] picture in this tragic glass," he had in mind little more, perhaps, than the trappings and tone of

tragedy: "the stately tent of war," which is to be his scene, and "the high astounding terms," which will be his rhetoric. But he brought such imaginative vigour and sensitivity to bear that melodrama is transcended, in terms reminiscent of high tragedy. Tamburlaine, a Scythian shepherd of the 14th century, becomes the spokesman, curiously enough, for the new world of the Renaissance—iconoclastic, independent, stridently ambitious. Just as the Greek tragedians challenged tradition, Tamburlaine shouts defiance at all the norms, religious and moral, that Marlowe's generation inherited. But Tamburlaine, although he is an iconoclast, is also a poet. No one before him on the English stage had talked with such magnificent lyric power as he does, whether it be on the glories of conquest or on the beauties of Zenocrate, his beloved. When, still unconquered by any enemy, he sickens and dies, he leaves the feeling that something great, however ruthless, has gone. Here once again is the ambiguity that was so much a part of the Greek tragic imagination—the combination of awe, pity, and fear that Aristotle defined.

In *Doctor Faustus* the sense of conflict between the tradition and the new Renaissance individualism is much greater. The claims of revealed Christianity are presented in the orthodox spirit of the morality and mystery plays, but Faustus's yearnings for power over space and time are also presented with a sympathy that cannot be denied. Here is modern man, tragic modern man,

CHRISTOPHER MARLOWE

(baptized Feb. 26, 1564, Canterbury, Kent, Eng.—d. May 30, 1593, Deptford, near London)

The British poet and playwright Christopher Marlowe was Shakespeare's most important predecessor in English drama. The son of a Canterbury shoemaker, he earned a degree from Cambridge University. From 1587 he wrote plays for London theatres, starting with Tamburlaine the Great *(published 1590), in which he established dramatic blank verse.* Tamburlaine *was followed by* Dido, Queen of Carthage *(published 1594), cowritten with Thomas Nashe;* The Massacre at Paris *(c. 1594); and* Edward II *(1594). His most famous play is* The Tragicall History of Doctor Faustus *(published 1604), which uses the dramatic framework of a morality play in its presentation of a story of temptation, fall, and damnation.* The Jew of Malta *(published 1633) may have been his final work. His poetry includes the unfinished long poem* Hero and Leander. *Known for leading a disreputable life, he died a violent death at age 29 in a tavern brawl. He may have been assassinated because of his service as a government spy.*

torn between the faith of tradition and faith in himself. Faustus takes the risk in the end and is bundled off to hell in true mystery-play fashion. But the final scene does not convey that justice has been done, even though Faustus admits that his fate is just. Rather, the scene suggests that the transcendent human individual has been caught in the consequences of a dilemma that he might have avoided but that no imaginative person *could* have avoided. The sense of the interplay of fate and freedom is not unlike that of *Oedipus.* The sense of tragic ambiguity is more poignant in Faustus than in *Oedipus* or *Tamburlaine* because Faustus is far more introspective than either of the other heroes. The conflict is inner. The battle is for Faustus's soul, a kind of conflict that neither the Greeks nor Tamburlaine had to contend with. For this reason, and not because it advocates

Christian doctrine, the play has been called the first Christian tragedy.

SHAKESPEAREAN TRAGEDY

Shakespeare was a long time coming to his tragic phase, the six or seven years that produced his five greatest tragedies—*Hamlet* (written c. 1599–1601), *Othello* (written c. 1603–04), *King Lear* (c. 1605–06), *Macbeth* (c. 1606–07), and *Antony and Cleopatra* (c. 1606–07). These were not the only plays written during those years. *Troilus and Cressida* (1601–02) may have come about the same time as or shortly after *Hamlet, All's Well That Ends Well* (1601–05) shortly before or after *Othello,* and *Measure for Measure* (1603–04) shortly before *King Lear.* But the concentration of tragedies is sufficient to distinguish this period from that of the comedies and history plays before and that of the so-called romances afterward.

Although the tragic period cannot entirely be accounted for in terms of biography, social history, or current stage fashions, all of which have been adduced as causes, certain questions should be answered, at least tentatively: What is Shakespeare's major tragic theme and method? How do they relate to Classical, medieval, and Renaissance traditions? In attempting to answer these questions, this proviso must be kept in mind: the degree to which he was consciously working in these traditions, consciously shaping his plays on early models, adapting Greek and Roman themes to his own purpose, or following the precepts of Aristotle must always remain conjectural. On the one hand, there is the comment by Ben Jonson that Shakespeare had "small Latin and less Greek," and John Milton in "L'Allegro" speaks of him as "fancy's child" warbling "his native wood-notes wild," as if he were unique, a sport of nature. On the other hand, Shakespeare knew Jonson (who knew a great deal of Latin and Greek) and is said to have acted in Jonson's *Sejanus* in 1603, a particularly Classical play, published in 1605 with a learned essay on Aristotle as preface. It can be assumed that Shakespeare knew the tradition. Certainly, the Elizabethan theatre could not have existed without the Greek and Roman prototype. For all its mixed nature—with comic and melodramatic elements jostling the tragic—the Elizabethan theatre retained some of the high concern, the sense of involvement, and even the ceremonial atmosphere of the Greek theatre. When tragedies were performed, the stage was draped in black. Modern studies have shown that the Elizabethan theatre retained many ties with both the Middle Ages and the tradition of the Greeks.

FROM COMEDY TO TRAGEDY

Shakespeare's earliest and most light-hearted plays reveal a sense of the individual, his innerness, his reality, his difference from every other individual, and, at times, his plight. Certain stock characters, to be sure, appear in the early comedies. Even Falstaff, that triumphant individual, has a prototype in the braggadocio of Roman comedy, and even Falstaff has his tragic side. As Shakespeare's art developed, his concern for the plight or predicament or dilemma seems to have grown. His earliest history plays, for instance (*Henry VI*, Parts 1, 2, and 3), are little more than chronicles of the great pageant figures—kingship in all its colour and potency. *Richard III* (1592–94), which follows them, focuses with an intensity traditionally reserved for the tragic hero on one man and on the sinister forces, within and without, that bring him to destruction. From kingship, that is, Shakespeare turned to the king, the symbolic individual, the focal man, to whom whole societies look for their values and meanings. Thus Richard III is almost wholly sinister, though there exists a fascination about him, an all but tragic ambiguity.

Although Shakespeare's developing sense of the tragic cannot be summed up adequately in any formula, one might hazard the following: he progressed from the *individual* of the early comedies; to the *burdened* individual, such as, in *Henry IV*, Prince Hal, the future Henry V, who manipulates, rather than suffers, the tragic ambiguities of the world; and, finally, in the great tragedies, to (in one critic's phrase) the *overburdened* individual, Lear being generally regarded as the greatest example. In these last plays, man is at the limits of his sovereignty as a human being, where everything that he has lived by, stood for, or loved is put to the test. Like Prometheus on the crag, or Oedipus as he learns who he is, or Medea deserted by Jason, the Shakespearean tragic heroes are at the extremities of their natures. Hamlet and Macbeth are thrust to the very edge of sanity; Lear and, momentarily, Othello are thrust beyond it. In every case, as in the Greek plays, the destructive forces seem to combine inner inadequacies or evils, such as Lear's temper or Macbeth's ambition, with external pressures, such as Lear's "tiger daughters," the witches in *Macbeth*, or Lady Macbeth's importunity. Once the destructive course is set going, these forces operate with the relentlessness the Greeks called Moira, or Fate.

SHAKESPEARE'S TRAGIC ART

At the height of his powers, Shakespeare revealed a tragic vision that comprehended the totality of possibilities for good and evil as nearly as the human imagination ever has. His heroes are the vehicles of psychological, societal, and cosmic forces that tend to ennoble and glorify humanity or infect it and destroy it. The logic of tragedy that possessed him demanded an insistence upon the latter. Initially, his heroes make free choices and are free time after time to turn back, but they move toward their doom as relentlessly as did Oedipus. The total tragic statement, however, is not limited to the fate of the hero. He is but the centre of an action that takes place in a context involving many other characters, each contributing a point of view, a set of values or antivalues to the complex dialectic of the play. In Macbeth's demon-ridden Scotland, where weird things happen to men and horses turn cannibal, there is the virtuous Malcolm, and society survives. Hamlet had the trustworthy friend Horatio, and, for all the bloodletting, what was "rotten" was purged. In the tragedies, most notably *Lear*, the Aeschylean notion of "knowledge through suffering" is powerfully dramatized. Although it is most obvious in the hero, it is also shared by the society of which he is the focal figure. The flaw in the hero may be a moral failing or, sometimes, an excess of virtue. The flaw in society may be the rottenness of the Danish court in *Hamlet* or the corruption of the Roman world in *Antony and Cleopatra*. The flaw or fault or dislocation may be in the very universe itself, as dramatized by Lear's raving at the heavens or the ghosts that walk the plays or the witches that prophesy. All these faults, Shakespeare seems to be saying, are inevitabilities of the human condition. But they do not spell rejection, nihilism, or despair. The hero may die, but, in the words novelist E.M. Forster used to describe the redeeming power of tragedy, "he has given us life."

Such is the precarious balance a tragedian must maintain: the cold, clear vision that sees the evil but is not maddened by it, a sense of the good that is equally clear but refuses the blandishments of optimism or sentimentalism. Few have ever sustained the balance for long. Aeschylus tended to slide off to the right, Euripides to the left, and even Sophocles had his hero transfigured at Colonus. Marlowe's early death should perhaps spare him the criticism his first plays warrant. Shakespeare's last two tragedies, *Macbeth* and *Antony and Cleopatra*, are close to the edge of a valueless void. The atmosphere of *Macbeth* is murky with evil. The action moves with almost melodramatic speed from horror to horror. The forces for good rally at last, but Macbeth steadily deteriorates into the most nihilistic of all Shakespeare's tragic heroes, saved in nothing except the sense of a great nature, like Medea, gone wrong. *Antony and Cleopatra*, in its ambiguities and irony, has been considered close to the Euripidean line of bitterness and detachment. Shakespeare himself soon modulated into another mood in his last plays, *Cymbeline* (c. 1608–10), *The Winter's Tale* (c. 1609–11), and *The Tempest* (1611). Each is based on a situation that could have been developed into

major tragedy had Shakespeare followed out its logic as he had done with earlier plays. For whatever reason, however, he chose not to. The great tragic questions are not pressed. *The Tempest*, especially, for all Prospero's charm and magnanimity, gives a sense of brooding melancholy over the ineradicable evil in humankind, a patient but sad acquiescence. All of these plays end in varying degrees of harmony and reconciliation. Shakespeare willed it so.

DECLINE IN 17TH-CENTURY ENGLAND

From Shakespeare's tragedies to the closing of the theatres in England by the Puritans in 1642, the quality of tragedy is steadily worse, if the best of the Greek and Shakespearean tragedies are taken as a standard. Among the leading dramatists of the period—John Webster, Thomas Middleton, Francis Beaumont, John Fletcher, Cyril Tourneur, and John Ford—there were some excellent craftsmen and brilliant poets. Though each of them has a rightful place in the history of English drama, tragedy suffered a transmutation in their hands.

The Jacobean dramatists—those who flourished in England during the reign of James I—failed to transcend the negative tendencies they inherited from Elizabethan tragedy: a sense of defeat, a mood of spiritual despair implicit in Marlowe's tragic thought; in the nihilistic broodings of some of Shakespeare's characters in their worst moods—Hamlet,

Gloucester in *Lear*, Macbeth; in the metaphoric implication of the theme of insanity, of a human pressed beyond the limit of endurance, that runs through many of these tragedies; most importantly, perhaps, in the moral confusion ("fair is foul and foul is fair") that threatens to unbalance even the staunchest of Shakespeare's tragic heroes. This sinister tendency came to a climax about 1605 and was in part a consequence of the anxiety surrounding the death of Queen Elizabeth I and the accession of James I. Despite their negative tendencies, the Elizabethans, in general, had affirmed life and celebrated it; Shakespeare's moral balance, throughout even his darkest plays, remained firm. The Jacobeans, however, were possessed by death. They became superb analysts of moral confusion and the darkened vision of humanity at cross purposes, preying upon itself; of lust, hate, and intrigue engulfing what is left of beauty, love, and integrity. There is little that is redemptive or that suggests, as had Aeschylus, that evil might be resolved by the enlightenment gained from suffering. As in the tragedies of Euripides, the protagonist's margin of freedom grows ever smaller. "You are the deed's creature," cries a murderer to his unwitting lady accomplice in Middleton's *Changeling* (1622), and a prisoner of her deed she remains. Many of the plays maintained a pose of ironic, detached reportage, without the sense of sympathetic involvement that the greatest tragedians have conveyed from the beginning.

Some qualities of the highest tragedians have been claimed for John Webster. One critic points to his search for a moral order as a link to Shakespeare and sees in his moral vision a basis for renewal. Webster's *Duchess of Malfi* (c. 1612–13) has been interpreted as a final triumph of life over death. Overwhelmed by final unleashed terror, the Duchess affirms the essential dignity of humanity. Despite such vestiges of greatness, however, the trend of tragedy was downward. High moral sensitivity and steady conviction are required to resist the temptation to resolve the intolerable tensions of tragedy into either the comfort of optimism or the relaxed apathy of despair. Periods of the creation of high tragedy are therefore few and short-lived. The demands on artist and audience alike are enormous. Forms wear out, and public taste seems destined to go through inevitable cycles of health and disease. What is to one generation powerful and persuasive rhetoric becomes bombast and bathos to the next. The inevitable materials of tragedy—violence, madness, hate, and lust—soon lose their symbolic role and become perverted to the uses of melodrama and sensationalism, mixed, for relief, with the broadest comedy or farce.

These corruptions had gone too far when John Milton, 29 years after the closing of the theatres, attempted to bring back the true spirit and tone of tragedy, which he called "the gravest, moralest, and most profitable of all other Poems." His *Samson Agonistes* (1671), however, is magnificent "closet tragedy"—drama more suitable for reading than for popular performance. Modeled on the *Prometheus*, it recalls Aeschylus's tragedy both in its form, in which the immobilized hero receives a sequence of visitors, and in its theme, in which there is a resurgence of the hero's spirit under stress. With Restoration comedy in full swing, however, and with the "heroic play" (an overly moralized version of tragedy) about to reach its crowning achievement in John Dryden's *All for Love* only seven years later (published 1678), *Samson Agonistes* was an anachronism.

NEOCLASSICAL ERA

The Neoclassical era may be best represented by the work of Pierre Corneille, who produced an astonishing variety of plays for nearly 40 years. He also prepared the way for a dramatic theatre that was the envy of Europe throughout the 17th century. His own contribution to this theatre, moreover, was that of master as much as of pioneer.

Corneille and Racine

Both Corneille and after him Racine also attempted to bring back the ancient form in France. The French Classical tragedy, whose monuments are Pierre Corneille's *Cid* (1637) and Jean Racine's *Bérénice* (1670) and *Phèdre* (1677), made no attempt to be popular in the way of the Elizabethan theatre. The plays were written by and for intellectual aristocrats, who came together in an elite theatre, patronized by royalty and nobility. Gone were the bustle and pageantry of the Elizabethan tragedies, with their admixtures of whatever modes and moods the dramatists thought would work. The French playwrights submitted themselves to the severe discipline they derived from the Greek models and especially the "rules," as they interpreted them, laid down by Aristotle. The unities of place, time, and action were strictly observed.

One theme, the conflict between Passion and Reason, was uppermost. The path of Reason was the path of Duty and Obligation (noblesse oblige), and that path had been clearly plotted by moralists and philosophers, both ancient and modern. In this sense there was nothing exploratory in the French tragedy; existing moral and spiritual norms were demanded. The norms are never criticized or tested as Aeschylus challenged the Olympians or as Marlowe presented, with startling sympathy, the Renaissance overreacher. Corneille's *Cid* shows Duty triumphant over Passion, and, as a reward, hero and heroine are happily united.

By the time of *Phèdre*, Corneille's proud affirmation of the power of the will and the reason over passion had given way to what Racine called "stately sorrow," with which he asks the audience to contemplate Phèdre's heroic, but losing, moral struggle. Her passion for her stepson, Hippolyte, bears her down relentlessly. Her fine principles and heroic will are of no avail. Both she and Hippolyte are destroyed. The action is limited to one terrible day; there is no change of scene; there is neither comic digression nor relief—the focus on the process by which a great nature goes down is sharp and intense. Such is the power of Racine's poetry (it is untranslatable), his conception of character, and his penetrating analysis of it, that it suggests the presence of Sophoclean "heroic humanism." In this sense it could be said that Racine tested the norms, that he uncovered a cruel injustice in the nature of a code that could destroy such a person as Phèdre. Once again, here is a world of tragic ambiguity, in which no precept or prescription can answer complicated human questions.

THE ENGLISH "HEROIC PLAY"

This ambiguity was all but eliminated in the "heroic play" that vied with the comedy of the Restoration stage in England in the latter part of the 17th century. After the vicissitudes of the Civil War, the age was hungry for heroism. An English philosopher of the time, Thomas Hobbes, defined the purpose of the type: "The work of an heroic poem is to raise admiration, principally for three virtues, valour, beauty, and love." Moral concern, beginning with Aeschylus, has always been central in tragedy, but in the works of the great tragedians this concern was exploratory and inductive. The moral concern of the heroic play is the reverse. It is deductive and dogmatic. The first rule, writes Dryden (following the contemporary French critic, René Le Bossu)

in his preface to his *Troilus and Cressida* (1679), is "to make the moral of the work; that is, to lay down to yourself what that precept of morality shall be, which you would insinuate into the people." In *All for Love* the moral is all too clear: Antony must choose between the path of honour and his illicit passion for Cleopatra. He chooses Cleopatra, and they are both destroyed. Only Dryden's poetry, with its air of emotional argumentation, manages to convey human complexities in spite of his moral bias and saves the play from artificiality—makes it, in fact, the finest near-tragic production of its age.

THE ECLIPSE OF TRAGEDY

Although the annals of the drama from Dryden onward are filled with plays called tragedies by their authors, the form as it has been defined here went into an eclipse during the late 17th, the 18th, and the early 19th centuries. Reasons that have been suggested for the decline include the politics of the Restoration in England; the rise of science and, with it, the optimism of the Enlightenment throughout Europe; the developing middle-class economy; the trend toward reassuring Deism in theology; and, in literature, the rise of the novel and the vogue of satire. The genius of the age was discursive and rationalistic. In France and later in England, belief in Evil was reduced to the perception of evils, which were looked upon as institutional and therefore remediable. The nature of man was no longer the problem; rather, it was the better organization and management of men. The old haunting fear and mystery, the sense of ambiguity at the centre of human nature and of dark forces working against humankind in the universe, were replaced by a new and confident dogma.

Tragedy never lost its high prestige in the minds of the leading spirits. Theorizing upon it were men of letters as diverse as Samuel Johnson, David Hume, Samuel Taylor Coleridge, and Percy Bysshe Shelley and German philosophers from Gotthold Lessing in the 18th century to Friedrich Nietzsche in the 19th.

Revivals of Shakespeare's tragedies were often bowdlerized or altered, as in the happy ending for *Lear* in a production of 1681. Those who felt themselves called upon to write tragedies produced little but weak imitations. Shelley tried it once, in *The Cenci* (1819), but, as his wife wrote, "the bent of his mind went the other way"—which way may be seen in his *Prometheus Unbound* (1820), in which Zeus is overthrown and a golden age, ruled by the power of love, is born. Goethe had the sense to stay away from tragedy: "The mere attempt to write tragedy," he said, "might be my undoing." He concluded his two-part *Faust* (1808, 1832) in the spirit of the 19th-century optimistic humanitarianism. It was not until the latter part of the 19th century, with the plays of a Norwegian, Henrik Ibsen, a Russian, Anton Chekhov, a Swede, August Strindberg, and, later, an American, Eugene O'Neill, that something of the original vision returned to inspire the tragic theatre.

A NEW VEHICLE: THE NOVEL

The theme and spirit of tragedy, meanwhile, found a new vehicle in the novel. This development is important, however far afield it may seem from the work of the formal dramatists. The English novelist Emily Brontë's *Wuthering Heights* (1847), in its grim Yorkshire setting, reflects the original concerns of tragedy: that is, the terrifying divisions in nature and human nature, love that creates and destroys, character at once fierce and pitiable, destructive actions that are willed yet seemingly destined, as if by a malicious fate, yet the whole controlled by an imagination that learns as it goes.

Another English novelist, Thomas Hardy, in the preface to *The Woodlanders* (1887), speaks of the rural setting of this and other of his novels as being comparable to the stark and simple setting of the Greek theatre, giving his novels something of that drama's intensity and sharpness of focus. His grimly pessimistic view of human nature and destiny and of the futility of human striving, as reflected in his novels *The Return of the Native* (1878), *Tess of the d'Urbervilles* (1891), and *Jude the Obscure* (1895), is barely redeemed for tragedy by his sense of the beauty of nature and of the beauty and dignity of human character and effort, however unavailing.

The work of the Polish-born English novelist Joseph Conrad provides another kind of setting for novels used as vehicles of the tragic sense. *Lord Jim* (1900), originally conceived as a short story, grew to a full-length novel as Conrad found himself exploring in ever greater depth the perplexing, ambiguous problem of lost honour and guilt, expiation and heroism. Darkness and doubt brood over the tale,

EMILY BRONTË

(b. July 30, 1818, Thornton, Yorkshire, Eng.—d. Dec. 19, 1848, Haworth, Yorkshire)

The English novelist and poet Emily Brontë (who published under the name Ellis Bell) produced a single, highly imaginative novel, Wuthering Heights *(1847), set on the Yorkshire moors. Emily was perhaps the greatest writer of the three Brontë sisters, but the record of her life is extremely meagre, for she was silent and reserved and left no correspondence of interest. Her single novel darkens rather than solves the mystery of her spiritual existence. Her mother died early. Together with her sister Charlotte, she attended the Clergy Daughter's School. Emily and Charlotte made an unsuccessful attempt to open a school. Their younger sister Anne, who died of tuberculosis in 1849 at age 29, was also a writer. Poems by Currer, Ellis and Acton Bell (1846), published jointly by the sisters (who assumed pseudonyms to avoid the special treatment that they believed reviewers accorded to women), contained 21 of Emily's poems. Many critics believe that she alone of the sisters wrote verse that reveals poetic genius. Though unsuccessful when published,* Wuthering Heights *later came to be considered one of the finest novels in English. Soon after its publication, Emily's health began to fail, and she died of tuberculosis at age 30.*

as they do over his long story *Heart of Darkness* (1899), in which Conrad's narrator, Marlow, again leads his listeners into the shadowy recesses of the human heart, with its forever unresolved and unpredictable capacities for good and evil.

DOSTOYEVSKY'S TRAGIC VIEW

In Russia, the novels of Fyodor Dostoyevsky, particularly *Crime and Punishment* (1866) and *The Brothers Karamazov* (1880), revealed a world of paradox, alienation, and loss of identity, prophetic of the major tragic themes of the 20th century. More than any earlier novelist, Dostoyevsky appropriated to his fictions the realm of the subconscious and explored in depth its shocking antinomies and discontinuities. Sigmund Freud, the founder of psychoanalysis, frequently acknowledged his indebtedness to Dostoyevsky's psychological insights. Dostoyevsky's protagonists are reminiscent of Marlowe's Doctor Faustus, caught between the old world of orthodox belief and the new world of intense individualism, each with its insistent claims and justifications. The battleground is once more the human soul, and the stakes are survival. Each of his major heroes—Raskolnikov in *Crime and Punishment* and the three Karamazovs—wins a victory, but it is in each case morally qualified, partial, or transient. The harmonious resolutions of the novels seem forced and are neither decisive of the action nor definitive of Dostoyevsky's total tragic view.

The American Tragic Novel

In the United States, Nathaniel Hawthorne's novel *The Scarlet Letter* (1850) and Herman Melville's *Moby Dick* (1851) are surprisingly complete embodiments of the tragic form, written as they were at a time of booming American optimism, materialistic expansion, and sentimentalism in fiction—and no tragic theatre whatever. In *The Scarlet Letter*, a story of adultery set in colonial New England, the heroine's sense of sin is incomplete. Her spirited individualism insists (as she tells her lover) that "what we did had a consecration of its own." The resulting conflict in her heart and mind is never resolved, and, although it does not destroy her, she lives out her life in gray and tragic isolation. Melville said that he was encouraged by Hawthorne's exploration of "a certain tragic phase of humanity," by his deep broodings and by the "blackness of darkness" in him, to proceed with similar explorations of his own in *Moby Dick*, which he dedicated to Hawthorne. Its protagonist, Captain Ahab, represents a return to what Melville called (defending Ahab's status as tragic hero) a "mighty pageant creature, formed for noble tragedies," whose "ponderous heart," "globular brain," and "nervous lofty language" prove that even an old Nantucket sea captain can take his place with kings and princes of the ancient drama. Shakespearean echoes abound in the novel. Some of its chapters are written in dramatic form. Its theme and central figure, reminiscent of Job and Lear in their search for justice and of Oedipus in his search for the truth, all show what Melville might have been—a great tragic dramatist had there been a tragic theatre in America.

Some American novelists of the 20th century carried on, however partially, the tragic tradition. Theodore Dreiser's *American Tragedy* (1925) is typical of the naturalistic novel, which is also represented by the work of Stephen Crane, James T. Farrell, and John Steinbeck. Though showing great sensitivity to environmental or sociological evils, such works fail to embody the high conception of character (as described to Melville) and are concerned mainly with externals, or reportage. The protagonists are generally "good" (or weak) and beaten down by society. The novels of Henry James, which span the period from 1876 to 1904, are concerned with what has been called the tragedy of manners. The society James projects is sophisticated, subtle, and sinister. The innocent and the good are destroyed, like Milly Theale in *The Wings of the Dove* (1902), who in the end "turns her face to the wall" and dies but in her death brings new vision and new values to those whose betrayals had driven her to her death.

The trend in American fiction, as in the drama, continued in the 20th century toward the pathos of the victim—the somehow inadequate, the sometimes insignificant figure destroyed by such vastly unequal forces that the struggle is scarcely significant. F. Scott Fitzgerald's Gatsby in his novel *The Great Gatsby*

(1925) is betrayed by his own meretricious dream, nurtured by a meretricious society. The hero of Ernest Hemingway's novel *A Farewell to Arms* (1929), disillusioned by war, makes a separate peace, deserts, and joins his beloved in neutral Switzerland. When she dies in childbirth, he sees it as still another example of how "they"—society, the politicians who run the war, or the mysterious forces that destroyed Catherine—get you in the end. The tone is lyric and pathetic rather than tragic (though Hemingway called the novel his *Romeo and Juliet*). Grief turns the hero away from, rather than toward, a deeper examination of life.

Only the novels of William Faulkner, in their range and depth and in their powerful assault on the basic tragic themes, recall unmistakably the values of the tragic tradition. His "saga of the South," as recounted in a series of novels (notably *Sartoris*, 1929; *The Sound and the Fury*, 1929; *As I Lay Dying*, 1930; *Sanctuary*, 1931; *Light in August*, 1932; *Absalom, Absalom!* 1936; *Intruder in the Dust*, 1948; *Requiem for a Nun*, 1951), incorporates some three hundred years of Southern history. At first regarded as a mere exploiter of decadence, he can now be seen as gradually working beyond reportage and toward meaning. His sociology became more and more the "sin" of the South—the rape of the land, slavery, the catastrophe of the Civil War and its legacy of a cynical and devitalized materialism. He increasingly saw the conflict as internal. The subject of art, Faulkner said in his 1949 Nobel Prize speech, is

"the human heart in conflict with itself." His insistence is on guilt as the evidence of the fate of humanity, and on the possibility of expiation as the assertion of human freedom. Compassion, endurance, and the capacity to learn are seen to be increasingly effective in his characters. In the veiled analogies to Christ as outcast and redeemer in *Light in August* and the more explicit Christology of *A Fable* (1954), the pastoral serenity following the anguish and horror in *Light in August*, and the high comedy of the last scene of *Intruder in the Dust*, Faulkner puts into tragic fiction the belief he stated in his Nobel speech: "I decline to accept the end of man."

TRAGEDY: TERMS AND CONCEPTS

Like comedy, tragedy has ancient roots. The selected terms that follow are largely the product of early criticism, though many, such as *catharsis* and *hubris*, have persisted into contemporary literature and criticism.

ANAGNORISIS

Anagnorisis (a Greek word meaning "recognition") is the startling discovery that produces a change from ignorance to knowledge. It is discussed by Aristotle in the *Poetics* as an essential part of the plot of a tragedy, although anagnorisis occurs in comedy, epic, and, at a later date, the novel as well. Anagnorisis usually involves revelation of the true identity of persons previously unknown, as when a father recognizes a stranger as his son, or vice versa. One of the finest occurs in Sophocles's *Oedipus Rex* when a messenger reveals to Oedipus his true birth, and Oedipus recognizes his wife Jocasta as his mother, the man he slew at the crossroads as his father, and himself as the unnatural sinner who brought misfortune on Thebes. This recognition is the more artistically satisfying because it is accompanied by a peripeteia ("reversal"), the shift in fortune from good to bad that moves on to the tragic catastrophe. An anagnorisis is not always accompanied by a peripeteia, as in the *Odyssey,* when Alcinous, ruler of Phaeacia, has his minstrel entertain a shipwrecked stranger with songs of the Trojan War, and the stranger begins to weep and reveals himself as none other than Odysseus. Aristotle discusses several kinds of anagnorisis employed by dramatists. The simplest kind, used, as he says, "from poverty of wit," is recognition by scars, birthmarks, or tokens. More interesting are those that arise naturally from incidents of the plot.

CATHARSIS

Catharsis is the purification or purgation of the emotions (especially pity and fear) primarily through art. In criticism, catharsis is a metaphor used by Aristotle in the *Poetics* to describe the effects of true tragedy on the spectator. The use is derived from the medical term *katharsis* (Greek: "purgation" or "purification"). Aristotle states that the purpose of tragedy is to arouse "terror and pity" and thereby effect the catharsis of these emotions. His exact meaning has been the subject of critical debate over the centuries. The German dramatist and literary critic Gotthold Lessing (1729–81) held that catharsis converts excess emotions into virtuous dispositions. Other critics see tragedy as a moral lesson in which the fear and pity excited by the tragic hero's fate serve to warn the spectator not to similarly tempt providence. The generally accepted interpretation is that through experiencing fear vicariously in a controlled situation, the spectator's own anxieties are directed outward, and, through sympathetic identification with the tragic protagonist, his insight and outlook are enlarged. Tragedy then has a healthful and humanizing effect on the spectator or reader.

HAMARTIA

The tragic flaw (or hamartia—from Greek *hamartanein* meaning "to err") refers to an inherent defect or shortcoming in the hero of a tragedy, who is in other respects a superior being favoured by fortune.

Aristotle introduced the term casually in the *Poetics* in describing the tragic hero as a man of noble rank and nature whose misfortune is not brought about by villainy but by some "error of judgment" (hamartia). This imperfection later came to be interpreted as a moral flaw, such as Othello's jealousy or Hamlet's irresolution, although most great tragedies defy such a simple interpretation.

Most importantly, the hero's suffering and its far-reaching reverberations are far out of proportion to his flaw. An element of cosmic collusion among the hero's flaw, chance, necessity, and other external forces is essential to bring about the tragic catastrophe.

In Greek tragedy the nature of the hero's flaw is even more elusive. Often the tragic deeds are committed unwittingly, as when Oedipus unknowingly kills his father and marries his own mother. If the deeds are committed knowingly, they are not committed by choice: Orestes is under obligation to Apollo to avenge his father's murder by killing his mother. Also, an apparent weakness is often only an excess of virtue, such as an extreme probity or zeal for perfection. It has been suggested in such cases, because the tragic hero is never passive but struggles to resolve his tragic difficulty with an obsessive dedication, that he is guilty of hubris (i.e., presumption of being godlike and attempting to overstep his human limitations).

HUBRIS

In Classical Athenian usage, hubris was the intentional use of violence to humiliate or degrade. The most famous example was the case of Meidias, who punched the orator Demosthenes in the face when the latter was dressed in ceremonial robes and performing an official function. *Hubris* could also characterize rape. Hubris was a crime at least from the time of Solon (6th century BCE), and

any citizen could bring charges against another party, as was the case also for treason or impiety. (In contrast, only a member of the victim's family could bring charges for murder.)

The most important discussion of hubris in antiquity is by Aristotle, in *Rhetoric*:

> *Hubris consists in doing and saying things that cause shame to the victim . . . simply for the pleasure of it. Retaliation is not hubris, but revenge. . . . Young men and the rich are hubristic because they think they are better than other people.*

Hubris fit into the shame culture of archaic and Classical Greece, in which people's actions were guided by avoiding shame and seeking honour. It did not fit into the culture of internalized guilt, which became important in later antiquity and characterizes the modern West.

Because Greek has a word for error, *hamartia*, but not for sin, some poets—especially Hesiod (7th century BCE) and Aeschylus (5th century BCE)—used *hubris* to describe wrongful action against the divine order. From this usage modern thinkers developed the idea that hubris meant overweening presumption leading to an impious disregard of the divinely fixed limits on human action in an ordered cosmos. Modern literary critics often seek to find in hubris the "tragic flaw" of the heroes of Greek tragedy. There are figures in Greek myth and history for whom this usage may be appropriate, such as

Oedipus in Sophocles' Oedipus the King, *drawing by Alfred Brennan, 1881.* Library of Congress, Washington, D.C.

the Persian king Xerxes in Herodotus's history of the Persian Wars, who tried to punish the sea for destroying his bridge over the Hellespont; Ajax in Sophocles' play *Ajax*, who told Athena to help other warriors because he did not need divine help; or Oedipus in Sophocles' *Oedipus the King*, who by unwittingly killing his true father and marrying his own mother fulfills the Delphic oracle's prophecy of

him. It is important to remember, however, that the modern connotation is not the usual meaning of the word *hybris* in Classical Greek.

REVENGE TRAGEDY

A drama in which the dominant motive is revenge for a real or imagined injury is known as a revenge tragedy. It was a favourite form of English tragedy in the Elizabethan and Jacobean eras and found its highest expression in William Shakespeare's *Hamlet*.

The revenge drama derived originally from the Roman tragedies of Seneca but was established on the English stage by Thomas Kyd with *The Spanish Tragedy* (c. 1590). This work, which opens with the Ghost of Andrea and Revenge, deals with Hieronimo, a Spanish gentleman who is driven to melancholy by the murder of his son. Between spells of madness, he discovers who the murderers are and plans his ingenious revenge. He stages a play in which the murderers take part, and, while enacting his role, Hieronimo actually kills them, then kills himself. The influence of this play, so apparent in *Hamlet* (performed c. 1600–01), is also evident in other plays of the period. In John Marston's *Antonio's Revenge* (1602), the ghost of Antonio's slain father urges Antonio to avenge his murder, which Antonio does during a court masque. In George Chapman's *Revenge of Bussy d'Ambois* (performed c. 1610), Bussy's ghost begs his introspective brother Clermont to avenge his murder. Clermont hesitates and vacillates but at last complies, then kills himself. Most revenge tragedies end with a scene of carnage that disposes of the avenger as well as his victims. Other examples are Shakespeare's *Titus Andronicus* (performed 1593–94), Henry Chettle's *Tragedy of Hoffman* (performed 1602), and Thomas Middleton's *Revenger's Tragedy* (1607).

SENECAN TRAGEDY

The body of nine closet dramas (i.e., plays intended to be read rather than performed), written in blank verse by the Roman Stoic philosopher Seneca in the 1st century CE are known as Senecan tragedies. Rediscovered by Italian humanists in the mid-16th century, they became the models for the revival of tragedy on the Renaissance stage. The two great, but quite different, dramatic traditions of the age—French Neoclassical tragedy and Elizabethan tragedy—both drew inspiration from Seneca.

Seneca's plays were reworkings chiefly of Euripides's dramas and also of works of Aeschylus and Sophocles. Probably meant to be recited at elite gatherings, they differ from their originals in their long declamatory, narrative accounts of action, their obtrusive moralizing, and their bombastic rhetoric. They dwell on detailed accounts of horrible deeds and contain long reflective soliloquies. Though the gods rarely appear in these plays, ghosts and witches abound. In an age when the Greek originals were scarcely known, Seneca's plays were mistaken for high Classical drama. The Renaissance scholar J.C. Scaliger (1484–1558), who knew both Latin and Greek, preferred Seneca to Euripides.

French Neoclassical dramatic tradition, which reached its highest expression in the 17th-century tragedies of Pierre Corneille and Jean Racine, drew on Seneca for form and grandeur of style. These Neoclassicists adopted Seneca's innovation of the confidant (usually a servant), his substitution of speech for action, and his moral hairsplitting.

The Elizabethan dramatists found Seneca's themes of bloodthirsty revenge more congenial to English taste than they did his form. The first English tragedy, *Gorboduc* (1561), by Thomas Sackville and Thomas Norton, is a chain of slaughter and revenge written in direct imitation of Seneca. Senecan tragedy is also evident in Shakespeare's *Hamlet*. The revenge theme, the corpse-strewn climax, and such points of stage machinery as the ghost can all be traced back to the Senecan model.

CONCLUSION

As this volume amply demonstrates, a plethora of ancient genres and subgenres have contributed to the immensely rich body of English-language literature. This book has been produced to help the reader understand how a portion of that literature—especially poetry and drama—developed through the centuries and came to be what it is today.

Drama is an ancient art. Some of the earliest extant tragedies and comedies still have the power to move a 21st-century reader to tears and laughter. This book has examined the origins of drama, its power to move, and its many variations.

Of the two principal genres included here, poetry (it is generally agreed) requires more effort to comprehend. It also often provides a greater reward. By use of it, ancient bards not only entertained their audiences, they disseminated history and gave their listeners an idea of their place in the world. They made clear what was expected of heroes, of the qualities to be admired and emulated as well as those to be avoided.

This early poetry, long since written down, is a different animal in the 21st century. Although its message has not changed, it is no longer conveyed by a respected leader to a group of willing listeners. Some of us have to be forced to read it. But with an open mind and a little quiet, the reading of poetry—ancient, modern, and in between—can be an intimate and gratifying experience when the solitary reader confronts the pattern of words on a page or even a computer screen. Knowing not just *what* a poem means, but (as the American poet and literary critic John Ciardi put it) *how* it means is a way of deepening your experience of life.

APPENDIX: POETS LAUREATE

POETS LAUREATE OF BRITAIN	
John Dryden	1668-89
Thomas Shadwell	1689-92
Nahum Tate	1692-1715
Nicholas Rowe	1715-18
Laurence Eusden	1718-30
Colley Cibber	1730-57
William Whitehead	1757-85
Thomas Warton	1785-90
Henry James Pye	1790-1813
Robert Southey	1813-43
William Wordsworth	1843-50
Alfred, Lord Tennyson	1850-92
Alfred Austin	1896-1913
Robert Bridges	1913-30
John Masefield	1930-67
Cecil Day-Lewis	1968-72
Sir John Betjeman	1972-84
Ted Hughes	1984-98
Andrew Motion	1999-2009[1]
Carol Ann Duffy	2009-

[1]Motion was the first to serve a fixed term.

POETS LAUREATE OF THE UNITED STATES	
Joseph Auslander	1937-41[1]
Allen Tate	1943-44
Robert Penn Warren	1944-45
Louise Bogan	1945-46
Karl Shapiro	1946-47
Robert Lowell	1947-48
Léonie Adams	1948-49
Elizabeth Bishop	1949–50
Conrad Aiken	1950–52[2]
William Carlos Williams	–[3]
James Dickey	1966-68
William Jay Smith	1968-70
William Stafford	1970-71
Josephine Jacobsen	1971-73
Daniel Hoffman	1973-74
Stanley Kunitz	1974-76
Robert Hayden	1976-78
William Meredith	1978-80
Maxine Kumin	1981-82
Anthony Hecht	1982-84
Robert Fitzgerald	1984-85[4]
Reed Whittemore	1984-85[5]
Gwendolyn Brooks	1985-86
Robert Penn Warren	1986-87[6]
Richard Wilbur	1987-88
Howard Nemerov	1988-90
Mark Strand	1990-91
Joseph Brodsky	1991-92
Mona Van Duyn	1992-93
Rita Dove	1993-95

Robert Hass	1995-97
Robert Pinsky	1997-2000[7]
Rita Dove, Louise Glück, and W.S. Merwin	1999-2000[8]
Stanley Kunitz	2000-01
Billy Collins	2001-03
Louise Glück	2003-04
Ted Kooser	2004-06
Donald Hall	2006-07
Charles Simic	2007-08
Kay Ryan	2008–

[1]Auslander's term was not fixed.

[2]Aiken was the first to serve two consecutive terms.

[3]Williams was appointed in 1952, but he did not serve.

[4]Fitzgerald was ailing when he was appointed. He served in a limited capacity and did not go to the Library of Congress.

[5]Whittemore was interim consultant in poetry.

[6]Warren was the first to be designated Poet Laureate Consultant in Poetry.

[7]Pinsky was the first to serve three consecutive terms.

[8]Dove, Glück, and Merwin were special bicentennial consultants.

GLOSSARY

arsis The lighter or shorter part of a poetic foot especially in quantitative verse.

ascetic Practicing strict self-denial as a measure of personal and especially spiritual discipline.

badinage Light and playful repartee or wit; banter.

bathos The sudden or unexpected appearance of the commonplace in writing or speaking otherwise elevated in style or content.

broadside A sizable sheet of paper printed on one side only; especially one publicizing a controversy or official proclamation.

broken rhyme A rhyme in which one of the rhyming elements is actually two words (i.e., "gutteral" with "sputter all").

coterie An intimate, often exclusive, group of persons having a binding common interest or purpose.

degenerate Having sunk to a lower class or standard or to a state below that normal to a type or to a thing.

end rhyme In poetry, a rhyme that occurs in the last syllables of two or more lines of a verse.

enjambment Also called run-on. In prosody, the continuation of the sense of a phrase beyond the end of a line of verse.

epitaph An inscription in verse or prose upon a tomb; and, by extension, anything written as if to be inscribed on a tomb.

foot In verse, the smallest metrical unit of measurement; the plural is feet.

gnomic Characterized by, or expressive of, aphorism or sententious wisdom, especially concerning human condition or conduct.

incremental repetition A device used in poetry of the oral tradition, especially English and Scottish ballads, in which a line is repeated in a changed context or with minor changes in the repeated part.

innuendo An oblique allusion, hint, or insinuation; a veiled or equivocal reflection on character or reputation.

internal rhyme Rhyme between a word within a line and another word either at the end of the same line or within another line.

irony Language device, either in spoken or written form, in which the real meaning is concealed or contradicted by the literal meaning of the words (verbal irony) or in a situation in which there is an incongruity between what is expected and what occurs (dramatic irony).

measure Poetic rhythm measured by temporal quantity or accent; metre.

meretricious Exhibiting synthetic or spurious attractions; based on pretence or insincerity.

metamorphosis Change of physical form, structure, or substance.

metaphor Figure of speech that implies comparison between two unlike entities. It is the fundamental language of poetry.

metre In poetry, the rhythmic pattern of a poetic line. Also spelled meter.

mosaic rhyme A type of multiple rhyme in which a single multisyllabic word is made to rhyme with two or more words.

overweening Arrogant, presumptuous.

poesy Artificial or sentimentalized poetic writing.

rhetoric The study of principles and rules of composition formulated by critics of ancient times, which can also involve the study of writing or speaking as a means of communication or persuasion.

rhyme The correspondence of two or more words with similar-sounding final syllables placed so as to echo one another. Also spelled rime.

ribald Characterized by or using coarse indecent humour.

simile Figure of speech involving a comparison between two unlike entities explicitly indicated by the words "like" or "as."

soliloquy Passage in a drama in which a character expresses his or her thoughts or feelings aloud while either alone upon the stage or with the other actors keeping silent.

strophe In poetry, a group of verses that form a distinct unit within a poem. The term is sometimes used as a synonym for stanza.

thesis The unstressed part of a poetic foot especially in accentual verse.

tout court Quite short; simply.

BIBLIOGRAPHY

The beginning reader of poetry may well be able to use some help in interpreting, such as a critical or explanatory anthology. Cleanth Brooks and Robert Penn Warren, *Understanding Poetry*, 4th ed. (1976, reprinted 2002), is still probably the best of its kind, as numerous imitations amply attest. Also useful are Tzvetan Todorov, *Introduction to Poetics* (1997; originally published in French, 1973), a comprehensive introduction to modern poetics; and John Ciardi and Miller Williams, *How Does a Poem Mean?*, 2nd ed. (1987).

General works on prosody include Alex Preminger, *Dictionary of Prosody* (1985); Donald Wesling, *The New Poetries: Poetic Form Since Coleridge and Wordsworth* (1985); and Thomas R. Arp and Greg Johnson (eds.), *Perrine's Sound and Sense: An Introduction to Poetry*, 13th ed. (2010).

H.M. Chadwick, *The Heroic Age* (1912); and H.M. Chadwick and N.K. Chadwick, *The Growth of Literature*, vol. 1, *The Ancient Literatures of Europe* (1932), are two classic works on European heroic poetries that are still valuable. Helen Damico and John Leyerle (eds.), *Heroic Poetry in the Anglo-Saxon Period* (1993), deals with Old English poetry. John G. Demaray, *Cosmos and Epic Representation: Dante, Spenser, Milton, and the Transformation of Renaissance Heroic Poetry* (1991), focuses chiefly on English poets. Karl Reichl, *Singing the Past: Turkic and Medieval Heroic Poetry* (2000), treats non-English sources. The subject of Homer is covered in Joachim Latacz, *Homer, His Art and His World* (1996, originally published in German); Ian Morris and Barry B. Powell (eds.), *A New Companion to Homer* (1997); and Barry B. Powell, *Homer* (2004). Sources on Beowulf include Craig Davis, *Beowulf and the Demise of Germanic Legend in England* (1996); and Stephen P. Thompson (ed.), *Readings on Beowulf* (1998). Among the books dealing with elements of Germanic epic are Brian Murdoch, *The Germanic Hero: Politics and Pragmatism in Early Medieval Poetry* (1996); and Joyce Tally Lionarons, *The Medieval Dragon: The Nature of the Beast in Germanic Literature* (1998). Michael Murrin, *The Allegorical Epic* (1980), is a survey of the European tradition.

F.J. Child (ed.), *The English and Scottish Popular Ballads*, 5 vol. (1882–98), is the canon of traditional balladry; the tunes for these are supplied in B.H. Bronson (ed.), *Traditional Tunes of the Child Ballads*, 4 vol. (1959-72; reissued 1980). A second edition, prepared by Mark F. Heiman and Laura Saxton Heiman, was issued in 2001. James Kinsley (ed.), *The Oxford Book* of Ballads (1989), is also a standard anthology.

Works on drama include Benjamin Bennett, *Theater as Problem: Modern Drama and its Place in Literature* (1990); and John Gould, *Myth, Ritual, Memory, and Exchange: Essays in Greek Literature and Culture* (2002). By far the vast majority of recent volumes on this subject—as well as on comedy and tragedy—focus on a specific dramatist, period, or sub-genre.

INDEX